Alfred Thomas Story

The Building of the British Empire

The Story of England's Growth from Elizabeth to Victoria

Alfred Thomas Story

The Building of the British Empire
The Story of England's Growth from Elizabeth to Victoria

ISBN/EAN: 9783337173043

Printed in Europe, USA, Canada, Australia, Japan

Cover: Foto ©ninafisch / pixelio.de

More available books at **www.hansebooks.com**

HER MAJESTY THE QUEEN IN 1859.
(After the painting by Winterhalter.)

Frontispiece.

THE STORY OF THE NATIONS

THE BUILDING OF THE BRITISH EMPIRE

THE STORY OF ENGLAND'S GROWTH FROM ELIZABETH TO VICTORIA

WITH UPWARDS OF ONE HUNDRED PORTRAITS AND
ILLUSTRATIONS FROM CONTEMPORARY PRINTS

BY

ALFRED THOMAS STORY

AUTHOR OF "THE LIFE OF JOHN LINNELL," "WILLIAM BLAKE: HIS LIFE
GENIUS, AND WORKS," "A BOOK OF VAGROM MEN," ETC.

IN TWO PARTS

1689–1895

G. P. PUTNAM'S SONS
NEW YORK & LONDON
The Knickerbocker Press
1898

COPYRIGHT, 1898
BY
G. P. PUTNAM'S SONS

The Knickerbocker Press, New York

CONTENTS.

BOOK III.

FIGHTING ON ALL THE SEAS.

CHAPTER		PAGE
I.	Results of the Revolution	1
II.	Progress of the New East India Company	20
III.	Fighting the French from Canada to the Ohio	35
IV.	Clive Begins his Career in India	56
V.	The French Driven out of the New World	85
VI.	The Conquest of Bengal	102
VII.	Quarrel with the American Colonies	123
VIII.	Driving the American Colonies to Revolt	141
IX.	Independence of the United States	169
X.	An Age of Development and Revolution	206

BOOK IV.

COMPLETING THE EDIFICE.

I.	A Titanic Contest	232
II.	A Struggle for Existence	263
III.	From War to Peace	296
IV.	Colonial Expansion	318
V.	A Peaceful Revolution	351
VI.	Mother of Nations	373
VII.	The Discovery of Gold	390
VIII.	The Chartered Companies	412
IX.	The Work Still to do	434
	Index	457

ILLUSTRATIONS.

	PAGE
HER MAJESTY THE QUEEN IN 1859	*Frontispiece*
After the painting by Winterhalter.	
WILLIAM OF ORANGE	3
BATTLE OF BARFLEUR, MAY 29, 1692	5
From an old print.	
BURNING OF FRENCH SHIPS IN THE HARBOUR OF LA HOGUE	9
From an old print	
THE SIEGE OF BARCELONA	11
From an old print.	
DUKE OF MARLBOROUGH	15
WILLIAM DAMPIER	18
THE NORTH GATE, OLD DELHI	25
From a painting by W. Daniels, R.A.	
THEATRE OF THE CONTEST WITH THE FRENCH	37
QUEEN ANNE	41
VIEW OF LOUISBOURG IN 1731	46
From a sketch in the Paris Archives.	
MADRAS	57
From an engraving by J. G. Martini.	
MAP OF INDIA	60
VIEW OF THE ROCK AT TRICHINOPOLY	79
From a drawing by Captain Trapaud.	

ILLUSTRATIONS.

	PAGE
WHITEFIELD PREACHING AT LEEDS	87
GENERAL WOLFE	92
THE TAKING OF QUEBEC	95
From an old print.	
DEATH OF GENERAL WOLFE	99
After the painting by Benjamin West.	
FORT GERIAH	107
From an old print.	
FORT WILLIAM	109
From an old print.	
LORD CLIVE	115
THE OLD STATE-HOUSE, BOSTON (1748), AS RESTORED IN 1881	149
LORD NORTH	153
THE EARL OF CHATHAM	173
FORTIFYING BUNKER HILL	177
From a design by F. O. Darley.	
ENGAGEMENT OFF USHANT, JULY 27, 1778, BETWEEN THE BRITISH FLEET UNDER ADMIRAL KEPPEL, AND THE FRENCH FLEET UNDER D'ORVILLIERS	183
From a print after a drawing by an officer on board the "Victory."	
ATTACK ON GIBRALTER BY SPANISH FLOATING BATTERIES, 1781	185
Redrawn from the "British Naval Chronicle."	
DEFEAT OF A SPANISH SQUADRON UNDER DE LANGARA, JANUARY 16, 1780	187
From a print after T. Luny.	
ENGAGEMENT ON THE DOGGER BANK, AUGUST 5, 1781, BETWEEN THE BRITISH SQUADRON UNDER VICE-ADMIRAL PARKER, AND THE DUTCH SQUADRON UNDER REAR-ADMIRAL ZOUTMAN	189

ILLUSTRATIONS.

	PAGE
COUNT DE GRASSE DELIVERING HIS SWORD TO ADMIRAL RODNEY	191
ADMIRAL RODNEY	193
GENERAL ELLIOTT	195
RAISING THE SIEGE OF GIBRALTAR	197
From an old print.	
BENJAMIN FRANKLIN	199
WARREN HASTINGS	203
GENERAL WASHINGTON	209
CAPTAIN COOK	217
THE "ENDEAVOUR" OFF TAHITI	218
DEATH OF CAPTAIN COOK	221
THE "SIRIUS" AND "SUPPLY" IN JACKSON'S BAY	225
THE "GLORIOUS FIRST OF JUNE," 1794	237
BATTLE OF ST. VINCENT, JULY 14, 1797	239
After a drawing by Lieut. J. Brenton, R.N.	
LORD NELSON, K.B.	241
After a painting by A. W. Devis.	
THE BATTLE OF THE NILE, 1798	243
Based on an old engraving.	
THE LAST EFFORT AND FALL OF TIPPOO SULTAN	251
From a painting by H. Singleton.	
SERINGAPATAM	256
PLAN OF THE FIELD OF ASSAYE	259
THE BATTLE OF TRAFALGAR, 1805	269
From the painting by C. Stanfield.	
THE DEATH OF NELSON	271
After the painting by Ernest Stingeneyer.	
WILLIAM PITT	273
WILLIAM WILBERFORCE	283
BATTLE OF COPENHAGEN, 1801	285

ILLUSTRATIONS.

	PAGE
FORMATION OF THE LINES OF BATTLE OF WATERLOO.	290
THE LAST CHARGE AT WATERLOO	293
From an engraving after the picture of Luke Clennell.	
CAPE OF GOOD HOPE	305
From an old print.	
CAPTAIN FLINDERS	325
SYDNEY IN ITS EARLY DAYS	330
AUCKLAND, THE FIRST CAPITAL OF NEW ZEALAND.	349
LORD BROUGHAM	355
EARL GREY, "REFORM PREMIER"	363
LORD DURHAM	371
MELBOURNE IN THE FORTIES.	395
SIR GEORGE GREY	407
RICHARD COBDEN	415
SIR ROBERT PEEL	417
RICHARD LANDER	425
SKETCH MAP OF SOUTH AFRICA	429
DAVID LIVINGSTONE	431
THE LATE SIR HENRY PARKES	455

THE BUILDING OF THE BRITISH EMPIRE

THE BUILDING OF THE EMPIRE.

BOOK III.

FIGHTING ON ALL THE SEAS.

CHAPTER I.

RESULTS OF THE REVOLUTION.

WITH the close of the seventeenth century England entered upon a new era of growth and development. By the Revolution the House of Commons was made paramount in regard to the government of the country. The "Divine right" was shifted from the shoulders of the King to the people; and in William III.—the last of our sovereigns to manifest any gift of statesmanship or military genius—was found a solution of the problem of constitutional monarchy. That was an enormous gain, and the result has been to cause the wheels of State to move with comparative ease ever since.

Nor was that all. Prior to the Revolution the whole of the supply for the public service had been at the disposal of the sovereign; but with William's accession it was decided that a definite sum should be set apart for the maintenance of the King and his Government, or what is now called the Civil List, the rest going for national defence and contingent expenditure. Estimates of the charges for the Army, Navy, and other services were henceforth to be submitted annually to Parliament; and the sums voted for these and other branches of the administration were limited to the specific objects for which they were granted. Hence it was no longer possible to avoid the assembling of Parliament year by year.

These and other constitutional changes provided for in the Bill of Rights were an immense step in advance towards popular government, and form practically the basis of the administrative machinery of the present day. The beneficial effects of these reforms were not long in manifesting themselves in nearly every department of the national life, but especially, in the course of a few years, in that of trade and commerce.

These effects would no doubt have been still more marked but for the expensive and destructive wars in which William III. and, afterwards, Anne found themselves engaged. It is curious to note that during these two reigns the Navy did not on all occasions justify its old renown. Indeed, at one time the French came very near winning the supremacy of the sea, and but for our Dutch allies might possibly have done so. This arose from no decadence in the qualities of British seamen, but rather from the corruption and incapacity of their officers.

WILLIAM OF ORANGE.

Through the indolence, if not from the actual treachery, of Admiral Herbert, who had been raised to the earldom of Torrington and the command of the fleet as the reward of his services at the Revolution, French privateers were enabled to sweep the seas; while in an action with a French squadron off Bantry Bay he allowed them to triumph after a half-hearted fight. It is said that James II., when told of this engagement, and that the French had defeated the English sailors, answered dryly, "It is the first time."

This was in 1689. In the following year Torrington allowed a French fleet under De Tourville to snatch a victory from the combined English and Dutch fleets off Beachy Head. The Hollanders, who led the van, fought with signal bravery, as did some of the English ships but others seemed to shirk the contest. In this action the English lost a couple of vessels, two of their captains, and some four hundred men; while the Dutch lost two Admirals, with a large number of men, and were besides obliged to sink several of their vessels to prevent them falling into the enemy's hands. Both commanders were blamed, Torrington for not fighting, the French Admiral for not following up his victory, which, indeed, from his failure to do so, profited the victors but little.

Two years later (May 19, 1692) another Naval engagement was fought, which fortunately put an end to all apprehension from the power of France at sea. James was determined to make one more effort to recover his throne, and Louis XIV. seconded the attempt with all his might. An army of thirty thousand men was gathered in Normandy in readi-

BATTLE OF BARFLEUR, MAY 29, 1692.
(From an old print.)

ness for a descent upon the English coast. Transports were provided to carry them over, and Admiral De Tourville was ordered to bring up his fleet from Brest to cover the passage. Great fears were entertained of Admiral Russell, who had succeeded Torrington in the command of the fleet, and whose Jacobite leanings were well known. Had he carried out the treason expected of him by that party, there would have been nothing to prevent the success of the deposed King's endeavour. Russell, however, was no Herbert, and whatever may have been the motives of his intrigues, he let his Jacobite friends know that, be his inclinations for James or for William, he was not going to suffer a defeat on his own element. "Do not think I will let the French triumph over us in our own seas," he said. "If I meet them I fight them, ay, though his Majesty himself should be on board."

The allied fleets, numbering in all ninety-nine vessels and manned by between thirty and forty thousand of the finest seamen of the two nations, fell in with the French off Barfleur, and at once engaged. The fleet under Admiral De Tourville, which counted but sixty-three ships, was no match for the English and Dutch, even though scarcely half their number could get a chance to engage. After a determined fight of five hours the French were obliged to retreat and make for the shelter of their ports. Twenty-two of their ships took refuge in St. Malo. The *Royal Sun*, celebrated as being the finest ship in the world, and two other three-deckers got safely into Cherbourg. The *Ambitious*, to which De Tourville had removed his flag in the latter part of the day, owing to the *Royal Sun* having been so badly damaged, with twelve other ships, found shelter in the bay of La Hogue. De Tourville's flagship and her two companions were attacked where they lay and burned to the water's edge by a British squadron under Delaval. Russell, with a large part of his fleet, did the like for the ships in La Hogue, blockading the port, and then sending in fire-ships and boats, which, on two successive days, burned first one half and then the other of the French ships, although they were protected by two strong forts. This latter daring feat was performed in sight of the army that was to have invaded England—in sight, too, of James II., who is said to have been rejoiced to behold the daring and prowess of his "brave English tars," even though their victory was the death-blow to his hopes of ever regaining the throne.

After this there was no more fear of invasion, partly because the Jacobite conspiracy was detected and suppressed, and partly because, though ship after ship was speedily built to replace those which had been destroyed, the confidence of the French sailors was broken, and even De Tourville did not again venture to challenge the supremacy of the English on the sea; although a year later, falling in with a combined English and Dutch squadron, which was convoying the Turkish fleet off Cape St. Vincent, he attacked them with his entire force, and made a great haul of merchantmen and men-of-war. A few months later Captain Benbow made an attack upon

St. Malo, when, after bombarding the town for three days, he, under cover of night, sent in a fire-ship to reduce it to ashes; but when within pistol-shot she struck upon a rock, and, being set fire to, blew up with such force that St. Malo was shaken as with an earthquake, and three hundred houses unroofed.

In the spring of 1694 the English fleet suffered another miserable reverse at Brest. Coming before that port with a powerful combination of land and naval forces, General Talmash was landed with the first six hundred men, who, however, found such formidable preparations made to receive them that they deemed it prudent to retire immediately to their ships. But the tide was going out, and the flat-bottomed boats were not able to get off. Most of those that landed were either killed or wounded, General Talmash being amongst the latter, and dying a few days later at Portsmouth. Soon after this disastrous affair the fleet under Lord Berkeley bombarded Dieppe, Havre de Grace, and Dunkirk, destroyed all the unprotected French fishing-boats and general shipping, and caused the utmost consternation along the whole coast. Although the devastation committed by these operations was so enormous, it was remarked at the time that their cost to the nation was almost equivalent to what the enemy had suffered by them.

In the course of the same summer another part of the Navy performed unquestionable service, Admiral Russell, with a fleet of sixty-five ships of the line, English and Dutch, not only clearing the Mediterranean of the French, but relieving Barcel-

BURNING FRENCH SHIPS IN THE HARBOUR OF LA HOGUE.
(From an old print.)

ona, blocking Toulon, compelling the States of Venice and Tuscany to recognise William's title, and causing the British flag to be respected from Gibraltar to the Dardanelles. Nor was this the whole of Russell's service. In place of coming home when he had completed this brilliant bit of work, he wintered at Cadiz, in order to prevent the annual junction of the Brest and Toulon fleets.

These signal services on the part of the Navy marked the turning-point of a new era in the maritime trade of England, which had been declining ever since the Revolution. The loss sustained by our commerce during those years in consequence of the activity of the French privateers had been very great, the East India Company especially being sufferers. In one year alone (1693) the captures of the French amounted to three hundred sail, as against 69 merchant vessels taken from that nation. The more purely naval record, however, was not nearly so favourable to the French; for when, in 1697, the Treaty of Ryswick was signed, it was found that during the war the French had lost 59 ships and 2224 guns, while the loss of the English had been 52 ships and 1112 guns.

With the victorious record of 1694, however, trade and commerce seemed to take a sudden leap forward, and a new and altogether unexpected spirit was infused into it in the course of a very few years. From the year 1708, the date of the new consolidating charter of the East India Company, to the year 1730, the imports of Great Britain, according to the realisation of the custom-house, in-

THE SIEGE OF BARCELONA.
(From an old print.)

creased from £4,698,663 to £7,780,019, and the exports from £6,969,089 to £11,974,135.[1]

This result is the more surprising when we consider the drain upon the finances of the country caused by the wars successively waged by William of Orange and Anne to curb the power of France. That country had never been so powerful as under Louis XIV., and it was only by William's persistent opposition and hostility to the designs of the "Grand Monarque," although nearly always defeated, followed by the brilliant triumphs of Marlborough and Prince Eugene under Anne, which had not been equalled since the days of Cressy and Agincourt, that the wings of Louis's towering ambition were clipped, and England was saved from sinking to a second-rate position among the nations of Europe.

The famous Treaty of Utrecht was the salvation of France. Exhausted rather than beaten in the struggle, she was glad to agree to terms of peace. The contrast betwixt the condition of that country on the accession of Louis and towards the close of his reign must have been painfully humiliating to that vain-glorious potentate. In the chief elements of national strength, France was at the former period in many respects superior to this country. In commerce, manufactures, and naval power she was equal; in public revenue greatly superior; while her population was double that of England, which at the Revolution is estimated to have been about five and a half millions.[2] At the close of the war

---

[1] Sir Charles Whitworth's Tables.
[2] Estimate of Gregory King, founded on the returns of Inhabited houses assessed to the hearth-tax in 1690.

she was in a miserably enfeebled state, her revenue greatly reduced, her currency depreciated, and her merchant and artisan classes weighed down with a burden of taxation that they alone had to bear, the clergy and nobility being exempt from all impost. The bill of costs piled up through Louis XIV.'s policy of *Gloire* was not finally liquidated until the French carried through their sanguinary imitation of our comparatively tame and colourless Revolution.

The gain to England from the famous treaty was that it recognised the Protestant succession, established her maritime supremacy, and left her the leading commercial country of Europe. Territorially her gain was considerable; Acadia, most of Newfoundland, Hudson's Bay (as already stated), and St. Christopher being ceded to her, besides the island of Minorca and the fortress of Gibraltar, which had been taken by the Confederate fleets in the month of July, 1704, chiefly by the dash and pluck of the sailors, who had to climb up rocks and scale precipices to come at the enemy. A very dubious condition of the treaty was one which granted to Great Britain the exclusive privilege of supplying the Spanish West Indies with negroes at the rate of 4800 slaves a year for the term of thirty years.

Other noteworthy events of this period that had a bearing on the growth of the Empire were the legislative union with Scotland in 1708, the establishment of the Bank of England, and the reorganisation of the currency, which did much towards placing English credit on a sound basis. The Bank of England was established in 1694, and the Bank of Scotland in the following year. These great chartered bodies were formed upon the model of those of Italy, Spain, and the Low Countries. The Bank of Scotland was projected by an Englishman named Holland, that of England by William Paterson, a Scotchman, who was afterwards engaged in the unfortunate attempt to establish a colony at Darien. A Scotch company was formed for that purpose, and fifty ships with 1200 men, who landed (November 4, 1698), made a settlement on the isthmus, and built a fort; but before the hot season was passed a large proportion of them had died of fever. The remainder abandoned New Edinburgh, as it was called, and made sail for the Hudson, which only about one half of them reached, the others having succumbed on the passage. Meanwhile a second consignment of colonists, larger than the first, sailed for Darien, to find, on their arrival, a ruined fort indeed, but no settlers and only the *débris* of the huts they had built for their habitation. With a resolution that did credit to their courage, they landed and set to work to re-establish New Edinburgh, but it soon became languid and soulless work, as death appeared with the heats of summer and laid them low like swathes of corn before the reaper. The end was visible enough to all, and it was not far off; but the Anarch was anticipated by the Spaniard, who appeared in the shape of a fleet, backed by a mongrel army from Panama, and constrained the New Caledonians to depart. A very small proportion of those who, flushed with hopes of wealth, had engaged in the adventure, lived to set eyes again upon their native land. Two of their

DUKE OF MARLBOROUGH.

ships foundered on their way home, while many of the emigrants, engaging themselves to the planters of Jamaica, found their graves in that island. Of all the colonisation schemes of the seventeenth century, there were few sadder and none madder than that of the isthmus of Darien.

Another matter which undoubtedly had its influence upon the development of the Empire—insignificant and almost unmarked at first though those influences were—was the growth of the newspaper press. The Licencing Act, passed soon after the Restoration, and founded upon the Star Chamber decree of 1637, expired in 1679. It was revived in the reign of James II., and was continued by renewals till the year 1694, when all restraints prior to publication ceased, with the exception to those on dramatic representations. A jesting paragraph, however, in a periodical called *The Flying Post*, appeared towards the end of 1696, reflecting on the credit of the Exchequer bills, and caused great excitement among the members of the House of Commons. They ordered the printer to be arrested, and gave leave to bring in a bill to prevent the writing, printing, or publishing news without a licence. But, on reflection, the House had the good sense to throw out the bill on the second reading, it appearing that less evils were likely to accrue from the abuses of the press than any legislative attempts to restrain them. This was the last open attempt to establish the censorship. The result of this liberty was that a number of weekly or twi-weekly newssheets were soon started, which, though they were small and at first but poorly furnished with news, laid the foundation of our present-day newspaper press, wielding a power that makes the world one vast judgment-hall, and to a large extent the initiative and *referendum* of all measures for the public good and the advancement of civilisation.

William of Orange was too busy with his wars against Louis XIV., and in support of the Protestant League, to have much time to think about extending the bounds of the realm over which he had been called to rule; but, unwittingly, he contributed his mite towards the establishment of those colonies in the Southern seas, the growth of which constitute one of the chief glories of her present Majesty's reign. In 1688 William Dampier, the famous buccaneer and navigator, had sailed along some part of the coast of Australia, which he described in his *Voyage Round the World*, published in 1697. That remarkable work attracted so much attention that in the following year he was appointed to the command of the *Roebuck*, a Royal sloop of war, which, on the 14th of January, 1699, sailed from the Downs on a voyage of discovery in the Australian seas.

New Holland, as it was then called, appears to have been first discovered by the Portuguese early in the sixteenth century. Between 1531 and 1542 they made known the existence of a land which they called Great Java, corresponding with Australia. The first authenticated visit paid to it, however, appears to have been made in 1601 by a Portuguese named Manuel Godinho de Eredia. Five years later the Spaniard Torres passed through the strait that now bears his name, between New Guinea and the larger island. Between that period and 1628 a considerable extent of the coast-line of Australia had been surveyed by Dutch navigators, and in

1664 the island-continent was named New Holland by the Dutch Government.

WILLIAM DAMPIER.

Dampier, who explored a large portion of the west and north-west coasts, appears to have been the first English navigator to visit Australia, and the account of his voyage,[1] which he published in 1703, the year after William III.'s death, was for long the only authentic account in English of that *terra incognita*. Although containing a very uninviting account of the country, it served to give great impetus to exploration in the South Pacific. Almost every discoverer who followed him, especially Dutch

[1] *New Voyage Round the World.*

and French, uniformly regarded Dampier with the warmest admiration, while Humboldt placed him "above those men of science who afterwards went over the same ground."[1] But notwithstanding the fact that his voyage resulted in many important additions to geographical knowledge, Dampier received neither reward nor promise of future employment for his pains, the circumstance that he lost the crazy vessel entrusted to his charge on his way home being allowed to overshadow all merit.

[1] *Life of William Dampier.*

CHAPTER II.

PROGRESS OF THE NEW EAST INDIA COMPANY.

AURENGZEBE, the last of the Great Moguls, had died in the forty-eighth year of his reign and the ninety-fourth of his age, the year before the consolidation of the two East India Companies. His empire had been weakened and greatly impoverished by constant hostilities against internal and external foes, but chiefly by the ceaseless warfare he was compelled to wage against the rising power of the Mahrattas in the Deccan, in Bijapur, in Hyderabad, and other parts of India. Powerful as he had been, and successful as he was on the whole in preserving the empire intact, his statecraft had consisted rather in the cunning to turn everything to his present advantage than in the wisdom to make the people happy and contented, and thus to consolidate the states under his dominion. His efforts to reform the finances of the realm had only resulted in throwing the revenues into greater confusion, the natural consequence being that the burthens under which the people were crushed were augmented in place of being decreased.

Himself a bigoted Mussulman, he treated the Hindus as a conquered and infidel people and subjected them to the invidious burthen of a poll-tax from which they had been previously exempted. Besides thus degrading them, he excluded all of their race and religion from office and preferment, and allowed their temples to be profaned, and, at times, mutilated and destroyed, by fanatics of his own creed. Moreover, not satisfied with these insults, he had caused their fairs and festivals to be suppressed. This treatment of a people who had been on the whole faithful and devoted subjects to Akbar and his successors, had stirred up a deep hatred in the breasts of the Hindus and an obstinate spirit of defiance to his rule.

Barely was the breath out of his body ere the usual struggle commenced amongst the heirs for the succession. His second son, Azim Shah, who was on the spot, was proclaimed in Hindustan. The eldest, who at an early age had received the title of Shah Aulum, was at Cabul, where for many years he had held the post of Governor. He at once collected his forces and marched to Agra, where, aided by his two sons, one of whom was Governor of Multan, the other of Bengal, he defeated his rival in a bloody battle, in which Azim and his two eldest sons lost their lives, and his youngest son, an infant, was taken prisoner.

Bahadur Shah, as he now called himself, had scarcely ascended the imperial musund, ere Kambuksh Shah, his youngest brother, who had recently been appointed to the government of Bijapur, decided to enter the contest for the sovereign power. Bahadur, even when near him with an irresistible army, invited the rash and inconsiderate young prince to enjoy in peace his kingdom of Bijapur, to which he offered to add that of Golconda; but the infatuated youth had been promised the throne by the astrologers, and hence rushed blindly to his destruction. Though deserted by his chief advisers, who saw through his light and inconstant character, as well as by most of his followers, he precipitated a battle near Hyderabad, and was defeated, dying of a mortal wound the same evening.[1]

Notwithstanding his victories, however, Bahadur Shah was so little sure of his strength that he was constrained to conclude an impolitic truce with the predatory Mahrattas, who had caused Aurengzebe so much trouble in the latter years of his reign, as well as to be content with a nominal allegiance on the part of the Rajpoots, who had been forced into revolt by the religious intolerance already referred to.[2]

He was driven to the acceptance of these compromises by a new and formidable enemy who was now threatening his borders. These were the Sikhs, a wild and fanatical sect whose history is one of the most curious of any of the Indian peoples. By them Bahadur suddenly found his diminished states invaded and ravaged as far as the neighbourhood of Lahore on the one side and the very capital itself on the other. Marching with all his force against these marauders, the Emperor succeeded in driving

[1] Mill.   [2] Mill.

them into the mountains beyond the Sutlej, and thus checking them for the time being, but by no means putting an end to them and to their depredations. That task was left for others, he dying suddenly in his camp near Lahore in February, 1712, after having reigned five years.

The four sons of Bahadur Shah contended for the throne. All of them were in the camp with their respective armies and followers. They were Moiz ad Dien Khan, the eldest; Azim Ooshaun, the second, and the favourite of his father; Ruffeh Ooshaun, the third; and Kojesteh Akter, the youngest. Azim Ooshaun, who had been able to possess himself of the treasure of his father, assumed the sceptre; but, having slighted Zulfeccar Khan, who had been the favourite general of Aurengzebe, he caused him to pass to the camp of Moiz ad Dien, where a union was formed of the three other brothers, who agreed to oppose Azim and afterwards divide the empire. A battle ensued, in which the latter was defeated, and in which he completely disappeared. His wounded elephant, it is supposed, rushed with him down the precipice into the river, where both sank to rise no more.

It remained for the surviving brothers to agree as to the division of the empire. Zulfeccar Khan, however, had other designs. It is curious to note the events that follow, they are so characteristic of the downward rush of the empire to dismemberment and ruin. By various artifices, Zulfeccar Khan contrived to secure the greater part of the late Emperor's treasure to Moiz ad Dien, whom it was his wish to raise to the throne. This roused the jealousy of Kojesteh Akter, who prepared for action; a battle ensured, in which the latter, deserted by his soldiers, was easily defeated. Ruffeh Ooshaun, confiding in the friendship of Zulfeccar Khan, stood aloof during the engagement, intending to fall upon the victor. During the night his design was communicated to the wily general, who quietly prepared to receive him. The result was the same as in the case of his younger brother; deserted by his army almost at the beginning of the battle, his cause was hopeless from the first, and he died on the field, fighting bravely amid a few followers.

So Moiz ad Dien triumphed and ascended the musund with the title of Jehander Shah. But he proved himself totally unworthy of his high fortunes, and in the course of a few months was defeated in battle by Feroksere, the son of Azim Ooshaun, and, together with the crafty Zulfeccar, ignominiously put to death. Feroksere, who now assumed the sceptre, proved a weak and despicable prince, and, after a reign of little more than six years, was forcibly deposed. During his tenure of the throne the empire was rent with division and disorder, both the Sikhs and the Mahrattas renewing their devastations and encroachments. Feroksere was succeeded by a consumptive prince of the blood, who survived his elevation but five months, and was in his turn succeeded by another youth, who died after a still shorter reign.

Mahomed Shah, a grandson of Jehander Shah, was the next to be set upon the throne. He was

THE NORTH GATE, OLD DELHI.
(From a painting by W. Daniels, R.A.)

seventeen years of age, and began his reign in 1720. Under him the empire of the Moguls sank to a depth of abasement it had never before witnessed. Serious conflicts had taken place between the Hindus and Mahomedans, and—in the very capital itself—between the two great Mussulman sects, the Shias and the Sunnis. The Deccan became almost independent under the Nizam-ul-Mulk; the Mahrattas grew ever bolder in their encroachments and devastations; and, amid the general anarchy, the Persians, under the famous Nadir Shah, invaded the country, and, penetrating as far as Delhi, defeated the effeminate Mogul, and ordered an indiscriminate massacre of the wretched inhabitants of the city. Nadir's sole object in invading India appears to have been loot, and he had no sort of scruple as to the way he obtained it. He first took possession of the imperial treasures and the jewels of the celebrated peacock-throne, valued at a million pounds. Turning then to the great nobles, he compelled them to surrender most of their effects. The inferior nobles, the state officials, bankers, and rich persons of every description were next fallen upon, and contributions enforced from them. Guards were stationed to prevent people leaving the city, and every man was obliged to declare the amount of his fortune, and to pay accordingly. " Every species of cruelty was employed to extort these contributions. Even men of consequence were beaten to draw forth confessions. Great numbers of the inhabitants died of the usage they received, and many destroyed themselves to avoid the disgrace and terror." [1]

[1] Elphinstone, *History of India*.

After holding possession of Delhi for thirty-seven days,[1] Nadir Shah " restored Mahomed to the exercise of his degraded sovereignty,"[2] and commenced his homeward march (April 13, 1739), taking with him treasure in gold, silver, jewels, and what not, to the value, it is estimated, of thirty-two millions sterling, or, according to Elphinstone, he carried away eight or nine millions in money, " besides several millions in gold and silver plate, valuable furniture, and rich stuffs of every description." Nor did this include the jewels, whose worth was inestimable.

Although the Great Mogul preserved his throne, he preserved little else. He was for a long time so stupefied by his calamities that he remained like one in a lethargy.[3] Whichever way he looked, there met his view nothing but the evidences of ruin and desolation; the empire seemed as if going to pieces, as, indeed, it was, and there was no help—the army gone, the treasury empty, and the sources of revenue all but exhausted.[4]

Even now the ill-starred monarch had not seen the last of his calamities. During these years of weakness and misgovernment a fierce tribe of Afghan warriors had settled upon the provinces east of the Ganges, from Oudh to the mountains, and almost wrested them bodily from the empire. They took their name from the district of Roh, bordering upon Cabul, and as Rohillas became a terror to the whole of the surrounding country, and

---

[1] Other accounts say fifty-eight days was the period of his stay.
[2] Mill.   [3] MacFarlane, *History of British India.*
[4] Elphinstone.

in the later history of India played no inconsiderable part. Though but a short period had elapsed since their rise to the position of a state, they had acquired such power that Mahommed Shah was obliged, in 1745, to take the field against them in order to compel them to a temporary submission.

Two years after this imperial expedition the wasting empire of the Moguls suffered the invasion of Ahmed Abdali, the founder of the present Afghan kingdom, who, after making himself master of Candahar and Cabul, turned his attention to the East, and speedily brought all the country up to the Indus under his sway. The Punjab was in such an unsatisfactory condition that it invited his advance. He received but little opposition from the Viceroy, who was in revolt. Pushing on, Ahmed seized Lahore and other towns on the road, and finally reached the Sutlej, where an army of the Mogul was coming to meet him. Making a detour, he got round this, and penetrated as far as Serhind, which he took and plundered. However, the Indian army now offered such determined opposition to the Durranis, as Ahmed had decided to call his people, that they were compelled to take their way back to Cabul. This was the last of the unhappy Mohammed Shah's earthly calamities. He only lived sufficiently long to learn the news of Ahmed's departure, dying in the thirtieth year of his reign and the forty-ninth of his age.[1]

Such was the condition of the great empire of the Moguls when the East India Company entered upon

[1] Mill.

the second century of its career. Every year saw some province wrested from the weakening hand of the central power; every year some ambitious feudatory made the attempt to carve for himself a kingdom out of the general wreck. Nor was the reigning Mogul as a rule unwilling to pay handsomely for any effective assistance, whether from a native or an outsider. But especially glad were these rebels and usurpers to get the foreigners on their side. The English, of course, were not slow to see their advantage in these quarrels and dissensions among the natives, and to turn them to the best account; although they were not the first to ferment and profit by them.

These native disturbances and disruptions benefited the English in another way. When everything in the native states was unsettled, and no man knew when his life or his goods were safe, many were not reluctant to take advantage of the protection, as well as the facilities for trade, offered by the Company's settlements; and hence at Surat, Bombay, Fort St. David, Calcutta, and other places, every year saw increasing colonies of natives, Mussulmans as well as Hindus, growing up under their protection.

At first, however, the unsettled condition of the empire, with its almost ceaseless internecine warfare, was a constant danger to the English. When they possessed but small settlements, ill able to defend themselves in case of attack, their property and their lives were always more or less at the mercy of neighbouring powers, whose hostility might at any moment be provoked either by jealousy of their presence, or envy of their wealth. Gradually, however, the Company was pushed forward in its career of territorial aggrandisement until it had everything to gain, and nothing to fear from the wars and rivalries of sects and princes.

According to Mill the official value of all the exports to India for the year 1708, the year in which the fusion of the two companies was completed, did not reach £70,000. The following year the exports rose in value to £168,357; but from this year they gradually decreased until, in 1715, they amounted to no more than £36,997. In 1716, however, they showed an increase, and the mean value of exportations during the twenty years subsequent to 1708 was a little over £92,000 per annum. The chief articles of export were lead, quicksilver, woollen cloths, and hardware. There was also a considerable exportation of bullion, the average annual value of which during the same years was £442,350.

The value of the Company's imports, which consisted chiefly of calicoes and other textile fabrics, raw silk, diamonds, tea, porcelain, pepper, drugs, and saltpetre, averaged during the twenty years, beginning with 1708, the sum of £758,042.

About this time the Company made a reform in their method of business which set free a considerable portion of their funds for direct trading. It had been their custom to build and own the ships engaged in their trade; but finding that they could economise by chartering vessels, they henceforth carried on the chief part of their commerce in hired bottoms, owning themselves only a few swift-sailing craft, called packets, which served the purpose of conveying intelligence rather than merchandise.

The business of the Company in India was at this period under the management of the three Presidencies of Bombay, Madras, and Calcutta, the latter of which had been created in 1707. These presidencies were independent the one of the other, and were accountable only to the board of directors in England. A presidency was composed of a President and a Council, both the direct appointment of the Company; the members of the Council being chosen from the civil servants according to rank and seniority. The President, or Governor, was also the Commander-in-chief of the military forces of his presidency, which were at this time of a very mixed character, consisting partly of the recruits sent out by the Company, partly of deserters from other European settlements in India, and partly, at least at Surat and Bombay, of half-breed Portuguese called Topazzes. But, in addition, the Company had already begun to employ natives, to whom the name Sepoys was given, in a military capacity, although as yet to a small extent only. They were at first armed in the native manner with sword and target, but trained to use the musket in case of need. Afterwards, however, they were armed and trained in the European manner, and, under British officers, became very efficient soldiers.

Next to the union of the two companies and the legislative confirmation of a period of monopoly, the event that most redounded to the prosperity of the Company was the Treaty of Utrecht. Delivered from the costly and destructive burthen of the war with France, the energies of the nation immediately began to manifest themselves in the rapid development of industry and commerce. Grants of commercial privileges were made the conditions of peace with the maritime powers, and territorial concessions were granted with a view to the interests of trade rather than power. Although the British Commissioners at Utrecht were blamed—and justly—for not taking sufficient advantage of the position in which the country was placed by the victories of Marlborough, it cannot be denied that the treaty they negotiated laid the foundation of the commercial superiority of Great Britain.

In 1713, the year of the above-mentioned treaty, which was also the first year of the Emperor Feroksere, the Presidency of Calcutta suggested to the court of directors the dispatch of an embassy to the imperial Durbar, in order, if possible, to secure greater privileges and protection. The directors having signified their approval, two of the Company's factors, who were accompanied by a doctor named Hamilton, set out for Delhi, where they arrived on the 8th of July, 1715. But in spite of the rich presents which they carried to Feroksere, the embassy was doomed to neglect, and its object might have entirely failed but for the public spirit of Dr. Hamilton. The emperor was suffering from a painful disorder, which the native physicians had utterly failed to relieve. He was, therefore, recommended to make trial of the English doctor's skill, which he did, with the best results. Dr. Hamilton was commanded to name his own reward, and in place of asking anything for himself he petitioned for certain important privileges for the Company, which were freely granted, although the negotiators did not return with the mandates signed by the emperor until more than two years had elapsed from the time of their arrival at Delhi. The privileges in question were that the cargoes of English ships wrecked on the Mogul's coasts should be protected from plunder; that a fixed sum should be received at Surat in lieu of all duties; that three villages contiguous to Madras, which had been granted autonomy and again resumed by the Government of Arcot, should be restored in perpetuity; that the island of Diu, near the port of Musilapatam, should be given to the Company for an annual rent; that they should have the privilege of introducing and conveying their merchandise from Calcutta through Bengal without duty or examination; and that the Company should be permitted to purchase the zemindarship of thirty-seven towns, in the same manner as they had been authorised by Azim Ooshaun to purchase Calcutta, Chutanuttee, and Govindpore.

The emperor's rescript produced its full effect in Guzerat and the Deccan; but the opposition of the Subadhar of Bengal was sufficient to deter the owners of the townships desired from selling to the Company, and so one of the most important privileges granted by the Emperor was rendered useless.

Nothing more of special importance in connection with the Company's affairs took place for well-nigh thirty years, beyond the schemings and intrigue to which the directors found it necessary to resort in order to secure the renewal of their monopoly, which became more and more difficult as more enlightened views in regard to trade gained ground. In 1732, by means of a bribe to the Government, they obtained an extension of their charter until 1769. But, ever on the alert to checkmate their opponents and score an advantage, in 1744 they secured a further extension to 1783 by the offer to the Government in the midst of the costly war with France and Spain of a million of money at three per cent. interest.

It is curious to note that, notwithstanding their monopoly and their many advantages, the Company never made the success of their trading that the Dutch East India Company did. While, in 1732, the English Company were obliged to reduce their dividend from eight to seven per cent. per annum, at which figure it remained until 1744, the Dutch Company during the same period never paid less than twelve and a half per cent. on their capital, and during most years it reached fifteen and even twenty-five per cent. It is possible that the privilege of carrying on private trade enjoyed by the servants of the English Company may account to some extent for the difference. This private trade was confined chiefly to India, and was carried on by ships from one native port to another, or by land from town to town and province to province. It was rendered necessary by the miserably small stipends paid to the Company's servants, who could not have existed without these extra earnings, which, in many cases, enabled the fortunate traders to retire in a few years with handsome fortunes.

CHAPTER III.

FIGHTING THE FRENCH FROM CANADA TO THE OHIO.

ALTHOUGH William of Orange directly did little or nothing towards the territorial expansion of Great Britain, he gave free scope to national energy and aspiration, and on sea and land, as far as his arms could reach, protected all that had a right to look up to the English flag. During his reign the American colonies made steady progress, even in the midst of war's insecurity and alarms. Very soon after his accession occurred the expedition of Sir William Phipps against the French in Canada. It was fitted out entirely by the New Englanders, who found that there could be no peaceful occupation of their homes and lands so long as the French were free to come and go along the great lakes and the inland waters as far as the Gulf of Mexico.

Early in their colonial history the French seem to have conceived the idea of possessing themselves of all the territory west and south of Canada, and of gradually driving the English into the sea. In the charter granted by Louis XIV. in 1662 to the West

India Company, which was to have free scope to win territory in all parts of North and South America, as well as in the neighbouring islands, from the Amazon to Hudson's Bay, that body was empowered to acquire possession of all lands and regions, " so far as the said Company may be able to penetrate, whether the countries may now appertain to France, or having been occupied by Frenchmen, or in so far as the said Company shall establish itself by exterminating or conquering the natives or colonists of such European nations as are not our allies."

The new Company was not allowed much time to carry out its programme before it became a thing of the past; but the policy of extermination or conquest was adopted by the French in Canada so thoroughly, and pursued with such unremitting ardour, that it is hardly to be wondered at if those they warred against gradually found it necessary to act in the same spirit. In 1678 La Salle had set on foot a scheme, the ultimate aim of which was to connect north and south with a chain of French settlements. In two years' time he had so far perfected his plans as to be able to make a start. Proceeding west as far as the Mississippi, he launched his frail canoes upon its bosom, and after months of toil and danger reached its mouth in the Gulf of Mexico. The State of Louisiana is to-day a monument of his ambition, he having taken possession of all the country watered by that vast river in the name of his sovereign, and called it after him. Subsequently he made an attempt to found a settlement in Florida, but was put to death by his mutinous followers, and it fell to others to carry on his grandiose design. This was done by inciting the Iroquois and other Indian tribes inhabiting those regions to ceaseless warfare against those nations who were

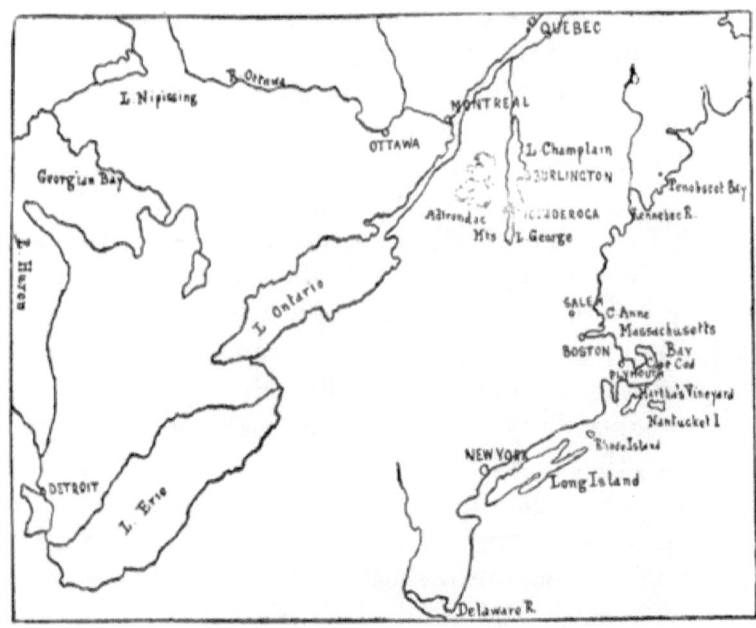

THEATRE OF THE CONTEST WITH THE FRENCH.

friendly with the English. This policy succeeded so well for a time that some of the English colonists "became alarmed at the success and increasing strength of the French, not only in Nova Scotia, where hostilities were almost incessant with the English at Massachusetts, but also by their occupation of the two great rivers, the St. Lawrence and the Mississippi, and their successful prosecution of the fur trade and fisheries, then deemed the chief source of wealth in North America. The population of Canada, which in 1674 did not exceed eight thousand, including the converted Indians, had rapidly increased; and the intermarriages of Frenchmen with the natives enabled the Governor of Quebec to command at all times a large force of Indian warriors."[1]

But this policy had its perils; and when, in 1689, the powerful tribe of the Illinois, the chief allies of the French, made their peace with the Iroquois, the strongest of the "Five Nations," and all the aborigines became friends of the British, the Canadians found themselves threatened with the very danger they had designed for others. Frontenac, Governor of Quebec, feeling that he must do something, prepared an expedition against the English of New York and the neighbouring colonies; while these, in retaliation, planned a combined Naval and Military attack on Nova Scotia and Canada. The Army was placed under the command of General Winthrop, and the naval armament, which consisted of a frigate of forty guns, two smaller vessels, and a number of transports for the conveyance of from eight hundred to a thousand men, was entrusted to the charge of Sir William Phipps, a man of considerable ability, who began life as a ship-carpenter, and, having learned his trade, built himself a vessel with which he went to the Bahamas in the hope of raising a sunken treasure-ship. He failed. Some years later the English Government put him on another job of the kind, with the same result; but it is pleasant to be able to relate that, five years afterwards, he was

[1] Martin, *The British Colonies.*

sent by the Duke of Albemarle, the Governor of Jamaica, to make a renewed attempt on the same wreck, reported to be enormously valuable, and that he actually succeeded in raising thirty-two tons of silver bullion, and a large quantity of gold, pearls, and jewels, which had been lying at the bottom of the sea for upwards of half a century. Knighted by James II., Phipps had previously conducted an expedition against Nova Scotia with ill results.

In the present venture he hoped to do better things, and did actually compel the surrender of Port Royal and other places in Acadia and Newfoundland, as well as several ports on the St. Lawrence. He had even reached within a few days' sail of Quebec before the alarm reached that place. Then, however, Frontenac made such dispositions, and the French colonials received the New Englanders so warmly that, after an attack extending over five days, Phipps and his troops were fain to re-embark, leaving behind their guns and ammunition. This little essay in conquest cost the colonists £140,000; and all that they had won by it was restored to the French by the Treaty of Ryswick (1697).

On the breaking out of the war of the Spanish Succession, in 1702, hostilities between the British colonies and the Canadians recommenced with increased bitterness, the former being now thoroughly possessed with the idea of grasping the whole of the territory of North America. The Count de Vaudreuil, who was now Governor, on his part, bent his efforts " to cut the English off from the fur trade, and gradually to hem them in between the highlands of

Nova Scotia and the Alleghany Mountains."[1] The English, calling upon their Indian allies to start afresh on the war-path against the French, were given to understand by one chief, that he thought both nations were drunk. Drunk or not, however, the New Englanders made preparations for the subjugation of Nova Scotia, and an assurance was obtained from the Crown " that if again conquered it should not be restored to France."[2]

With this encouragement from Queen Anne, tiny emulator of the great Queen Bess, two successive expeditions were sent against the devoted colony; but it was so ably defended by Subercase, the French commander, that the assailants had twice to raise the siege of Port Royal and retire with a heavy loss. Undaunted by these reverses, however, the New England colonists set to work to prepare a third expedition. It took them two years to get ready; but then, with the aid of the home Government, an armament was enabled to sail (September, 1710) under the command of General Nicholson, and Subercase, after a short siege, was compelled to surrender Port Royal. The capitulation was signed on the 2d of October, " and," says Montgomery Martin, " is memorable as the commencement of the permanent annexation of Nova Scotia to the British Crown," in honour of which event the name of Port Royal was changed to Annapolis.

The Grand Monarque had his hands too full with his antagonists in Europe to be able to spare men or money for the reconquest of Nova Scotia; but every

[1] Martin. [2] Ibid.

inducement was given to others to make the attempt, and through the exertions of De Vaudreuil there was

QUEEN ANNE.

a renewal of hostilities, which, however, were soon put an end to by the peace of 1713. By the Treaty of Utrecht Louis XIV. not only ceded Nova Scotia to the British, and relinquished his designs upon the Mississippi Valley, but abandoned all claim to sovereignty over Newfoundland, where, for years, as well as in Nova Scotia, a most destructive warfare had been going on intermittently between the two peoples.

On the rupture of amicable relations between England and France following his elevation to the throne, William III. had made it the subject of one of his complaints "that of late the encroachments of the French upon Newfoundland and his Majesty's subjects' trade and fisheries there, had been more like the invasions of an enemy than becoming to friends who enjoyed the advantages of that trade only by permission." To this Louis XIV. replied to the effect that he had as good a right to Newfoundland as the English, and that he intended to make his claim effective. Whereupon, for the period of the war, the island was the scene of frequent hostilities and much misery. In 1692 the British made a futile attack upon Placentia; four years later the French retaliated by sending two squadrons to Newfoundland, the second of which succeeded in taking and destroying St. John's, and wasting with fire and sword all the British stations, except Bonavista and Carbonier, on Conception Bay, which were successfully defended by the settlers. A strong British force was then sent out to expel the French; but, the command being in weak hands, it effected nothing; and so matters went on until the Treaty of Ryswick (1697), which left things very much as they had been before the war.

During the few succeeding years of peace the French did all they could to encourage emigration to Newfoundland, whilst our Government did everything in its power to check it; so that when, in 1702, the war of the Succession broke out, Newfoundland, "instead of having a hardy native population to resist or overwhelm their ambitious and restless neighbours, had to depend on the occasional presence of ships of war." Again the island was subjected to the miseries attendant on ever-recurring hostilities. A squadron was sent by Queen Anne to make a clean sweep of the French; but Sir John Leake was not the man to do that, albeit he destroyed several French settlements and captured some vessels. He was followed, in 1703, by a fleet under Admiral Graydon, who did nothing. Two years later the French garrison at Placentia, reinforced by five hundred men from Canada, ravaged the whole island, taking several settlements, though they failed in an attempt upon St. John's. In the following year the tide of war turned in favour of the English, the enemy being expelled by Captain Underdown from their recent acquisitions, and otherwise put to defeat and check. But two years later (January, 1708), St. Ovide, the commander at Placentia, surprised and completely destroyed St. John's, afterwards seizing every British station except Carbonier, which was again stoutly defended by the settlers.

"The news of this misfortune produced great excitement in England," says Martin, "as the possession of the fisheries had ever been considered a point of immense importance, and an expedition was ordered . . . to attempt to dispossess the French; but little was effected beyond the destruction of a few fishing-stations." The fact is, the Government at home was so fully occupied with the warlike operations proceeding on the Continent, that they could bestow but little attention on so small a matter as a fishing colony three thousand miles away. However, some sort of amends were made by the brilliant successes of Marlborough and Prince Eugene, which placed England in a position to exact at Utrecht the favourable terms already referred to.

After this, until the breaking out of war between France and England in 1756, Newfoundland enjoyed a period of great prosperity, only interrupted by occasional disputes with the French, who had retained the right to cure and dry fish on the coast between Bonavista and Point Riche, and to occupy the small islands of St. Pierre and Miquelon, with a garrison of fifty men in each. In 1729 the island, which had been under the direction of the Governor of Nova Scotia, was formed into a separate province. Gradually administrative machinery was introduced and improved, and the lawlessness that had arisen from the long neglect to which the colony had been subjected brought under effective control. When the war broke out in which France lost all her American colonies, advantage was taken of the defenceless state of the island by a French squadron, which succeeded in taking St. John's, Carbonier, and the village of Trinity. The captors, however, were speedily dislodged by Lord Colville, who was in command of the British fleet in those waters.

Like Newfoundland, Nova Scotia also was for many years after its cession in an extremely unsettled state, partly on account of the resident French population, who, though they were treated with great leniency, neither rents nor taxes being required of them, were constantly suspected of inciting the Indians to acts of hostility, and partly on account of those aborigines themselves, who were very numerous, especially in the western portion of the province, and constantly breaking out into acts of depredation and outrage. At length the British colonists solicited aid from Massachusetts, and a well-planned attack was made (1724) upon a fort on the Kennebec, the chief stronghold of the Indians, which was taken with great slaughter, and served to overawe them for some time.

With the renewal of war in 1744, De Quesnal, the Governor of Cape Breton, surprised and took Canso, and twice laid ineffectual siege to Annapolis. The New Englanders retaliated by preparing a formidable armament for the reduction of Louisburg, the chief town of Cape Breton, which had been fortified at enormous expense by the French, with a view to the protection of their navigation and fisheries in those waters. This "Dunkirk of America" was protected by a rampart from 30 to 36 feet high and a ditch 80 feet wide. Its bastions and batteries contained embrasures for 148 cannon and 16 mortars, whereof only 45, however, were mounted. On an island at the entrance of the harbour was a battery of 30 guns, carrying 28-pound shot, while at the bottom of the harbour was another battery, called the Grand or Royal, of 28 guns, most of them 42-pounders. The entrance to the town was at the west gate over a drawbridge, near which was a circular battery, mounting sixteen 14-pounders.

Embarking for Canso in April, the colonial force was there joined by Commodore Warren with the fleet from the West India station, and on the 30th of the month arrived in view of Louisburg, and, coming upon the place by surprise, they easily effected a landing. A portion of the troops at once got round to the north-east harbour and burned the naval stores, the smoke whereof, driven into the Grand Battery, compelled the detachment holding it to retire into the town. The battery was occupied the next morning, and the spiked guns having been drilled, were turned with good effect upon the city. While the besieged were being thus entertained, the colonial forces were engaged during fourteen nights dragging the cannon over a morass. The siege was now pressed with vigour, and several unsuccessful attacks were made on the island battery. In the meanwhile Commodore Warren captured a French frigate of 74 guns, with a reinforcement of 560 men, and a large quantity of military stores. This seems to have decided Duchambon, the Governor, to surrender (June 16th), just as preparations were being urged forward for a grand assault. It was a splendid achievement for the colonials, and elated them immensely, especially Governor Shirley, whose con-

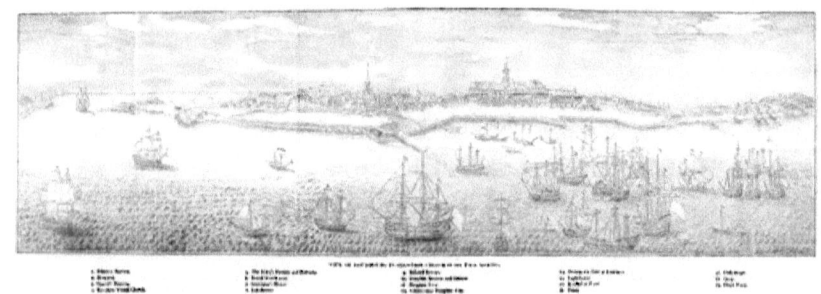

ception it was, and who now, rewarded by a baronetcy, made a still bolder bid for fame by submitting to the authorities in London a plan for the conquest of the whole of the French colonies in America. But, although the scheme was approved by the Government, and instructions were given to prepare land forces to co-operate with a fleet, nothing came of it.

In the meantime the operations of England against the Spanish possessions in America had been anything but successful, although one brilliant exploit had characterised the war. Admiral Vernon, having captured the important city of Porto Bello, on the American isthmus, induced Walpole to send out a large armament against the Spanish colonies. Vernon with a fleet, and Lord Cathcart with a powerful land force, were to assail the possessions of Spain on the side of the Atlantic, while Commodore Anson sailed round Cape Horn to ravage the coasts of Chili and Peru. The death of Cathcart and the incapacity of his successor rendered the operations on the Atlantic almost fruitless, although fifteen thousand men fell victims to the climate. Commodore Anson, in the meantime, was so buffeted by storms in getting round Cape Horn that he lost one of his ships, while two others were obliged to return. With his diminished squadron, however, he captured several prizes off the coast of Chili, and sacked the town of Paita in Peru. Reduced at length to one ship, the *Centurion*, with only 227 men out of 961 with which he left England, he captured the Spanish galleon, laden with treasure, that sailed annually from Manila to Acapulco (June 20, 1743). The value of the prize was enormous; and Anson, satisfied that nothing more was to be done, returned to England by the Cape of Good Hope, anchoring at Spithead on the 15th of June, 1744. The treasure was paraded through the streets of London in thirty-two waggons, guarded by the ship's company, with flags flying and music playing.

The news of the conquest of Cape Breton, and the reduction of the island of St. John—now Prince Edward Island—which soon followed, created an immense stir in France, and occasioned the despatch of a fleet for the recovery of those possessions such as the American waters had not yet seen. It was composed of seventy sail, carried 3150 disciplined troops, and was commanded by the Duke d'Anville, an officer of approved experience and ability. Sailing from Brest early in the summer of 1746, D'Anville was successful in eluding the vigilance of Admiral Martin, who had been sent out to watch his movements. After that his good fortune deserted him; his voyage was protracted by storms, and when he arrived at Chebucto—now Halifax—four of his largest ships were so shattered that they were obliged to return to France. These disappointments, with others, so preyed upon the Duke's mind that he died within a week of his arrival. His place was now taken by the Vice-Admiral, Distournelle. He suggested an immediate return to France, but was opposed by La Jonquière, the Governor of Canada, who was for making an immediate attack upon Annapolis. The harass and worry of the situation drove the poor Vice-Admiral out of his mind, and he ran himself through with his sword. La Jonquière now assumed the command; but he seemed to be blessed with little better luck than his predecessors. Rounding Cape Sable on his way to Annapolis, his ships were so shattered by storms and weakened by discord amongst the officers that everybody was glad to turn his back upon the fateful shore and get back to France; while the New Englanders, who had been greatly alarmed at this armament, sent up prayers of thankfulness for their deliverance.

This, however, was not the end of D'Anville's fleet. Upon its arrival in France, La Jonquière was immediately sent with thirty-eight sail to Nova Scotia, where he was so handled by Admirals Anson and Warren that he was thankful to get away with the loss of one of his men-of-war, from four to five thousand prisoners, and six richly laden Indiamen which were under his convoy.

It was a bitter pill for the colonists that, by the Treaty of Aix-la-Chapelle in the following year (1748), they were obliged to restore Cape Breton to France, the British Ministry having agreed to do so on condition of the Low Countries being given up to Maria Theresa, to maintain "the balance of power in Europe." Nova Scotia, however, was maintained, and as the peace left a vast number of military and naval men without employment, it was decided by the Government to offer inducements for a large contingent of them to settle in this province.

The idea was seized upon with avidity, and in May, 1749, between three and four thousand emigrants of this description, with their families, landed at Chebucto harbour, under the direction of the Hon. Edward Cornwallis, who had been appointed Governor. The town of Halifax was built and its harbour fortified; and Nova Scotia began to rise rapidly in importance.

The French, who had hitherto regarded the province as little better than a barren waste, commenced now to raise disputes concerning its boundaries; and the settlers, from both countries, did not always arrange their differences by amicable means. Of still greater moment were the differences which arose in respect to the interior, where, notwithstanding the Treaty of Utrecht, which relinquished such claims, the French still aimed at sovereignty. They were naturally anxious to establish a communication between the Canadas in the north and Louisiana in the south. This could only be effected by depriving the English of rights they had obtained west of the Alleghany Mountains. The Pennsylvanians had carried on trade with the Indians of the Ohio Valley for many years; they were followed by gentlemen of Virginia and Maryland, who obtained from the Government a grant of five hundred thousand acres west of the Alleghanies, between the Monongahela and the Kanawha. The company was chartered under the name of the Ohio Company, and preparations made for a settlement. But before any active steps could be taken the French interfered. The Governor of Canada sent his brother with three hundred men to the banks of the Ohio, to assert the French claims and to set the Indians against the English. He ordered the Pennsylvanian traders to quit the country, and wrote to the Governor of that colony, informing him that any one found there in future would be severely dealt with. Several servants of the Ohio company were taken prisoners and sent to a fort on Lake Erie. Following up these measures, the French built forts on the banks of the Ohio and Niagara, and, in short, completed the chain of fortified posts from the St. Lawrence to New Orleans.

News of these doings having reached England, the Government required that the fort at Niagara should be destroyed, and other encroachments put a stop to. The French government promised to observe their treaty engagements, but apparently only with a view to gain time; for De Bienville, the Governor of Canada, not only increased the number of his forts, but incited his people to acts of hostility against the English all along the frontier, from Nova Scotia to Ohio. This state of things could not long exist without leading to war, and war soon followed. Hostilities were commenced by the colonial authorities.

The Governor of Virginia, judging that it was time to act, sent a missive to the commander of the fort of Au Beuf, demanding, in the name of the King, that he should desist from his operations. The bearer was George Washington, then a young Virginia planter, who, with a single attendant, made his way in the depth of winter a distance of two hundred miles, through a country infested by Indians of a treacherous character.[1] The officer in charge of the fort answered that he was under the command of the Governor of Canada, and that he must carry out his instructions.

It was now decided to build forts to oppose those of the French, and a regiment was raised in Virginia and placed under the command of Washington, then only twenty-one years of age, with which he marched into the disputed territory. He found the French at work on a fort, and, considering that they had invaded British territory, he surprised them in their camp at night and compelled them to surrender. He then proceeded to erect a fort on the spot, which he called Fort Necessity; and, being reinforced by two companies from New York and North Carolina, marched to dislodge the enemy from Fort Du Quesne, which had been newly erected. Finding, however, that it had been largely reinforced, he deeemd it advisable to fall back on Fort Necessity, which he had scarcely gained before it was attacked by De Villiers, and, after a day's fighting, compelled to surrender, Washington and his little garrison going out with all the honours of war.

Divided counsels now breaking out amongst the colonies, the Ministry saw that it was time to take the matter vigorously in hand; and in January, 1755, a force was despatched under General Braddock to dislodge the French from the frontiers of Pennsylvania and Virginia, and from the Valley of the Ohio. Owing to the rashness of that com-

[1] Irving, *Life of Washington*.

mander, and his refusal to profit by the local knowledge of the provincial officers, the British suffered a severe defeat. Falling into an ambuscade of French and Indians, Braddock, instead of endeavouring to extricate himself, attempted to make a stand. At length he was slain, while vainly striving to rally his men, and the regular troops fled with disgraceful precipitation. It is deserving of remark that the provincial militia, commanded by Washington, now Major, did not share the panic of the Royal troops, but displayed great coolness and presence of mind.

Somewhat earlier than these unfortunate events, Colonel Monckton had reduced all the French forts within the limits of Nova Scotia. These operations were effected with a force which had been rapidly got together in New York. His first capture was a fort named Beau Sejour, recently erected by the French on the narrow neck of land connecting Nova Scotia with New Brunswick, which was obliged to surrender after four days' bombardment. On the following day Monckton drove the enemy from another stronghold, situated upon the river Gaspereaux, taking a large quantity of provisions and other stores. Other posts were abandoned without a blow. Two other expeditions, against the Forts of Niagara and Crown Point, were not so successful, although General Johnson, who commanded that against the latter, gained a victory over the hostile army. At sea the British arms were more effectually displayed. Two sail of the line were taken by Admiral Boscawen off Newfoundland, and more than three hundred merchant vessels were brought as prizes into the ports of Great Britain.

One act of signal cruelty marked these hostilities between the two nations. The French population of Nova Scotia, which greatly outnumbered the British, were a cause of great anxiety. Their sympathies naturally were with their own people; and though the large proportion of them were peaceful and docile subjects, there were others who were the reverse, and who, there was reason to apprehend, would be only too ready to assist the French should they attempt an invasion of the colony. Seeing that the Acadians numbered between 17,000 and 18,000, while the British were only about 5000, it cannot be said that their alarm was unreasonable. Nevertheless, it is hard to justify the course which the authorities decided to take. Assembling them in their respective settlements, under the pretence of making some communication relative to their welfare, they then, without giving them time for any preparation, forced the Acadians on board a number of vessels provided for the purpose, and dispersed them over the colonies of New England, New York, and Virginia. Every one knows the story, as told by Longfellow, in his pathetic poem of *Evangeline;* and if the Acadians who were thus heartlessly exiled in 1755 did not all exhibit the pastoral innocence and simplicity of the poet's people, they were far from deserving the fate that befell them. But, as Haliburton puts it in his *History of Nova Scotia*, " if the Acadians had to lament that they were condemned unheard, that their accusers were also their judges, and that their sentence was disproportioned to their offence, they had also much reason to attribute their misfortunes to the intrigues of their countrymen in Canada, who seduced them from their allegiance to a Government which was disposed to extend to them its protection and regard, and instigated them to a rebellion which it was easy to foresee would end in their ruin."

Notwithstanding these various acts of hostility, a formal declaration of war was delayed. Its publication was the signal for one of the fiercest struggles wherein modern Europe had yet been involved.

CHAPTER IV.

CLIVE BEGINS HIS CAREER IN INDIA.

WHEN with the fall of Walpole his pacific policy was changed for one of war with France, hostilities were not long in spreading to India, where the French, from their stronghold at Pondicherry, were pushing their fortunes with ever-increasing boldness. Several officers of approved ability were now sent out, in the hope that they would be able to strike a blow at the English settlements. The chief of these was Labourdonnais, a man of high character and singular ability, who had risen from a low rank in the French Navy to be Governor of the islands of Mauritius and Bourbon. On the 14th of September, 1746, he suddenly appeared off Madras with a squadron and 3600 men, a large number of whom were Europeans, the rest being Sepoys and natives of Madagascar, and commenced an attack upon it.

The settlement of Madras, which had for a hundred years been the chief station of the English on the Coromandel coast, extended five miles along the shore and about a mile inland. The town consisted of three sections. The first, which was called

MADRAS.
(From an engraving by J. G. Martini.)

the White Town, numbered about fifty houses, and was inhabited by the English and other Europeans under their protection. It contained also the warehouses and other buildings of the Company, including two churches, and was surrounded by a wall, strengthened by bastions and four batteries, but of no great strength. Adjoining Fort St. George, as it was designated, on the north was the division in which resided the Armenian and the richer of the Hindu traders, who, on their northern border, were flanked by a wide district inhabited by natives in the miserable huts of the country. These two sections were known as the Black Town. The whole population of the Presidency numbered about 250,000; of these, the English did not exceed 300 men, while 200 of them constituted the garrison of the fort, the remainder consisting of Armenians, Mahomedans, and Hindus, the last being by far the most numerous. With the exception of Goa, Madras was the most important European settlement in India, both as regards size and opulence.

It may be imagined that, with its small garrison and slender defences, it was but ill-prepared to sustain an attack, and, after a bombardment of five days, it capitulated, Labourdonnais pledging himself on his honour to restore the settlement on payment of a fixed ransom. On these terms it was received into the town. So far as the captor was concerned, he scrupulously observed the terms of the capitulation, protecting the persons and property of the inhabitants, but taking possession of the magazines and warehouses of the Company.

At this time the French colonies in the East consisted of the Isles of Bourbon and France (now Mauritius), on the eastern side of Madagascar, and the town and territory of Pondicherry, with the factories of Mahé, Karical, and Chandernagore, on the mainland. They were under the control of the respective presidencies or governments of the Isle of France and Pondicherry. These governments were similar in constitution to the English presidencies, although the Governor was allowed to exercise a much greater share of power than was the case in the English settlements. Labourdonnais was the Governor of the islands (appointed in 1745), and M. Duplaix the Governor of Pondicherry, and upon them more than on any one else depended the fortunes of the French in India. Both were remarkable men, both possessed exceptional powers for organisation and command; and it is hardly too much to say that, had they been able to work together in harmony, the future of India might have been very different from what it is; but they could not, and so the French lost their chance.

Joseph François Duplaix, whose influence proved so momentous to the destinies of Hindustan, was the son of a director of the French East India Company, and a farmer-general of the revenues. His interest secured the younger Duplaix a place in the Council of Pondicherry in 1720. Devoting himself with great assiduity to the business of his office, he soon became minutely acquainted with the commerce of the country, and was thus enabled greatly to enrich himself by private trade. After ten years at

Pondicherry, he was transferred to Chandernagore, in Bengal, where, as superintendent of the Company's affairs, he soon brought about such a transformation as to make that settlement, which had been in a languishing condition, a scene of the greatest activity and prosperity. Besides thus raising the condition of Chandernagore, M. Duplaix established a new factory at Patna, and generally so stirred up French commerce in Bengal that it was the envy of other European colonies.[1]

From this post he was recalled to Pondicherry as Governor in 1742. The Company was then in debt, and he was required as his first duty to reduce expenses. It was also represented to him that war was impending between France and the maritime powers. This information caused Duplaix to turn his attention to the fortifying of Pondicherry, which was entirely open to the sea, although he was expressly forbidden to do so by his instructions. He had, however, his own views in regard to the future of France in India, and he proceeded with the work of fortification as a primary duty. He was still struggling to put the place in a defensible position when Labourdonnais arrived—he, too, with his views of a French empire to be carved out in the East.

The two men, however, were quite different in character. Although Duplaix was undoubtedly a man of great business ability and of wide views, he appears to have been of a low and sordid turn of mind, and incapable of carrying out a lofty ambition because of a jealousy and vanity that could not

[1] Mill.

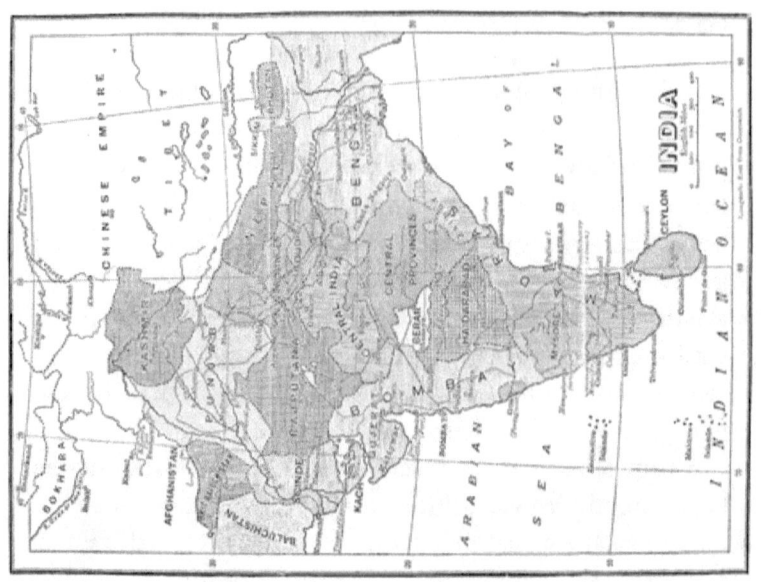

allow others to shine before or in conjunction with himself. This was the reason of his working so inharmoniously with Labourdonnais, whose higher qualities and superior ability he doubtless perceived from the first. Even previous to his capture of Madras, Duplaix had shown the pettiness of his spirit by hampering and thwarting his colleague in every possible way.

He now carried his malignancy to still further lengths. It was in consequence of the distinct orders of the directors that Labourdonnais agreed to the restoration of Madras. Duplaix, with his ambitious views, was greatly averse to such an abandonment of the place, and did everything he could—going even to the extent of using threats— to turn the former from his purpose. Labourdonnais, however, would not hear of any departure from the agreement into which he had entered, and proceeded with his arrangements to evacuate Madras by the 15th of October. This opposition exasperated Duplaix beyond bounds, and he refused all assistance or co-operation to get the things removed before the arrival of the storms which accompany the change of monsoon. In these disputes valuable time was lost, and the very thing the brave sailor tried to obviate befell: a storm arose on the night of the 13th of October, which drove the ships to sea, wrecking two, and terribly shattering the rest. Even in the midst of these calamities, Duplaix remained inexorable. At length it was suggested that the terms of the treaty should be so far altered as to give time to the French for the removal of the goods. Labourdonnais and the English agreed, though not without misgivings, to extend the period of evacuation from the 15th of October to the 15th of January. This was all that the Governor of Pondicherry desired. He knew that in the meanwhile Labourdonnais would be required elsewhere, and that Madras would have to be delivered into his hands—to keep or relinquish, as he chose.

The remainder of Labourdonnais's career is an apt exemplification of the fact that truth and honour do not always prevail. After sailing to the islands to put the affairs of his government in order, he took passage in a Dutch ship for Europe, in order to make his defence, or answer the accusations of his enemies. By the declaration of war the vessel was forced into an English harbour, and Labourdonnais was recognised and made prisoner. The story of his doings at Madras had already reached England, and caused him to be received with favour and distinction by all classes of society. In order that he might return to France, a director of the East India Company offered to be security for him with his person and property; but the Government, with equal generosity, declined the offer, requiring no other security than the word of Labourdonnais. Very different was his treatment at home. "The representations of Duplaix had arrived: a brother of Duplaix was a director of the East India Company; Duplaix had only violated a solemn treaty; Labourdonnais had only faithfully and gloriously served his country; and he was thrown into the Bastile. He remained in that prison three years;

though the vindication which he published of his conduct, and the authentic documents by which he supported it, fully established his innocence, and the ardour and ability of his services. He survived his liberation but a little time, and left a memorable example of the manner in which a blind government encourages desert;" thus Mill. Voltaire, among other praises, says of him: "Il fit plus; il dispersa une escadre Anglaise dans la mer de l'Inde, ce qui n'etoit jamais arrivé qu'à lui, et ce qu'on n'a pas revu depuis."[1]

Labourdonnais had scarcely taken his departure from Madras ere the Nawab of Arcot, who was the ally of the English, sent an army to drive out the French. It happened, however, that the brave sailor, in consequence of the disaster that befell his ships, was obliged to leave behind him about twelve hundred Europeans, whom he had carefully disciplined. With these the French met the Hindus, and gave them so sharp an encounter with their artillery, that they speedily broke and fled, although vastly more numerous than the victorious force. This was the first time for more than a century, says Orme, that "any of the European nations had gained a decisive advantage in war against the officers of the Great Mogul," and its effect was of the most momentous importance, since it broke the spell by which the Europeans had been held in a sort of superstitious awe of the native powers.

Duplaix now—as was all along his intention—annulled Labourdonnais's treaty, and gave orders to his

[1] *Frag. Hist. sur l'Inde.*

officers at Madras to seize every article of property except the clothes of the wearers, the furniture of the houses, and the jewels of the women. His commands were executed without the slightest compunction; and to this betrayal was added the indignity of carrying the Governor and the principal inhabitants prisoners to Pondicherry, where they were paraded by Duplaix in a sort of triumph. All who were left in Madras were required to promise not to commit any act of hostility against the French.

Some of the inhabitants, with several of the military officers, determined not to give the parole that was demanded of them, and, escaping out of the town at night, made their way to Fort St. David. The Company had here a larger territory than that of Madras. The fort, which was situated near the sea, was twelve miles south of Pondicherry. Though small, it was stronger than any of its size in India. About a mile to the south of it was situated the town of Cuddalore, in which many natives resided, including some of the principal Indian merchants. Three of its sides were defended by walls flanked with bastions; the fourth side, toward the sea, was open, although protected by a stream, which was separated from the sea by a mound of sand. To the westward of the fort, and within the Company's territory, were several populous villages, inhabited by natives. The government of Fort St. David was dependent on that of Madras; but on the breach of Labourdonnais's treaty, the Company's agents there took upon themselves the general administration of affairs on the Coromandel coast.

M. Duplaix was resolved to take Fort St. David, and sent a force composed of Europeans and natives for that purpose. It consisted of 1700 men, of whom fifty were cavalry. Their artillery comprised six field-pieces and as many mortars. They arrived within a mile and a half of the fort, but were then surprised, while resting at a country house belonging to the Governor, by the Nawab's Army, under the command of his sons Maphuse Khan and Mahomed Ali, and compelled to retreat to Arioncopang with a loss of twelve Europeans killed and one hundred and twenty wounded. This took place, according to Orme, on the 9th of December.

Not to be turned from his purpose, M. Duplaix now formed a project to take Cuddalore by surprise, at the same time entering into negotiations with the Nawab to induce him to withdraw his troops. Five hundred men were embarked in boats at Arioncopang, with instructions to seize Cuddalore from the river at break of day; but no sooner were their craft through the surf than the wind became so high that the expedition had to put back.

The French again marched against Fort St. David on the 2d of March; an engagement took place between them and the English garrison and a troop of horse at the crossing of the river Panua. The French succeeded in passing the river, and the English retired to the fort. The next day, however, perceiving a number of ships approaching from the north, the French recrossed the river and made all haste back to Pondicherry. The ships proved to be the British squadron under Admiral Griffin, with reinforcements. While the ships remained on the coast no further attempts were made against the English.

In the month of January, 1748, Major Lawrence arrived from England at Fort St. David, commissioned to take charge of all the Company's forces in India. Some time later, while Admiral Griffin was in pursuit of a French squadron which had appeared off the coast, M. Duplaix determined to take advantage of his absence and make another attack upon Cuddalore. Eight hundred Europeans, with one thousand Sepoys, marched from Pondicherry, and arrived within three miles of the town, where they rested during the day, designing to take the place by surprise at night. Major Lawrence, hearing of this intention, ordered the garrison to march and the cannon to be removed to Fort St. David, his purpose being to make the French believe that he could not hold the place. But at nightfall the garrison, greatly augmented, returned with the guns to Cuddalore, precaution being taken to prevent the enemy from learning of their stratagem.

In due course the French advanced with their scaling-ladders; but no sooner had they begun to place them against the walls than they received the fire of all the musketry from the ramparts, together with that of four or five guns laden with grape-shot. This unexpected reception threw the whole force, officers as well as men, into a panic, and they fled, many of them throwing away their arms, and not stopping until they reached the bounds of Pondicherry.

The home Government, deeply concerned by the disaster which had befallen the English in India, and at the growing ascendency of the French in the Peninsula, despatched a formidable armament to the East, consisting of nine ships of war, under the command of Admiral Boscawen. It set sail from England towards the end of 1747, accompanied by eleven ships of the Company carrying stores and troops. Boscawen was instructed to take the island of Mauritius on his way; but, after examining the coast and its defences, he resolved to leave it alone, and proceeding on his way to India, arrived at Fort St. David in August. This squadron, joined to that under Griffin, formed the largest naval armament that any European power had yet sent to India.

Preparations were now made to advance on Pondicherry; but the military genius which was never afterwards lacking in India, was as yet conspicuous by its absence, and the whole of the operations against the French stronghold miscarried in such a way as to give Duplaix the opportunity to boast of a signal victory over the English, and to cause the English to be regarded by the natives " as only a secondary and inferior people."[1]

At this juncture the intelligence arrived that an armistice had taken place between England and France; and this was shortly after followed by the news of the peace of Aix-la-Chapelle (October 7, 1748). By that treaty Madras was restored, and it was delivered up in the month of August following. At the same time the town of San Tomé, formerly

[1] Mill.

belonging to the Portuguese, and the Catholic priests of which had been found to be hostile to the English, was taken, and the mischievous part of the inhabitants compelled to leave.

In the meanwhile events had been taking place which opened an entirely new chapter in the history of the East India Company. Duplaix had for some time been intriguing with the native princes, with the most extensive views in his head in regard to French domination. The knowledge of these schemes, and the activity with which the Governor of Pondicherry was pushing them, seems to have roused the jealousy and distrust of the English, and, perhaps, was a largely exciting cause of what now happened.

Sahujee, a Hindu, who had some years before acquired and lost the throne of Tanjore, proposed to the English at Fort St. David that they should assist him against his brother, Pretaupa Sing, who had dethroned him, offering to reward them with the fort and country of Devicotta if he were successful, and the payment of all expenses. The English closed with the offer; and in April, 1749, a force, composed of Europeans and Sepoys, marched from Fort St. David into Tanjore, which was a small Rajahship covering little more than the space enclosed and intersected by the mouths of the river Cauvery. The Coleroon, the northernmost branch of that river, bounded it in that direction, and upon it stood Devicotta, at a point where the channel, within the bar, was capable of receiving ships of the largest burthen, while there was not another port from Cape Comorin to Masulipatam which could receive a vessel of three hundred tons. The troops proceeded by land, while the cannon and provisions were conveyed by sea. There seemed to be a complete lack of plan and organisation, and the expedition miscarried.

Ashamed of such a miserable result, the rulers of Madras resolved to make a second attempt. A new expedition was therefore fitted out, again commanded by Major Lawrence, and, proceeding wholly by sea, was this time successful. But its success was due as much to the ingenuity of a common ship's carpenter as to anybody else. After a three days' bombardment a breach was made in the fort; but no advantage could be taken of it till the river was crossed. The passage was dangerous both from the rapidity of the stream and the number of soldiers in the thickets lining the opposite shore. In this dilemma John Moore, the carpenter, constructed a raft capable of carrying four hundred men, and then swam the river in the night, fastened a rope to a tree, carefully concealed it in the bushes and water, and returned without being perceived. Before the raft began to move, several guns directed their fire to the spot where the rope was tied, compelling the enemy to remove too far away to perceive it. The raft was then sent across several times, and the whole of the troops landed on the opposite bank.

A young man who had been brought up to the pen rather than the sword, offered to lead the attack. This was Clive, who had been in the Company's employ in a civil capacity. But war no sooner broke out than he elected to go into active service. He had given signal proofs of his courage at the siege of Pondicherry; he did the like now. Leading the attack with a platoon of Europeans and seven hundred Sepoys, he allowed himself, at the head of the former, to be separated from the Sepoys, and narrowly escaped with his life.[1]

Shortly after the taking of the place, a truce was concluded; the reigning Rajah of Tanjore, Pretaupa Sing, agreeing to surrender to the English the town and fort, together with the adjoining territory; and they, on their part, undertaking not only to renounce the support of the pretender to the throne, for whom they had entered into the contest, but to secure his person, so that he might give no more trouble to his Royal brother. It was not a nice business; and Sahujee was lucky to escape from the clutches of the rulers at Madras, who do not seem to have been people at all nice in their notions of right and wrong.

While the English were employing themselves over this small acquisition, the French had been busily carrying out an intrigue which effected a complete revolution in the Carnatic, and so greatly involved the English in its throes that henceforth the history of Hindustan becomes almost a part of the history of Great Britain. The series of events which led up to the existing condition of affairs in the Carnatic need not be recapitulated; suffice it to state that on the death of the Nizam-al-Mulk, the Subahdar of the Deccan, in 1748, at the age of one hundred and four, there arose a rivalry for the government

[1] Orme.

of the Carnatic, which was dependent upon that of the Deccan. An'war-ad-Dien held the reins; but he was unpopular, and a strong desire prevailed to depose him and put in his place Chunda Sahib, who belonged to the Sadatullah family, which had ruled in the Carnatic for many years prior to the advent of An'war-ad-Dien, whom the Nizam-al-Mulk had raised temporarily to the Nawabship. Chunda Sahib was the only member of the Sadatullah family who possessed the ability necessary for so onerous a position; and Duplaix seems to have early marked him out as a convenient instrument for his ambition.

But while Chunda Sahib and An'war-ad-Dien were rivals for the government of the Carnatic, there were also competitors for the throne of the Deccan. These were Nazir Jung, the second son of the late Nazir-al-Mulk, and Mirzapha Jung, a grandson, whom, it was given out and believed, the old man had appointed to be his successor. Chunda Sahib threw in his fortunes with Mirzapha; both regarded Duplaix as an invaluable ally, while he, by becoming the means of raising to power a Subahdar of the Deccan and a Nawab of the Carnatic,[1] counted upon reaping the greatest advantages for himself as well as for his country. Chunda Sahib prevailed on Mirzapha Jung to commence operations in the Carnatic, and they proceeded thither with an army of forty thousand men, which was augmented by a French force of four hundred Europeans and nearly two thousand Sepoys, under the command of M. d'Auteuil. An'war-ad-Dien was encountered (Au-

[1] Mill.

gust 3, 1749) fifty miles west of Arcot, the capital of the Carnatic, and, after a stubborn fight, defeated and slain. His eldest son was taken prisoner, his second, Mahomed Ali, escaping with the wreck of the army to Trichinopoly, of which he was Governor.

Contrary to the advice of Duplaix, as he affirms,[1] the conquerors wasted time at Arcot, which surrendered at the first summons, instead of proceeding at once to Trichinopoly. They then spent some weeks at Pondicherry, and finally, towards the end of October, directed their march to the City of Tanjore, with the object of plundering the Rajah, who, in addition to a demand for arrears of tribute, was squeezed to the extent of two lacs of rupees and eighty-one villages—these by way of payment for the assistance of the French.[2] In this operation of raising supplies precious time was allowed to slip by, until, with the end of December, news came that Nazir Jung, the Subahdar, was on his march to attack them. In the greatest alarm they broke up their camp and made their way back to Pondicherry.

The invasion of the Carnatic and the defeat of An'war-ad-Dien happened while the English were engaged in the Tanjore affair, and seem to have struck them with consternation, the more so as Boscawen, with the fleet and troops, had been allowed to leave for home at the end of October. However, the arrival of Nazir Jung at the head of a large army inspired them with renewed courage. They had already, in response to Mahomed Ali's appeal for

---

[1] *Memoir pour Duplaix.*
[2] Sir John Malcolm, *Life of Lord Clive.*

help, sent some small detachments to Trichinopoly, as well as afforded some assistance to the Rajah of Tanjore. Nazir Jung now summoned Mahomed Ali to join him, and at the same time solicited the aid of the English at Fort St. David. The Company's agents appear at first to have had some doubts as to the possibility of complying with this request, seeing that England and France were at peace; they finally gave their consent, however, and Major Lawrence, determining to follow the example of the French in representing the English as mere auxiliaries, joined the Subahdar with six hundred Europeans.

The two armies were now almost face to face with each other, and a battle seemed imminent, when suddenly the whole aspect of affairs was changed through the resignation of thirteen French officers, who were angry at not having shared in the spoils of Tanjore. D'Auteuil, who was again in command—Duplaix himself always keeping at a discreet distance from danger, because the sound of firing disarranged his ideas—feeling that it would be unwise to risk a fight with men thus disaffected, withdrew in the night, and made for Pondicherry. Mirzapha Jung and Chunda Sahib were now at their wits' ends, and, not knowing what else to do, the one gave himself up to his uncle, who at once placed him in fetters, while the other, with his troops, went after the French to Pondicherry.

Thus, as it were at a whiff, the whole scene was changed, and the allies of the English seemed triumphant; but a squabble with Nazir Jung about some territory near Madras, which had been promised to the English in recompense for their aid, caused Major Lawrence to return with his men to Fort St. David. In the meantime Duplaix, ever ready with a new scheme and fresh intrigues, had been at work in the victorious army. While on the one hand he offered terms of peace to the Subahdar, on the other he was instigating some of his disaffected chiefs to mutiny and murder. He had already pacified the French officers and restored the spirit of his little army, so that D'Auteuil was able to take the field again, and with three hundred men to effect an entrance into the Subahdar's camp by night and inflict so grievous a loss upon him that he was glad to withdraw from the neighbourhood of so crafty an enemy, and take refuge in Arcot.

The French now followed up this success by several others. A small body of troops sailed to Masulipatam, at the mouth of the river Kistna, and took it by a night attack with but little loss; another detachment seized the pagoda of Trivadi, about fifteen miles to the west of Fort St. David; while a third force advanced against the famous rock-fortress of Gingee, deemed the strongest in the Carnatic. This daring exploit seemed to strike terror into the natives,[1] and at last brought Nazir Jung out of his harem at Arcot. He moved with his army towards Gingee, at the same time putting himself in communication with Duplaix. But the Frenchman had now completed his terms with the mutinous Patan chiefs; they sent the concerted summons to the commander at Gingee, who at once

[1] Orme

marched to meet the Subahdar with four thousand men, who broke into his camp, and were joined by the traitors, a couple of bullets from whom, as he was mounting his war-elephant, settled the affairs of Nazir Jung.

The revolution effected by these Patan shots freed Mirzapha from his imprisonment and invested him with the coveted Subahdarship. To reward the French, he gave them a large share of Nazir Jung's treasures, and appointed Duplaix Governor of all the Mogul dominions on the Coromandel coast from the river Kistna to Cape Comorin, with Chunda Sahib as his deputy at Arcot.

One thing, however, the new Subahdar and his powerful ally had failed to do: they had not satisfied the Patan chiefs for their perfidy; and when, in the month of January, 1751, Mirzapha Jung set out from Pondicherry *en route* for Hyderabad, his capital, accompanied by a body of French troops, under the command of M. Bussy, who above all others had signalised himself in the late transactions, they had barely gone sixty leagues ere a disturbance, apparently accidental, broke out among a portion of the troops. It was the Patans in revolt again; they had seized a defile through which the army had to pass, and were disposed to force the Subahdar to give them better terms for their treachery. The French fought their way through with great spirit, using their artillery to great advantage; but Mirzapha died as his predecessor had done, and almost before his body was cold the energetic M. Bussy— the "French Clive," as he has been called—appointed a new Subahdar in the person of Salabut Jung, who happened to be in the camp, and continued his march to Hyderabad.

This sudden change of affairs, together with the apparently helpless condition of the English, caused Mahomed Ali to contemplate joining the French and giving up Trichinopoly. Fortunately, Duplaix had been rendered haughty and exacting, and Mahomed, receiving some timely support from the presidency of Fort St. David, was encouraged to persevere in his defence. The English contingents, however, badly commanded, were almost useless, while the siege of Trichinopoly was being pressed by Chunda Sahib, with some French assistance.

Trichinopoly, famous in the annals of the British in India, is situated on the south side of the river Cauvery, at a distance of about ninety miles from the sea. For an Indian city it was fortified with extraordinary strength. A few miles above Trichinopoly the Cauvery divides into two branches, which, some fifteen miles below the city, are only prevented from again uniting by a narrow mound, forming a peninsula, which is known as the Island of Seringham, "celebrated," says Mill, "as containing one of the most remarkable structures, and one of the most venerable pagodas, in India."

While the Council of Fort St. David were doing all they could to support Mahomed Ali, albeit to little purpose, young Clive suggested a plan for relieving Trichinopoly, which he was willing to execute, and which, in a lucky hour, the presidency adopted. This was no less than to make a sudden attack upon Arcot, Chunda Sahib's capital. To effect this daring object, Clive was furnished with two hundred Europeans and three hundred Sepoys, who were commanded by eight officers, six of whom had never been in action, while four were young men newly drafted from the mercantile service of the Company. For artillery they had three field-pieces. With this slender force Clive, now Captain, set out from Madras on the 25th of August, 1751. On the 31st they halted within ten miles of Arcot. Natives who had come across them, reported with awe that they had seen the English marching without concern in the midst of a terrific storm of thunder, lightning, and rain. The news struck terror into the garrison, and they at once abandoned the fort, although in numbers they were three times the strength of the force which was advancing against them. On taking possession, the English found their slender artillery augmented by eight guns, besides food for them in the form of lead and gunpowder.

Anticipating a siege, Clive exerted himself to the utmost to supply the fort with provisions and place it in a defensible condition; and, as the erewhile garrison remained in the vicinity, he harassed them by frequent attacks, beating up their camp at night, and thus keeping both them and the natives generally in awe of his daring and audacity.

The possession of Arcot soon produced the effect Clive had anticipated. Chunda Sahib despatched four thousand of his best troops from Trichinopoly, under his son, Rajah Sahib, to lay siege to the fort.

Being joined by the forces already in the neighbourhood, by a hundred and fifty French from Pondicherry, and other bands, Rajah Sahib found himself in command of an army of upwards of eight thousand men, with which he hoped to be more than a match for Clive and his handful of English and Sepoys.

Clive resolved to make an effort to drive the enemy out of the town; but, after a long fight in the streets, in which he lost fifteen of his English soldiers and one of his officers, he was compelled to fall back by the French artillery. "The next day," says Mill, "the enemy were reinforced with two thousand men from Vellore. The fort was more than a mile in circumference; the walls in many places ruinous; the towers inconvenient and decayed, and everything unfavourable to defence; yet Clive found the means of making an effectual resistance. When the enemy attempted to storm at two breaches, one of fifty and one of ninety feet, he repulsed them with but eighty Europeans and a hundred and twenty Sepoys fit for duty; so effectually did he avail himself of his feeble resources, and to such a pitch of fortitude had he exalted the spirits of those under his command. During the following night the enemy abandoned the town with precipitation, after they had maintained the siege for fifty days. A reinforcement from Madras joined him on the following day; and, leaving a small garrison in Arcot, he set out to pursue the enemy. With the assistance of a small body of Mahrattas, who joined him in hopes of plunder, he gave the enemy, now

VIEW OF THE ROCK AT TRICHINOPOLY.
(From a drawing by Captain Trapaud.)

greatly reduced by the dropping away of the auxiliaries, a defeat at Arni, and recovered Conjeveram, into which the French had thrown a garrison, and where they had behaved with barbarity to some English prisoners." After strengthening the garrison at Arcot, Clive returned to Fort St. David about the end of December.

By these successes of the daring young commander, Mahomed Ali, in place of being besieged in Trichinopoly, saw a great part of the Carnatic brought under his dominion, and ready to acknowledge him as Nawab. But the enemy, though checked, were not beaten, and, in fact, soon had another force in the field, with which they began to lay waste the Company's territory. Reinforced by some troops which had unexpectedly arrived from Bengal, Clive sallied out in February, 1752, to meet them. The French numbered 400 Europeans and 4500 natives, horse and foot, with a train of artillery; the English mustered only 1680, of whom 1300 were Sepoys, with six field-pieces. But such was the terror inspired by Clive's name that the enemy were afraid to join issue with him, and abandoned one position after another on his approach. However, at Covrepank, he came up with them, and, after a determined fight, gave them a signal thrashing. Nine guns were taken, and sixty French soldiers. Nearly as many of that nation were found dead on the field, besides three hundred native troops. After this disaster the enemy dispersed, and Clive returned to the presidency.

It was now resolved to send Clive to Trichinopoly,

and in a few days he was ready to start. But Major Lawrence, who in the meanwhile had been to England, on the 26th of March returned to Madras, and took command of the reinforcements, which consisted of four hundred Europeans and eleven hundred Sepoys, with eight guns and some military stores. An attempt was made to intercept the force on its way to Trichinopoly, but it proved unavailing. As Mahomed Ali had prevailed on the Hindu government of Mysore to send an army twenty thousand strong to his assistance, and this force was further augmented by five thousand Tanjorines, the French were seized with dismay, and, to the annoyance of Chunda Sahib, it is said, resolved to break up their camp before Trichinopoly and pass over to the island of Seringham. Moreover, in the hurry of their retreat, being unable to carry over a large portion of their provisions, it had to be burned.

Of these stores they were soon in need; for, at his own suggestion, Clive was sent across the Coleroon to intercept supplies from that side; and so effectually did he do the work that, though Duplaix sent succour and aid to his people, D'Auteuil, who was in command of the reinforcements, was driven to take refuge in an old fort, and finally constrained to surrender. The same fate soon befell his countrymen on the island. In sore distress for provisions, their camp mercilessly cannonaded by the English, and finally deserted by Chunda Sahib and his troops, the French at length capitulated and surrendered themselves prisoners of war. Chunda Sahib, deserted by his troops, gave himself up to the commander of the Tanjorine forces, who, after promising him protection, cut off his head and sent it to Mahomed Ali, in order to settle a dispute which arose between the latter, the Rajah of Mysore, some Mahratta chiefs who were in his pay, and the Tanjorines, as to who should have his person. Thus ended Chunda Sahib, in the good old Indian way.

A contention now arose amongst the successful leaders as to the spoils of war; but ere any satisfactory settlement could be arrived at, Major Lawrence was called upon to combat the French in other quarters. Contrary to his advice, he was required first of all to reduce Gingee; but in that enterprise he suffered a reverse with loss. However, he was enabled to take his revenge very soon after by inflicting a severe defeat upon a French force which had ventured within two miles of Fort St. David.

Clive was now sent to drive the French out of the fort of Covelong, about twenty miles south of Madras. Although the place mounted thirty pieces of cannon, and was garrisoned by fifty French and three hundred Sepoys, Clive succeeded in taking it with four 24-pounders, five hundred newly raised Sepoys, and two hundred raw recruits, said to be " the very refuse of the gaols of London," of whom he made heroes. After reducing Covelong, Clive defeated a force coming from the fort of Chingleput to its relief, and then, marching forty miles, compelled the commander of that stronghold to surrender.

Clive now returned to Madras, and, finding his health, never very robust, greatly impaired by the enormous labours and fatigues to which he had been subjected in the late campaigns, he proceeded to England by the first ship that sailed.

As Clive may almost be called the maker of India, Mill's brief account of his striking career will not be out of place here. "This young man," says he, "was the son of a gentleman of small fortune in Shropshire. From the unattractableness of his disposition, or the unsteadiness of his father's, he was moved from one to another through a great variety of schools. At school he was daring, impetuous, averse to application, and impatient of control. At the age of nineteen he was appointed a writer in the service of the East India Company, and sent to Madras. There his turbulence, though he was not ill-natured, engaged him in quarrels with his equals; his dislike of application and control prevented his acquiring the benevolence of his superiors. When the capitulation with Madras was violated, Clive made his escape in a Mohammedan dress to Fort St. David, and when the siege of Pondicherry was undertaken, he was allowed to enter into the military service, with the rank of an ensign. At the siege of Pondicherry, and the enterprise against Devicotta, he rendered himself conspicuous by courting posts of danger, and exhibiting in them a daring intrepidity. The discerning, however, along with his rashness, perceived a coolness and presence of mind, with a readiness of resource in the midst of danger, which made Lawrence, at an early period, point him out as a man of promise. Upon the conclusion of the affair at Devicotta, Clive returned to his civil occupation, but no sooner did his countrymen resume the sword than his own disposition and the scarcity of officers again involved him in operations far better suited to his restless, daring, and contentious mind."

CHAPTER V.

THE FRENCH DRIVEN OUT OF THE NEW WORLD.

No war, perhaps, produced greater triumphs for England, or had more momentous results upon the history of the world than the Seven Years' War, which broke out in 1755. Since the close of the wars of Anne, which had been so barren of results, England, especially under the peaceful administration of Walpole, had made enormous strides in commercial and industrial activity. Exports had grown from six millions at the beginning of the century to double that amount by the middle of it.[1] The colonial trade had developed enormously, causing Liverpool to spring from a small country town to the rank of the third port in the kingdom. Bristol also leapt into renewed prosperity; while places like Manchester, Birmingham, and Sheffield, whose manufactures were coming into great demand, were more than doubling their population. Indeed, with the practical settlement of the succession by the accession of the House of Hanover, and the union of Scotland with England, there had come a fresh burst

[1] Green.

of energy into the national life, which was showing itself in almost every sphere of human activity. Even in religion it was manifesting itself in a way that it had not done since the Restoration corrupted manners and caused sincerity to become unfashionable; and John Wesley and his Methodists, aided by men like Whitefield, were planting a leaven which was destined, ere he had ended his career, to cause a thorough revolution in the manners of the people of these islands, who, when he began his career, were degraded to the lowest degree and brutal almost beyond belief.

There were manifold causes at work to produce the outbreak of the Seven Years' War; but not the least was the critical state of affairs in America, where the inactivity of the British Generals stood in striking contrast to the energy of Montcalm, who was in command of the French forces. Masters of the Valley of the Ohio by the defeat of Braddock, the French now drove the English garrison from the forts which commanded lakes Ontario and Champlain, and for a brief season looked on an unbroken possession that stretched from the St. Lawrence to Louisiana. There were spirits in the old country who were depressed almost to the verge of despair by the outlook of things generally; and when France made vigorous exertions to carry on the war, even threatening England with invasion, something like a panic took place, and Hessian and Hanoverian mercenaries were brought over to protect the Kingdom, as though it had been a fold of sheep. The loss of Minorca, chiefly through the fault of the

WHITEFIELD PREACHING AT LEEDS.

unlucky Admiral Byng, who fled from the encounter of a French fleet, was followed by the ill-success of the military operations in America, where a second series of expeditions against the French forts signally failed, while Montcalm captured Oswego, where the British had deposited the greater part of their military stores, including a park of artillery. The news of this disaster upset all the offensive plans of the British, putting a stop to expeditions that were on the point of moving against Fort Duquesne, Crown Point, and the Kennebec.

A sort of temporary paralysis seemed to fall upon the country. Pennsylvania, Virginia, and Maryland stood on the defensive. A fort was hastily constructed on the Tennessee, named Fort Loudoun, after the Commander-in-chief, and, with Forts George, Moore, Frederic, and Augusta, was garrisoned by Royal troops, for the protection of Carolina and Georgia, the latter being the last formed of the British colonies in America, the first settlement having been planted there in 1733, under a grant of territory from the Crown.

In the following summer, with six thousand American troops, Loudoun proceeded to Halifax, where Admiral Holborne had arrived with a powerful squadron and five thousand troops under the command of Lord Howe. The reduction of Louisburg was the object in view; but the French were again too quick for the British, and Loudoun returned to New York. In the meanwhile, however, Montcalm had taken advantage of his absence, and laid siege to Fort William Henry, at the south end of Lake George, with a force of nine thousand men, against a garrison of three thousand American and English, under a British officer named Munro. It was supposed to be strengthened by the proximity of Fort Edward, fourteen miles away, on the east of the Hudson, which was held by four thousand men under General Webb. Munro sent to the latter for aid, but for sole reply received the advice to surrender. Munro was forced to yield; but, in marching out with the honours of war, his troops were set upon by the Indian allies of the French, and fifteen hundred of them either massacred or taken prisoners, Montcalm being unable to check his savage followers. The French then destroyed the fort and all the British shipping on the lake, and carried off an immense booty in arms, ammunition, and provisions.

Failures hardly less disastrous and disgraceful had taken place likewise in Europe. They would have proved fatal to the new Ministry which had just come into power, with William Pitt (afterwards Earl of Chatham) as its leading spirit, had it not been generally understood that the officers, whose cowardice or incapacity had led to such inglorious results, were the choice of their predecessors, and were maintained in their positions by Court favour. This conviction proved favourable to Pitt; George II. was compelled to grant full powers to his Ministers, and the underhand intrigues by which the Cabinet was controlled were rendered powerless for a time. The enterprising spirit of "the Great Commoner," freed from these trammels, diffused some of its confidence and vigour through the Empire, and in especial animated the officers of the Army and Navy. A number of French ships of war were captured by the British; an armament, destined for North America, was dispersed and driven on shore by Sir Edward Hawke, whose fleet rode triumphant in the Channel. This success was followed by two expeditions against the coast of France, one of which effected the destrution of Cherbourg, though at a loss of life out of all proportion to the advantage gained.

But it was North America in which the new spirit most triumphantly showed itself. There, with the removal of the Earl of Loudoun from the command, the main cause of the apathy and incapacity which had brought disgrace on the British arms, and the appointment of General Abercrombie in his place, a complete change was brought about in the fortunes of war. Then with a foresight and generosity only possible to a "Great Commoner," the sympathies of the colonies were won by an order conferring on provincial officers equal rank with those of the regular Army while in the field. The effect was immediately seen in the alacrity with which the colonists —never backward when there was stirring duty to be done—responded to the call for men. Twenty thousand were soon ready for the field, Massachusetts and Connecticut alone mustering twelve thousand, while New Hampshire, Rhode Island, New York, and New Jersey all contributed their proportion. To co-operate with these a powerful armament sailed on the 19th of February, 1758, from Plymouth for the harbour of Halifax. With the provincial troops the total force amounted to fifty thousand men.

The final object was the complete subjugation of Canada; but as a first measure, for the protection of British commerce, it was resolved to take Louisburg, which had ever been a harbour of retreat and refuge for French privateers. Simultaneously with the attack on this stronghold, an expedition was to proceed against Crown Point and Ticonderoga, the latter situated on the isthmus between the north end of Lake George and the south shore of Lake Champlain, and about fifteen miles from Crown Point, on the latter lake; and a third against Fort Duquesne. General Amherst, with fourteen thousand men, laid siege to Louisburg, and, aided by the talents of Brigadier-General Wolfe, who was fast rising into eminence, compelled that fortress, though defended by a garrison of upwards of five thousand men, to a capitulation. This was followed by the entire reduction of the island of Cape Breton, and the inferior stations which the French occupied in the Gulf of St. Lawrence.

In the meantime Abercrombie had marched in person against Ticonderoga, with a force of fifteen thousand men and a long train of artillery. Crossing Lake George by means of boats and rafts, the troops were formed into four columns and marched to the attack. Getting entangled and somewhat confused in the thick woods, however, they were suddenly set upon by the enemy, and, in an almost hand-to-hand conflict, Lord Howe was killed. A small port was captured within two miles of Ticonderoga, and Abercrombie resolved on an instant assault. But, deceived in the strength of the place, he launched his forces against it in vain, and was finally compelled to abandon the expedition, and recrossed Lake George with a loss of two thousand men.

GENERAL WOLFE.

In order to redeem in some sort the disgrace of their failure, Bradstreet proposed an expedition against Fort Frontenac, the key to the communication between Canada and Louisiana. It was completely successful; the fort was taken and destroyed, and the stores intended for Fort Duquesne carried off. The expedition against the latter place was equally triumphant. It started from Philadelphia under General Forbes early in July, and, guided and animated by the genius of Washington, reached Fort Duquesne, after a protracted march and the conquest of almost insuperable difficulties, in November. There was nothing more to be done: the garrison, deserted by their Indian allies, had evacuated the place the previous night, and fled down the Ohio. In honour of the Minister who had been the means of opening the West to them, the colonists renamed the place Pittsburg.

Thus, in spite of the failure of the attack on Ticonderoga, the campaign had been favourable to the British arms. The capture of Frontenac and Duquesne had thoroughly broken the power of the French in Ohio. At the same time the effect upon their Indian allies was such that a peace was concluded with the tribes between Ohio and the lakes. The colonists were inspired with new courage and ardour, especially when they learned that the great Minister's programme was not yet complete, but that it included the total subjugation of Canada.

The plan of operations was similar to that just carried out. Three powerful Armies were to fall upon the enemy simultaneously at three different points. Wolfe was to ascend the St. Lawrence and lay siege to Quebec; Amherst, who had succeeded Abercrombie in the chief command, was to advance against Ticonderoga and Crown Point, and, having reduced them, join Wolfe; while General Prideaux, with the third Army, was to reduce Fort Niagara, and then, embarking on Lake Ontario, to sail down the St. Lawrence and take Montreal.

It was an astounding programme, that hardly any one but a Pitt would have put in motion, and—still more astounding—it was carried out, not without a hitch, but without a single failure. Perhaps it owed something of its success to the fact that the master-mind that planned it had to some extent prepared the Canadians for a change of rulers by the politic protection granted to the French settlers in Guadaloupe, which had been taken possession of early in the year (1758), and by the guarantee given to the inhabitants for the enjoyment of religious liberty. When, therefore, General Wolfe ascended the St. Lawrence, he met with very little serious opposition from the Canadians, who, probably worn out with the constant drain upon feeble resources, had come to regard the possible result with indifference.

While Wolfe was making his way to Quebec, General Amherst compelled the evacuation of Ticonderoga and Crown Point, and Sir William Johnson, succeeding to the command on Prideaux's death, gained possession of the important fortress of Niagara, after defeating a strong force sent to its relief. Unfortunately, Amherst was unable to form a junction with General Wolfe, who was thus compelled to proceed with a hazardous enterprise with very inadequate means. It was the end of June when Wolfe, with eight thousand veteran troops landed on the Isle of Orleans, a little below Quebec, and from thence surveyed the extent and difficulty of his task. The city stands on the north bank of

THE TAKING OF QUEBEC.
(From an old print.)

the St. Lawrence, and consists of an upper and a lower town. The latter lies on the flat betwixt the river and a precipitous wall of rock, running parallel to it westward. At the summit of the precipice is the upper town, situated on a level plain. East of the city is the St. Charles River; at a short distance from it the Montmorency, and between the two, stretching from one river to the other, lay the French army, strongly entrenched, and somewhat stronger than the British. Montcalm possessed also a few vessels of war and some fire-ships, with which an attempt was made to destroy the English squadron; but they were caught with grappling-irons by the British tars, and towed safely out of harm's way.

The strength of Montcalm's defences was tested by General Wolfe when, after a short skirmish, he occupied Point Levi, on the south bank of the St. Lawrence, opposite Quebec, in the hope thence of being able to bombard the city; and again when, on the 31st of July, he made an attack on the entrenchments at Montmorency, but was compelled to fall back with a severe loss in killed and wounded. The boats, it is said, in which the British landed were accidently delayed; the Grenadiers then rushed forward too impetuously, and the enemy, strongly posted, poured in upon them so destructive a fire that they were compelled to retire. This check so disappointed Wolfe that it brought on a fever which for some time prevented his taking the field. However, all this time he was maturing plans for another attempt; and on the 13th of September, an hour after midnight, embarking with five thousand men in flat-bottomed boats, he dropped silently down the stream. " Qui va la ? " demanded a French sentinel. " La France," was the response. " A quel régiment ? " " De la Reine," again came the answer, the speaker giving the name of one of De Bougainville's detachments. " Passe! " returned the sentinel, and the boats glided swiftly on till they arrived at the spot which has ever since borne the name of Wolfe's Cove. The landing-place was so narrow, and the ascent so precipitous, that Wolfe doubted for a moment whether it was practicable. But he soon perceived that where one could go, two could go, and where two a hundred; and so, animating his soldiers by his own heroic spirit, he led the way. His men followed, pulling themselves up by means of shrubs and jutting rocks, and when the day broke they had all reached the Heights of Abraham, and stood in ordered ranks before Quebec. It is said that the audacity of the action was too much for Montcalm's patience, and on his attention being called to the English, who had, in fact, cut off his supplies, he exclaimed, " Oui, je les vois, ou ils ne doivent pas être; je vais les écraser."

A battle was, of course, inevitable, and both generals prepared for the contest with equal courage. The Armies were almost equally weak in artillery, the French having but two guns, and the English a light cannon which had been dragged up the rocks by means of ropes. On the part of the French the first advance was made by fifteen hundred light infantry and some Indian riflemen, who harassed the British with a desultory fire. Wolfe, however, forbade his men to return a single shot until the enemy were within thirty yards. The withering volley with which they were then met, followed by an impetuous onslaught with the bayonet, may be said to have decided the day. The tide of victory was just beginning to turn in favour of the British when Wolfe received his third and mortal wound. His fall only roused the English soldiers to redoubled exertions; their attack with the bayonet had broken the French lines, and the confusion was speedily turned into a complete rout by the charge of a body of Highlanders with their broadswords. As the dying General lay in a partial swoon, he heard some one near him cry, " They run! See how they run!" " Who run ?" demanded Wolfe, as though just awakened from sleep. " The enemy," was the answer; " they give way everywhere." Then, having given an order to cut off the enemy's retreat, and learned that it had been obeyed, the hero turned on his side, and murmuring, " God be praised! now I shall die happy!" calmly passed away.

General Montcalm met with the same fate. He was not inferior to his rival in skill and bravery, nor did he encounter death with less intrepidity. When told after the battle that his hurts were mortal, he replied, " So much the better; I shall not live to witness the surrender of Quebec." Five days after the battle, that city opened its gates to a British garrison. The French bravely contested the issue for another year, and then, surrounded by the English at Montreal, the Marquis de Vaudreuil was compelled to sign a capitulation (September 8, 1760),

DEATH OF GENERAL WOLFE.
(After the painting by Benjamin West.)

surrendering to the victors the whole of Canada, which has ever since remained an integral part of the Empire.

The population of Canada at this time amounted to about sixty-nine thousand, including between seven and eight thousand converted Indians,[1] and are described as a frugal, moral, and industrious race. Civil and religious liberty was soon granted to the people; and it is gratifying to be able to record, in the words of the author of the *Political Annals of Canada*, that " previous history affords no example of such forbearance and generosity on the part of the conquerors towards the conquered — forming such a new era in civilised warfare that an admiring world admitted the claim of Great Britain to the glory of conquering a people, less from views of ambition and the security of her other colonies, than from the hope of improving their situation, and endowing them with the privileges of freedom."

When we think of what so soon after followed, we have to take this pious utterance with deductions; but the moral greatness of Great Britain is an inconstant quality, changing with the character of the men who are at the helm.

These stirring events in Canada were speedily followed by others of equal moment in other parts of the world. A secret understanding between the Bourbons had joined together the fortunes of France and Spain, and Pitt, in order to anticipate the hostile designs of the Court of Madrid, proposed to seize the plate-fleet, laden with the treasures of Spanish-

[1] Martin.

America. But his colleagues, already offended by his imperious manners, refused to sanction such bold measures, and he resigned the seals of office. The new Ministry, however, headed by the Earl of Bute, found it necessary to declare war against Spain (1762). This was immediately followed by a campaign in Portugal, in which the British arms were in the end successful, as also in an attack upon the enemy's possessions in the West Indies. The islands which the French still retained there, Martinique, St. Lucie, Grenada, and St. Vincent, were seized, while the Spaniards suffered the more considerable loss of Havana, the capital of Cuba, and the large fleet that lay in its harbour, captured by Admiral Pococke and Lord Albemarle. Nor was this the least alarming of the consequences that resulted from the unwise interference of Spain; an armament from Madras, under the command of Admiral Cornish and General Draper, capturing Manila, while the fall of that city involved the fate of the whole of the Philippine Islands.

CHAPTER VI.

THE CONQUEST OF BENGAL.

AFTER Clive's departure for England in 1753, things went from bad to worse in India. Duplaix was no sooner checked in one direction than his enterprising genius found vent in another. Foiled in his attempts on Trichinopoly through the aid given to the English by the Rajah of Mysore, he made advances to that ruler, with the result that his alliance with the English was suddenly broken. The Mohammedan Governor of Vellore, Morari Rao, and the Mahratta, speedily followed his example. Aided by the forces of these new allies, the French once more laid siege to Trichinopoly. Major Lawrence threw himself into that place on the 6th of May, 1753, and from that day until the 11th of October, 1754, he held the city against the united forces of the French and their Indian allies, although he was unable to compel them to raise the siege. In the meanwhile an attempt was made by Duplaix to arrive at an amicable arrangement with Mr. Saunders, the Governor of Madras (January, 1754). The subject of negotiation was as to who should be acknowledged Nawab of the Carnatic; but no satisfactory decision could be arrived at, and the negotiations for a basis of peace between the two Companies, broken off in Asia, were transferred to Europe. As the result of the arrangements then come to, M. Godheu was sent out to supersede Duplaix, and that gentleman, arriving at Pondicherry on the 2d of August, was able so to settle matters with Mr. Saunders as to bring about a suspension of arms on the 11th of October; and, on the 26th of December, a provisional treaty, to be confirmed or altered in Europe, was signed at Pondicherry.

"By this treaty," says Mill, "everything for which they had been contending was gained by the English." Mahomed Ali was left Nawab of the Carnatic; while the important acquisitions obtained by M. Bussy in recognition of his services to Salabat Jung, the Subahdar of the Deccan, consisted of the five important provinces of Ellore, Rajamundry, Chicacole, Condapilly, and Guntoor. These provinces, called the Northern Circars, "made the French masters of the sea-coast of Coromandel and Orissa in an uninterrupted line of six hundred miles from Medapilly to the Pagoda of Juggernaut."[1] Colonel Wilks adds that they "not only afforded the requisite pecuniary resources, but furnished the convenient means of receiving reinforcements of men and military stores from Pondicherry and Mauritius; and thus enabled Bussy to extend his political views to the indirect or absolute empire of the Deccan and the South."[2] These advantages—and they were

[1] Orme.   [2] *Political Sketches.*

certainly no insignificant ones—were now sacrificed by M. Godheu in the interests of peace.

The successful conclusion of these negotiations coincided with the termination of Duplaix's career in Asia. On the 14th of October he departed for Europe, where he received similar treatment to that which he had been the means of inflicting upon the gallant Labourdonnais. "He was reduced," says Voltaire, "to the necessity of disputing the last miserable remnants of his fortune with the Company of India, and of soliciting audiences in the antechambers of his judges, which caused him soon after to die of chagrin." Such was the end of the man of whom, Orme says: "Had he been supported from France in the manner necessary to carry on the extensive projects he had formed, there is no doubt but that he would have placed Chunda Sahib in the Nawabship of the Carnatic, given law to the subah of the Deccan, and, perhaps, to the throne of Delhi itself, and have established a sovereignty over many of the most valuable provinces of the empire."

Notwithstanding the treaty with the French Company, in which both parties had agreed not to interfere in the affairs of native princes, the English continued to give military aid to Mahomed Ali in extorting overdue tribute and in reducing rebellious chiefs to submission. But in view of the striking events which now took place in other parts of India, these minor actions sink into insignificance. Suffice it to note only the expedition which was despatched under Admiral Watson to destroy a nest of pirates who for fifty years had harassed the Malabar coast with their depredations. Angria, the chief of these corsairs, was of the Mahratta race, and nominally acknowledged the Peshwa, or supreme head of the Mahrattas; but he and his people had of late given such offence to that Prince that he was eager for their destruction, and joined his fleet to Watson's squadron. The English ships drove the pirates from two of their strongholds, and took possession of them; but it was not until the early part of the following year (1756) that their chief place, the fort and harbour of Geriah, was attacked.

By this time Clive had returned to Madras as Governor of Fort St. David, with the rank of Lieutenant-Colonel in the British Army, which had been given him by George II. He joined Admiral Watson in his expedition, the forces of which consisted of eight ships and some bomb-ketches, carrying eight hundred Europeans and one thousand native troops. The robber-fortress, strong as it was, and nearly surrounded by the sea, was soon stormed and carried, and its fleet burned—the pirates, indeed, when it came to the push, offering but a feeble resistance. Angria, their chief, fled to the camp of the Mahrattas, who had contributed a land force. Booty to the value of £150,000 sterling was divided between the Royal Navy and the Company's troops.[1]

Returning now to Madras, Clive took over the Governorship of Fort St. David on the 20th of June—a day ever memorable in the annals of India as that on which happened an event that changed the current of Empire in India, and within a few

---
[1] Sir John Malcolm, *Life of Clive.*

months was to call forth all the energies of Clive's bold and masterful spirit.

The Company's settlement at Calcutta had grown into the most considerable one in the Peninsula, thanks to the natural wealth of Bengal, and to the friendliness of Aliverdy Khan, the Viceroy, who had been conspicuous amongst native rulers for his kindness and consideration to the English. He died in 1756, and the Nawabship descended to his grandson, Surajah Dowlah, a youth under twenty years of age, who possessed all the vices and none of the virtues of an Oriental despot. His intellect, naturally feeble, had been still further weakened by debauchery, and his enervated body was a fit receptacle for his mind. This creature had from his childhood hated the English, and hence was not long in finding an excuse to quarrel with them. Because the Company's servants at Calcutta had dared, without permission, to strengthen their defences in anticipation of war with France, and because they had refused to give up a rich native whom he wished to plunder, Surajah Dowlah advanced with a great army against Fort William. Those who were there to command and to defend the place immediately lost their heads, and fled to the ships, and the fort, feebly defended, was soon taken. A great number of the English fell into the hands of the tyrant, and all the world knows what happened.

The captives—one hundred and forty-six in all—were driven at the point of the sword into a dungeon only twenty feet square, with air-holes so small and

FORT GERIAH.
(From an old print.)

obstructed that the place would have been oppressive for one person alone at that season of the year—the summer solstice—when, with every aid and convenience, it is hardly possible to make the climate tolerable for Europeans. What it must have been for the one hundred and forty-six crushed into it the imagination can hardly conceive. It is too painful even to dwell upon. Only twenty-three came out alive; the rest had died in agonies of thirst and suffocation—had died, many of them, raving mad. Such was the tragedy of the Black Hole of Calcutta.

The news of the catastrophe did not reach Madras until August. It naturally roused feelings of the fiercest resentment; and before twenty-four hours had passed away an expedition was resolved upon, with Admiral Watson in command of the naval armament, and Clive in charge of the land forces, these latter to consist of nine hundred British infantry and fifteen hundred Sepoys. Even this small force took some time to get together. It finally sailed on the 16th of October, but in consequence of adverse winds did not reach Bengal until December. On the 22d of that month they reached Fulta, twenty miles below Calcutta, where the fugitives from that place had taken refuge. After an encounter with the Nawab's troops at Budge-Budge, Clive advanced to Calcutta, and on the 2d of January, 1757, Admiral Watson brought his ships to anchor close off the fort. The Nawab's general had already fled, and it required but a few shots to make the three thousand undisciplined troops which formed the garrison scamper after him. Thus without the

FORT WILLIAM.
(From an old print.)

loss of a single life the English recaptured the fort and town. Within a few days Clive advanced upon the important town of Hugli, which, though defended by a fortress bristling with guns, was taken after a short cannonade, yielding to the conquerors a booty of £15,000.

At this time news reached Calcutta of the breaking out of the Seven Years' War, which made Clive anxious to arrange a peace with Surajah Dowlah, fearing lest the French at Chandernagore, who had a force of three hundred Europeans and a train of field artillery, might join the Nawab. The latter, although he pretended to be willing to treat, marched from Moorshedabad, his capital, with a large army, and on the 3d of February appeared before Calcutta. Clive, who had taken up a position to the north of the town, and hastily fortified his camp, watched his opportunity, and at three o'clock on the morning of the 5th, reinforced by some sailors with matchlocks, penetrated into the Nawab's camp, marched right through with part of his force, and attacking at once both at front and rear, threw the enemy into confusion and gained a signal victory. Clive's loss, however, considering his small force, was very heavy, consisting of one hundred and twenty Europeans and a hundred Sepoys. The loss inflicted on the enemy, however, was far greater; and the effect upon Surajah Dowlah was such that he at once sued for peace, and on the 9th of February a treaty was signed by which the Nawab agreed to restore to the Company their factories, and all the privileges they had formerly enjoyed, to permit them to fortify

Calcutta, and to make compensation to them for the losses they had sustained. This treaty was followed two days later by an offensive and defensive alliance between Surajah Dowlah and the English.

It was soon found, however, that no reliance could be placed upon the Nawab. Almost immediately after the signing of the treaty he was found to be intriguing with the French at Chandernagore, and inviting M. Bussy, who was still with Salabat Jung, the Subahdah of the Deccan, to hasten to protect Bengal against the English. Under the circumstances, Chandernagore was considered a standing menace to Calcutta, and it was therefore decided to take it. The place was strong, and the French garrison made a valiant defence; but it had no chance against Clive and the British squadron, and after a bombardment of fifteen days it was obliged to surrender.

Events now marched quickly. It is needless to go into all the details. For one thing, it was known that a French fleet was on its way to India, and the authorities at Madras, anticipating that they would be the first to receive a visit, were anxious to have Clive back. Clive, on his part, perceived with the eyes of a statesman that there could be no security for the English with such a weak and unstable Prince at the head of affairs in Bengal, and the French only too ready to incite and aid his schemes of revenge. There was a conspiracy amongst some of the Nawab's own people to dethrone him and put another in his place. The Company's agents at Moorshedabad were sounded, and the subject was discussed at Calcutta. Clive was strongly in favour of acting with the conspirators, and his voice in the end prevailed.

It is generally conceded that Clive was right, and that, not only for the safety of the English, but for the good of his own people, it was best that Surajah Dowlah should be deposed. But some of the means to which he had recourse to bring about that end cannot be justified. One man who was found a useful agent in the transactions was a Bengalee merchant named Omichund, who had influence at the Court of Moorshedabad, and was employed to lull the Nawab's suspicions. But he proved treacherous, and threatened to disclose everything unless his promised reward was largely increased. Under the circumstances Clive considered that it was perfectly justifiable to meet cunning with cunning. He therefore had two treaties drawn up, one of which granted to Omichund the £300,000 he demanded, the other made no mention of the matter. The latter was signed by both Clive and Admiral Watson; but to the false document, which was written on red paper, Watson declined to put his signature. It was therefore subscribed for him—Macaulay says by Clive himself. But whether Clive signed Watson's name himself, or got some one else to do it, the guilt was very much the same. It was an immoral and degrading act, and no one can know how degrading it was so well as the perpetrator himself came to know, when in after years it dogged him like an avenging Nemesis.

When everything was ready Clive wrote to Surajah Dowlah, setting forth the grievances of the English, and offering to submit the points in dispute to Mir Jaffier. Mir Jaffier was the principal commander of the Nawab's troops, and the man who had been selected to take his place. Having done this, and given the Nawab to understand that it was a question of unqualified submission or war, Clive moved his army from Chandernagore in the direction of Moorshedabad. On the 16th of June he halted at Patlee, and despatched Major Coote to Cutwa, where he found rice enough to provision a native army of ten thousand men for a whole year.

In the meanwhile the Nawab had assembled a large force and marched to encounter the English. It had been agreed that Mir Jaffier should join Clive with his whole force at Cutwa. But as the decisive moment drew near, when everything must, as it were, turn on the cast of a die, Clive became doubtful of his confederate. He had advanced to Cosimbuzar; in front of him lay a river which, though easy enough to cross, none of his little force might be able to repass should anything go wrong. The issues at stake were so great, the features of doubt so many, that for once in his life Clive was irresolute. Could he have been certain that Mir Jaffier would keep his part of the agreement and join him with his three thousand horse, all would have been well. But he could not; and in his consequent state of uncertainty and indecision he called a council of war, which decided against an advance. Clive agreed with the decision; but still doubtful whether the prudent way was the wise one, he retired to an adjacent grove, and after passing an hour there alone he came to the determination to risk everything, and gave his orders for the passing of the river the next morning.

At sunrise the Army was put in motion, and by four in the afternoon all had crossed the river. Marching then rapidly for Plassey, where the Nawab's army had been entrenched for some time, they reached that place late at night, and encamped within a mile of the enemy. All night Clive was prevented from sleeping by the drums and barbaric music of the enemy, kept up to dispel drowsiness, as well as by his own thoughts, which could not but speculate anxiously on the issue of the morrow. By daybreak the Nawab's army was in motion. It did not wait for the attack of the English, but began at once to move towards the grove in which they had fixed their camp.

It looked as though they might overwhelm the British with numbers. They counted in all forty thousand foot and sixteen thousand horse; and they had fifty pieces of heavy ordnance, each drawn by a team of white oxen and pushed on from behind by an elephant, besides some light field-pieces in charge of a company of about forty French soldiers. To oppose this formidable host Clive had but three thousand foot; nearly a thousand of them, however, were English, while all were led by English officers, and all thoroughly disciplined in the European manner. Their artillery consisted of eight field-pieces. The battle began towards eight o'clock in the morning with a sharp cannonade in which the Nawab's artillery did scarcely any execution, while that of the English, served coolly and with effect, caused some havoc amongst Surajah Dowlah's officers.

LORD CLIVE.

Mir Murden, one of his chief officers, was mortally wounded, and the disaster greatly alarmed the Nawab, although he was in his tent at a safe distance. One of the conspirators took advantage of his terror, and advised him to retreat. The suggestion fell in so aptly with his own feelings that he gave orders for his army to fall back. This was about two o'clock in the afternoon, and presently the whole of his host was seen retreating through the camp.

From that moment Surajah Dowlah's fate was sealed. Clive no sooner saw the movement than he ordered his troops to advance, and the retreat soon became a disorderly rout. The little company of Frenchmen, and a few who were inspired by their bravery, alone attempted to stem the English advance; but it was not for long. When the advance began, a cloud of cavalry hovered on the flank of the English. Clive thought they might be Mir Jaffier's three thousand horse; but as he received no sign, he detached some troops of the line to watch them. At length, instead of joining the Nawab's army, they moved altogether off the field; and then Clive was convinced that it must be Mir Jaffier, and that he was doing something in his dubious, half-hearted way to decide the contest. Seeing the end now before him, Clive fell upon the plucky band of Frenchmen, who, finding themselves deserted by the natives, soon took to flight, leaving their field-pieces behind them.

That was the last rally. In one hour from the time when Clive gave the order to advance, the Nawab's army was utterly broken and in precipitate retreat towards Moorshedabad. Only five hundred of the enemy had been slain; but their camp, with tents, baggage, artillery, white oxen, and the whole paraphernalia of battle—altogether a considerable booty—fell into the hands of the victors. The loss of the English had been twenty-two soldiers killed and fifty wounded. Amongst Clive's little army of heroes, the 39th British Regiment had specially distinguished itself, and it to this day bears on its colours the name of "Plassey," and the motto *Primus in Indis*. The English forces pursued the fugitives for about six miles, and then halted for the night at Daudpore.

Such was the battle of Plassey, certainly one of the "decisive battles of the world," since it placed at the feet of the conqueror a country larger and more populous than Great Britain.

Mir Jaffier, who had done so little to secure the victory, no sooner saw how things had turned than he sent a letter of congratulation to Clive, and next morning presented himself at the English quarters. He was received with every mark of respect, and at once saluted as Subahdar of the Provinces of Bengal, Orissa, and Bahar. In the meantime Surajah Dowlah was hastening with all speed to Moorshedabad, which he reached, by means of a fleet dromedary, in less than twenty-four hours. His councillors were immediately summoned, and their advice taken; some suggested that he should throw himself upon the mercy of the English, others that he should again try the fortune of war. He decided upon the latter course, and gave orders to that effect; but in the meanwhile Mir Jaffier arrived, and the news threw him into such a paroxysm of dread that he let himself down from one of the palace windows in the dead of night, and with a casket of jewels and two attendants, fled by river to Patna.

A few days later Clive arrived at Moorshedabad, and Mir Jaffier was at once installed with all the customary ceremonies in the Subahdarship. He was then called upon to fulfil the engagements into which he had entered with his fellow-conspirators, and a conference took place at the house of Jugget Seit, a great Hindu banker. Omichund presented himself with the rest, eager to touch some of the lacs of rupees that had been promised to him as his share of the rewards. But at the suggestion of Clive he was at once told of the trick that had been played upon him, and that he was to have nothing. Mill says that when "told that he was cheated, and found that he was a ruined man, he fainted away, and lost his reason"; and that reason, which had been so strong and clear before, never returned. Macaulay is very severe on these acts of duplicity and wrong committed by Clive, and no one with a nicely adjusted conscience can doubt that his judgment is the right one. Mill's comment on the transaction is: "Not an Englishman, not even Mr. Orme, has yet expressed a word of sympathy or regret." Clive's biographer[1] excuses his hero in every act of this transaction, and only regrets the necessity there was to resort to means so liable to abuse as forgery. This is an attitude that has been too common in the past in the dealings of the English with subject races. In short, in the building up of the British Empire as it is to-day they have often enough sunk right in expediency; but if that empire is to continue to stand it will only be by buttressing it on every side with justice.

[1] Sir John Malcolm.

Another victim of the revolution received even less mercy, and undoubtedly deserved less, than Omichund. Surajah Dowlah had reached Rajmahal, when, hiding in a garden, he was recognised by a man whom he had treated with cruelty, and who instantly betrayed him to the Governor. He was carried to Moorshedabad, and brought into the presence of Mir Jaffier, who, it is affirmed, pitying his abject condition, was inclined to spare his life, but that his son, a creature as abject as Surajah Dowlah, insisted that he should be put to death, in order to make his own succession the more secure. The murder was carried out at his instigation in one of the distant chambers of the palace.

It appears that when the Bengal treasury came to be examined, it was found to contain far less wealth than had been anticipated. This was a great disappointment to all concerned; and the Company's agents were obliged to consent to an arrangement by which payment of the compensation agreed upon was extended over three years. However, on the 6th of July, Clive and the English committee received as a first instalment coined silver amounting in English money to £800,000; and before the 9th of August very little short of the half of £2,750,000, the total amount of " the restitution, with the donations to the squadron, the army, and the committee," [1] was " delivered and discharged," and sent down to Fort William in the boats of the squadron, " with banners flying, and music sounding." Clive's share of the " donations " was between two and three hundred thousand pounds. In short, in one

[1] Orme.

brief campaign, the poor clerk of a few years back was raised to almost undreamed-of opulence.

In addition to their pecuniary compensation, the Company received a number of valuable concessions, which put their trade on an entirely new footing, including a right to establish their own mint at Calcutta.

While these matters were being transacted at Moorshedabad, Captain Coote was in pursuit of M. Law, who had escaped from Chandernagore with a small French force, and was now in Behar, where he hoped to sell his services to Ramnarrain, the Governor of that province. Although Coote failed to overtake the nimble Frenchman before he crossed into Oude, he struck terror into Ramnarrain and other native rulers, and made them take oaths to be faithful to the new Subahdar. This was the closing scene of a campaign which established the supremacy of the British in Northern India, where their power has never since been shaken.

While Clive was thus employed establishing British supremacy in Bengal, the Presidency of Madras continued to have its hands full trying to foil the efforts of the French in the Carnatic. In the month of September, 1657, a squadron of twelve French ships appeared off Fort St. David, but disappeared in the course of two or three days, frightened away, it is affirmed, by the report that Admiral Watson was on his way thither—poor Admiral Watson, who had died of jungle fever nearly a month before!

In the month of April following another French squadron, numbering twelve ships, arrived on the coast, under the command of Count d'Aché. It brought a regiment of infantry, a corps of artillerymen, and a number of officers of distinction, all under the command of Count Lally, who, with the appointment of Governor-General of all the French possessions and establishments in India, came out with special instructions to commence operations by the reduction of Fort St. David. It is not necessary to follow in detail the doings of this officer, any more than of any other who afterwards left his mark on the history of Hindustan. Suffice it to say that, possessing more courage than prudence, he threw himself into enterprises beyond his means, and especially frittered away his limited resources in a futile attack on Madras. Colonel Coote, who was placed in command of the British forces, was inferior to his adversaries in numerical strength, but he was backed by ample pecuniary resources, and altogether excelled Lally, both as a general and a statesman. The two came to a decisive engagement at Wandewash on the 21st of January, 1760, in which the French were completely defeated, and what remained of their influence in the Carnatic destroyed. A year later India saw the fall of Pondicherry, and with it the last stronghold of the French in India. During the campaign, Admiral Pococke, who had twice before failed to bring M. d'Aché to a decisive engagement, finally fell in with him off the coast of Ceylon, and, although inferior both in number of ships and guns, administered a severe defeat. This victory rendered the British masters of the Indian seas. About the same time (1759) a

Dutch armament arrived in the Hugli, under strong suspicion of being in communication with Mir Jaffier. Notwithstanding England and Holland were at peace, Clive ordered it to be attacked by land and sea. The Dutch were forced to surrender, and ample apologies were made by the Government of Holland for this infraction of treaties. A few months subsequent to this (February, 1760), Clive returned to England, where he was received with every honour, and raised to the Irish peerage, as Baron Clive of Plassey.

CHAPTER VII.

QUARREL WITH THE AMERICAN COLONIES.

WHEN Clive reached home, England was on the eve of momentous changes. George II. lived long enough to raise him to the Irish peerage as Baron Clive of Plassey; but before the year was out he was dead, and the accession of George III., to be followed ere long by the formation of the Cabinet of Lord Bute, in place of that of Pitt, brought into power men " who knew not Joseph." Bute hastened to bring the war with France to a close, preliminary articles being signed at Fountainebleau on the 3d of November, 1762. By the articles of this treaty England gave up nothing of which she was possessed at the commencement of the war, and obtained Canada from France and Florida from Spain. Pondicherry and the other conquests from the French which had been made in the East Indies were restored; but England retained Senegal in Africa and several West India islands. Clive was greatly mortified that he was not consulted as to Indian affairs by the new Ministry, and predicted that, whenever war again broke out between England and France, there would be another fierce struggle for supremacy in the East. Not only, however, was the hero of Plassey ignored in these affairs, but the Bute Administration leagued themselves with some of the directors of the East India Company to deprive him of his wealth.

Great Britain was then, and had been since the time of William III., ruled by a number of aristocratic families, who, with few exceptions, regarded the interests of the country as subordinate to their own, who considered place and power, with the emoluments accruing therefrom, as their right and privilege, and whose arrogance from a supposed superiority of birth was only equalled by their contempt for new men like Clive, whom they envied for their wealth and prosperity, and only recognised when they could be advantageously used. The struggle now, and for some years to come, was to rescue the Government from what was little better than an aristocratic oligarchy, whose divisions and feuds were influenced less by national concerns than by family ambition and personal gain. England could not continue to thrive under such a condition of things; unfortunately, however, before any improvement could be effected, the country was to suffer one of the most disgraceful reverses to be met with in the whole course of its history. The lesson proved a salutary one in the long run, though purchased at an enormous cost. But before giving an account of the quarrel with the American colonies, it will be necessary to refer briefly to Clive's third visit to India.

While the conqueror of Bengal was being involved in legal disputes, and the East India Company were contending with the man who had re-established their declining power in Hindustan, intelligence reached England of a most lamentable disaster to one of their settlements. After Clive's return to England, the government of Calcutta was entrusted to a Council, whereof Mr. Vansittart was appointed President. The rapidity with which, since the death of Aliverdy Khan, the English had achieved supremacy in Bengal, inspired the servants of the Company with feelings of the most supreme contempt for the natives. This soon led to angry disputes with Mir Jaffier, or Jaffier Khan, as he now called himself. At length the Council of Calcutta, for a bribe of £200,000, consented to the deposition of Jaffier and to the elevation of his son-in-law, Cossim Ali Khan, to the Subahdarship in his stead. But Cossim soon proved to be less tractable and more dangerous than his predecessor. The Company's servants claimed an exemption from all duties on commerce, and thus ruined the native traders. The Subahdar, after vainly remonstrating with Mr. Vansittart and his people, did away with the transit duties altogether; and this act of equity to his own subjects, to which he was forced by necessity, was vehemently condemned as an infringement of his engagements with the Company. Two agents were sent to Moorshedabad to demand the abrogation of the offensive decree. While the matter was still under consideration, the English resident at Patna seized the citadel of that place, and though it was immediately recaptured by the Subahdar, he was rendered so furious by the treatment of the English, who now saw nothing better to do than to restore old Jaffier Khan to the throne, that he ordered the execution of his English prisoners, soldiers and servants of the Company, to the number of a hundred and fifty.

A war now broke out fiercer and more determined than ever, which lasted from 1763 until the 3d of May, 1765, when General Carnac, in a pitched battle near Corah, defeated the last hostile force which was in the field against the English. This consisted of the forces of Sujah Dowlah, the Nawab of Oude, and a powerful army of Mahratta horse under Rao Holkar; but the combination was powerless to resist the coolness and organisation of the British attack, and the entire confederate army was broken and driven across the Jumna.

At this time Jaffier Khan had been some few months dead, and in consideration of a bribe of £140,000, divided amongst a number of the most powerful servants of the Company, an infant son of the deceased Subahdar had been placed on the throne.[1] Clive arrived at Calcutta the very day of Carnac's victory, and it fell to his lot, as Governor and Commander-in-Chief of the British possessions in Bengal, to conduct the negotiations for a peaceful settlement of affairs. A treaty was signed at Allahabad, where the British camp was stationed, by the terms of which the Mogul, Shah Alum, granted to the English the diwani, or fiscal adminis-

[1] Macaulay's essay, *Lord Clive*.

tration of Bengal, Behar, and Orissa; in return for which he was to receive, in addition to the revenues of Allahabad, Corah, and Douab, twenty-six lacs of rupees a year. Along with the right to this revenue, which practically constituted the Company the sovereign power in the extensive regions named in the deed, the Mogul confirmed the rights of the Company to all the territory which they held in other parts of India. By the same treaty Sujah Dowlah, besides being established in the Subahdarship of Oude, was reappointed Vizier to Shah Alum; while he, on his part, engaged to defend the frontiers of Bengal against the Mahrattas and other foes in return for English assistance in case of invasion.

No sooner had this business been completed than Clive set to work to cleanse the Augean stable of abuses which had grown up among the servants of the Company. The fertile province of Bengal was converted into a desert by the corruption of those into whose hands its destinies had fallen; friendly princes were turned into adversaries by the ceaseless extortion practised by men eager to get rich; and to complete the Governor's difficulties, his proceedings were subject to control by a committee who had been used to carrying matters with a high hand, and hence were not inclined to take a subordinate position. There was at first an attempt to oppose his reforming hand, and to defy his power to check abuse; but in the end all obstacles had to bend before his firm resolve and indomitable will.

The first outbreak of opposition was a general meeting of the officers of the army, who were supported by a large subscription from the civilians in Calcutta. They thought Clive would be forced to give way before such a storm. But he met the difficulty by calling up as many officers from Madras as could be spared, and by giving commissions to suitable men in the civil service of the Company who were disposed to serve him. The leaders in the conspiracy were put on their trial and cashiered; the rest, humbled and ashamed, begged to be allowed to return to their duty. In short, Clive's firmness restored order in Calcutta; but his reforming zeal raised up a host of enemies, who, though they were rendered powerless to hurt at present, did not store up their hatred in vain. In the course of a year and a half his task was accomplished, and he quitted India for the last time (January, 1767), having in that short period done a work almost as great as the original subjugation of Bengal—having, indeed, as Macaulay puts it, " effected one of the most extensive, difficult, and salutary reforms that ever was accomplished by any statesman." Soon after, the substitution of British rule for the native vice-royalties in Bengal did away with a fertile source of intrigue and peculation, although it opened the way to other and by no means lesser evils.

While these transactions were taking place in India a more perilous crisis was approaching in the American provinces. The Peace of 1763, which restored tranquillity to the transatlantic colonies, also released Europe from a long and sanguinary war, in which the arms of Britain, though at first miserably foiled, had in the end been everywhere triumphant. George III. had ascended the throne in the full tide of victory, and amidst all those circumstances that dazzle and win the popular mind. Everything, indeed, looked bright and prosperous; but these fair appearances were for the most part delusive and dangerous. The people as a mass were extremely ignorant, and almost as brutal as they were ignorant; all classes alike were addicted to the coarsest pleasures and the lowest vices; and the worst of it was that, as is ever the case with demoralised people, they were incapable of seeing very far beyond their own selfish concerns. It is true that the religious influences which have already been mentioned were steadily at work infusing a better leaven into the minds of the people; but the effect so far had not been such as to produce any great change.

To this condition of the nation must be attributed in the main the unwise policy which was now pursued, and the disastrous results that presently flowed from it. The young King had given his confidence to men who were as unfitted to guide the instincts and desires of the people as they were unwilling to seek or be influenced by their sympathies. The business of government is to govern; and the act of government consists as much in finding out how the governed would have a good done to them as in doing that good. He is but a fool of a policeman who is forever using the rough side of his tongue, or handling his bludgeon. Yet of some such type were the statesmen who at this period guided the counsels of George III. They ever chose rather to insult, irritate, and defy the people, than to soothe their passions, illumine their reason, and so keep them within the bounds of justice and moderation. What they did at home, that they did also in the colonies.

When, by the Treaty of Paris, peace was restored to the colonies, the British settlers, from New England to Georgia, were perfectly loyal subjects. They had borne a no mean share in the struggle, freely pouring out their blood, as well as contributing towards the cost of the war. This they had done as a whole cheerfully, glorying not a little in the common heritage and the British name. It would not have been greatly surprising if it had been otherwise, considering how large a proportion of the original colonists had been driven from England by tyranny and persecution, and how little aid they had received from the mother-country in building up homes for themselves in a wild country, infested by the wiliest and most truculent of savages. Moreover, not only had they been scanted of almost everything in the way of help, but they had been subjected at every turn to the whims and caprices of unwise kings and their too often merely time-serving courtiers and ministers. It was only when they had made themselves, as it were, a nation that England began to regard them seriously, and look upon them as a valuable and important part of the Empire. The thing was then done effectually, as we have seen, and at enormous cost to the nation. The benefit to the colonies was exceedingly great, and they commenced to increase so rapidly in wealth that it was thought they ought to share in the burden of taxation.

By their charters the colonists were bound to pay to the Crown a percentage on all goods imported; and some commercial regulations had afterwards been established with a view to increasing the revenue. But this was not deemed enough, and taxation began its career when, by an Act passed in the sixth year of George III., duties were imposed on sugar, rum, and molasses imported into the colonies—an act which, though not openly resisted, was in a great measure evaded by smuggling. So extensively was this illicit traffic carried on that a number of small ships of war were sent out expressly to watch and put it down. The commanders of these craft did not always show the highest amount of tact and discretion; sometimes they forgot even the dictates of humanity, the inevitable result being that the feelings of merchants were needlessly wounded and their minds gradually alienated from the home Government.

This irritation, however, had not gone to any great depth, nor was it at all widely extended when, in the spring of 1764, a Bill was passed by Parliament, and received the Royal assent, imposing certain duties on coffee, indigo, East India silk, French lawns, and some other articles imported into the colonies. These duties were required to be paid in specie. The provisions of this Act, being chiefly of the nature of commercial regulations, passed the Imperial Parliament without any particular notice being taken of them; they were, however, regarded with a jealous eye in the colonies.

Another Act which became law in the same session of Parliament caused much greater annoyance, though more in some provinces than in others. During the late war the colonial Assemblies had adopted the plan of issuing bills of credit to meet the needs of the hour; and, with a view to making them of more value, they constituted them a legal tender in payment of debt. This paper currency was issued in such quantities as to become extremely detrimental to commerce; and, in order to put a stop to the evil—chiefly by reason of the complaints of merchants in England—the colonial Assemblies were restrained from making their bills a legal currency.

Prior to the above-mentioned enactment, imposing duties on merchandise, the usual method of raising supplies in the colonies had been by requisition from the Crown, through the Governors, to the several Assemblies; but at the time of passing this Act, Mr. Grenville, who was then at the head of affairs, moved a resolution, " that towards further defraying the expense of protecting and securing the colonies, it may be proper to charge certain stamp duties in the colonies." But, although this resolution was adopted, with but one dissentient voice, that of the Hon. H. Seymour, no Bill founded upon it was introduced in that session of Parliament. It was intended at once as a feeler and an intimation of what the colonists might expect; and there was possibly a thought also that, as the Americans were sensitive on the point of taxation, it might be the means of working off some of their heat before the actual measure was passed. The projected impost roused universal indignation throughout the American provinces. Though the colonists had submitted to the regulation of their commerce by the House of Commons, they had constantly denied the right of Parliament to impose internal taxes on them without their consent, taking their stand upon the principle that a Parliament in which they were not represented could not claim the right of taxing them. In taking this position, however, they did not deny the right of the King to supplies from them towards protecting the colonies, but affirmed their willingness to vote such aids when applied for in a constitutional way—that is, by representing his needs and trusting to their free grants.

To the plea that the colonists were not represented in Parliament, the upholders of the measure replied that they were virtually represented in the House of Commons, in the same way as many of his Majesty's subjects in Britain who had no vote in the election of members of the legislature. One can hardly imagine reasonable men returning such an answer seriously; for, though large numbers of the population were not directly represented in Parliament, the members of the House had themselves to bear their share of the taxes they imposed; whereas, if allowed to tax the colonies, they would be imposing burdens on others from which they themselves would not only be free, but by which they might greatly reduce their own burdens. The colonists were quick to see and to raise this objection.

However, remonstrance was vain. The Bill had

been determined upon, and it must be passed. Accordingly, on the 29th of January, 1765, the Minister, in a committee of the House of Commons, moved fifty-five resolutions for imposing stamp duties on certain papers and documents used in the colonies; and soon after introduced a Bill founded on these resolutions. It was vigorously opposed by a few members; but, notwithstanding their arguments and representations, it was carried through both Houses by large majorities, received the Royal assent on the 22d of March, and was to take effect on the first day of November following. By the terms of the Act, all contracts, bills, notes of hand, marriage certificates, and other legal documents must be on stamped paper, which the home Government was to furnish at high rates, or those contracts would not be valid in law. A heavy tax was thus laid on every civil transaction, and, to make matters worse, the penalties incurred by the violation of the Act were recoverable in the Courts of Admiralty. Words are inadequate to express the burst of indignation with which the measure was received throughout the American colonies; and the surprise on the English side of the water was something akin to dismay when it was seen that the first determined note of opposition came from Virginia, which had hitherto been regarded as the most loyal of the provinces.

Hitherto the people of New England, and especially those of Massachusetts, had been the foremost in opposing taxation by the Imperial Parliament; and they were so decided in their views, and so determined to make them known, that they spared no pains to bring the other colonies to their way of thinking. Their efforts were powerfully seconded by the proceedings of the home Government; for, by one enactment or another, they managed to give offence to all the colonies, and made the Southern planters as bitter in their denunciations of the oppressor as the Northern merchants and farmers. The restrictions on paper currency had been particularly offensive to the Southern colonies, where there was not a sufficient supply of the precious metals to serve the needs of a circulating medium. Moreover, the restraint placed upon them had tended to lower the value of their paper money; and, as they did not perceive its ultimate utility, they regarded the Act as a wanton interference to the detriment of their interests and prosperity.

In like manner the measures that had been taken to suppress smuggling had put an end to the trade between the colonies and the Spanish possessions, from whence came their supply of gold and silver. Another Act that proved similarly disadvantageous was that which required the duties to be paid in specie, and transmitted to the English treasury before being applied to colonial purposes, thus tending to drain the settlements of the precious metals. The united operation of these various measures so greatly incommoded the colonists, and stood in the way of their interests, that they would have been more than human if their resentment had not been deeply roused.

Such was the state of public feeling, from the hills and forests of Maine to the marshes of Georgia, when copies of the Stamp Act, with an account of the debates to which it had given rise in Parliament, reached the colonies. The two together acted like a live match thrown into a litter of straw. Aware, as the Ministry undoubtedly were, of the ferment in the colonies, they calculated that the ebullition would cool down before a want of unanimity among the colonists and the warm loyalty of some of the provinces. Imagine, then, their chagrin when the news came that the first outburst of opposition occurred in Virginia. The General Assembly was sitting when a copy of the inauspicious Act, with the information that it had become law, reached Williamsburg. The subject soon found its way into the Assembly, and gave rise to one of the most violent debates that had ever been known in that province. A young lawyer, named Patrick Henry, rose and declared that the General Assembly had the exclusive right and power to levy taxes and impositions on the inhabitants, and that whoever maintained the contrary should be deemed an enemy to the colony.[1] As a result of the discussion, the Assembly agreed to four resolutions, which were inserted in the journals of the House on the 29th of May, 1765. The substance of these resolutions was: (1) that their ancestors brought with them from England, and transmitted to their posterity, all the rights, privileges, and immunities enjoyed by British subjects; (2) that those privileges were confirmed by two Royal charters granted by James I. ; (3) that they had ever enjoyed the right of being governed by their own

---

[1] *Life of Patrick Henry.*

Assembly in the matter of taxes and internal police, which right had not been forfeited or yielded up, but had been recognised by the King and people of Great Britain; (4) that the General Assembly of Virginia, with his Majesty, or his substitute, had the only exclusive right and power to levy taxes and impositions on the inhabitants of the colony, and that every attempt to invest such a power in any person or persons whatsoever, other than the General Assembly aforesaid, was illegal, unconstitutional, and unjust, and had a manifest tendency to destroy British as well as American freedom.

It is worthy of remark that, while the Assembly of Virginia based its opposition to the obnoxious Act on its charters, that of Massachusetts had the previous year gone straight to that unwritten charter of which the world was to hear so much a few years later—the natural rights of man.

The resolutions passed by the Virginia Assembly so startled the Governor that he at once dissolved the House. But that step was of little avail. The Assembly had pronounced the Stamp Act unconstitutional and illegal, and so was understood, in a measure, to have sanctioned resistance to its enforcement. The news of this revolt spread through the colonies with incredible rapidity, and, in the course of the next few months, one Assembly after another entered in their books resolutions similar to those of the premier colony. Then, at the suggestion of the General Assembly of Massachusetts, a Congress was held in October at New York, when delegates from nine of the provinces appeared, New Hampshire,

Virginia, North Carolina, and Georgia not being represented. The Assemblies of the three last-named colonies were not in session when the letters from Massachusetts arrived, and the Governors took care to put off their meeting until the day for opening the Congress was passed, consequently they were not able to appoint delegates. The Assembly of New Hampshire, while sending no representatives, approved the object of the Congress, and intimated its willingness to join in any petition which the deputies of the other colonies might determine upon.

After two weeks spent in deliberation, the Congress agreed to a number of resolutions setting forth their rights and their grievances. In these, whilst acknowledging the allegiance to the King and all the subordination to Parliament, they affirmed that they were entitled to the same rights and privileges as the people of Great Britain; that no taxes can be imposed on a free people except with their consent or that of their representatives; that all supplies to the Crown were free gifts from the people, and that therefore it was unreasonable that the Parliament of England should vote away the property of the inhabitants of the colonies; that the Stamp and other Acts, by imposing taxes, and extending the jurisdiction of the Courts of Admiralty beyond the ancient limits, had a tendency to subvert the rights and privileges of the colonists; that the prosperity of the colonies depended on the free enjoyment of their rights and privileges, etc. When these resolutions had been agreed to, and petitions had been drawn up in accordance therewith to the King and both Houses of Parliament, the Congress was dissolved (October 25, 1765).

The Congress was of momentous importance in more ways than one. Not only were leading men brought to know each other who would not otherwise have met, but they discovered common grounds of interest that had not before been manifest, the result being that the colonies were drawn closer together, and began to act henceforth more in unison. One of the first effects of the gathering was that associations were formed in all the colonies against the introduction of British manufactures, agreements being entered into not to import such merchandise after the first day of January next ensuing until the repeal of the Stamp Act.

As the day approached for carrying the Stamp Act into effect, riots occurred in Boston and elsewhere, and persons who had to put the Act in force, or who were in favour of it, were obliged to flee for their lives, and, in some cases, suffered the destruction of their houses. On the day when it should have come into force, there were no stamps, no one to distribute them, and nobody who durst have used them even if they had been at hand.

Business was in consequence almost entirely suspended; cargoes could not be cleared, ships could not proceed to sea, and the civil courts were at a standstill. In some cases the difficulties were overcome by temporary expedients; but in no colony did they venture to meet the crisis so boldly as in Massachusetts, where the Council and Assembly declared it lawful to continue to transact business as formerly.

English merchants and manufacturers soon began to feel the effects of this state of affairs in the colonies, with the result that petitions were presently being sent up to Parliament against the mischievous Act. Matters had now gone so far that there were only two ways out of the difficulty: either the Act must be repealed, or force employed to compel its observance. Fortunately, a change of Ministers favoured the peaceful alternative. Mr. Grenville, the patron of the Stamp Act, and his friends were dismissed from office, and the Marquis of Rockingham and his adherents appointed to take their place. These men had opposed the unfortunate measure in its progress through Parliament, and they resolved, therefore, to repeal it. This was accordingly done on the 18th of March, 1766. But, in taking this step, the Premier felt compelled to pass a resolution asserting the right of the King and Parliament to enact laws for the colonies in all cases whatsoever.

However, not much notice was taken of this "Declaratory Act" at the time, so great was the rejoicing at the repeal of the measure which had roused so much bitterness and conflict. Even in London the church bells were rung and the houses illuminated in honour of the occasion, while in the colonies "addresses of gratitude and professions of loyalty everywhere abounded."[1]

[1] *Popular History of America.*

CHAPTER VIII.

DRIVING THE AMERICAN COLONIES TO REVOLT.

WHILE the American colonists generally were rejoicing over the repeal of the Stamp Act, some of those who saw further than others deemed it wise to give their fellow-burgesses a word of caution not to be over-sanguine about this victory. Lord Rockingham's "Declaratory Act" was to them a sign that the struggle was not yet at an end, and that it was incumbent upon them not to relinquish their watchfulness. Hence, while the courts of law resumed their sittings, the provincial Assemblies met again for business, and congratulations passed between them and their Governors, notes of jealousy and distrust were not by any means wanting.

Causes of irritation were soon forthcoming. In accordance with a requisition of Parliament, the Governors of provinces desired the Assemblies to grant compensation to such persons as had sustained loss in the riots occasioned by the obnoxious statute. With this request Maryland readily complied; not so the Assembly of Massachusetts. Finding fault with the manner in which Governor Bernard had expressed the requisition, they told him that they would take an early opportunity to consider the recommendation. In the course of a few days they granted the compensation, but accompanied it with a clause indemnifying the rioters. The Assemblies of New York and Rhode Island, the only other colonies in which loss had occurred, manifested a similar spirit of independence.

In the same session of Parliament which had seen the repeal of the Stamp Act some innovations were made, by means of a clause in the Mutiny Act, in regard to the provision for soldiers stationed in America. They were to be supplied with certain necessaries by the colonies, and the Assemblies were ordered to provide the requisite funds. When the Governor of New York informed the Assembly of this provision of the Amended Act, and required them to make provision for certain troops on their way to the city, they, after some delay, told him that they would provide for the soldiers as formerly. The Governor remonstrated, but the colonists remained firm, contending that, while they were ready to make the usual provision for marching troops, it was unjust to expect them to do the same for stationary forces. It required an Act suspending the powers of the Governor and Assembly of New York to bring them to terms. A like spirit of resistance to the measure was manifested in other colonies, particularly in Massachusetts.

Notwithstanding these and other indications of the determination on the part of the Americans to maintain their independence and their rights, the

Ministers of King George could not be induced to withhold their hands from law-making, and see what quietude and the persuasions of time might do. The Rockingham Ministry was followed by that of the Earl of Chatham; but wisdom did not come with the change. Determined to draw a revenue from the American colonies, they obtained an Act of Parliament, levying duties on glass, paper, white lead, painters' colours, and tea, payable on the importation of those articles into the colonies. The funds arising from these imports were to be applied in making provision for the administration of justice and the maintenance of civil government. By a clause in the Act, the King was empowered to establish a general civil list in America, with salaries, pensions, and appointments, to the full extent of the colonial revenues, the residue, if any, to be at the disposal of Parliament. This Act, which was passed in June, in conjunction with one authorising the establishment of a customs board, whose headquarters were fixed at Boston, where the Commissioners arrived in the autumn, had the effect of reawakening all the irritation that had been partially allayed by the repeal of the Stamp Act.

It should be explained, as to some extent a justification of this measure, that during the discussions on the repealed Act a distinction had been drawn by the opponents of the Bill between what were called external and internal taxes; that is, between revenue raised by duties on imported or exported goods, and taxes levied in the way proposed by the Stamp Act. The Government thought, therefore, that they were quite safe in taking this new step. They were mistaken, however. Since the question of taxation had been first raised the colonists had had time to discuss and consider the subject in all its bearings, and they had come to the conclusion— or their leading minds had—that, in conformity with the British Constitution, they possessed the right of being taxed by their own representatives, and by them alone, and that the new Acts were a violation of such right. It is necessary to bear this fact distinctly in mind, because, throughout the whole of these unfortunate proceedings, this was the firm ground whereon the Americans took their stand, and from this time forward they were consistent in the position they took.

As usual, Massachusetts led in opposition to the new measures. The inhabitants of that province saw an insidious principle at work in the desire to draw from them a fund, independent of the annual grants of the colonial Assemblies, for paying the salaries of Crown officers, appointed without their consent, and over whom they could have no control. Meetings were accordingly held, clubs formed, and resolutions taken to encourage colonial manufactures and to refrain from purchasing any of the articles scheduled in the new Act. This was in the autumn of 1767.

When the General Assembly met, in the month of January of the following year, it at once drew up a petition to the King, complaining not merely of the Acts of the past session, but of all the Acts levying duties on the colonies since 1763. Having done this, the Assembly next addressed a circular letter to each of the other colonial Assemblies, explaining the step they had taken, and expressing a wish that they would all adopt similar measures. In this document, after referring to the violation of the constitutional rights of the colonies, the Assembly pointed with indignation to the fact that, by the new Act, the colonial judges were not independent of the Crown, as in England; and affirmed that freedom and justice were not safe in the hands of civil functionaries holding office directly from the King, and subject to no sort of control on the part of the Assemblies or the people.

This letter, which was dated the 11th of February, 1768, caused considerable alarm in England. It especially annoyed the Ministry, and the Secretary for American Affairs was instructed to send letters to the colonial Governors, to be placed before the Assemblies, warning them to be on their guard against the mischievous policy of the General Court of Massachusetts, and to treat their letter with contempt. Massachusetts was required to rescind their letter; but the Assembly refused to do so. The other colonies were equally uncompliant; and, acting on the suggestion of Massachusetts, transmitted to England petitions similar to that of the General Court.

Up to this time the unity of opinion among the colonies had not been very great; the Middle and Southern provinces were far from reciprocating the independent notions and unyielding principles of New England, and, had there been anything like an approach to wisdom in the minds of the aristocratic oligarchy that governed Great Britain, those differences might have been used as a foil to the uncompromising attitude of Boston. But they did not even possess the cunning of the ordinary politician; the opportunity was consequently lost, and the provinces that were at first much more inclined for conciliation than Massachusetts and its neighbour colonies, when it came to choosing between the pretensions of the Cabinet of King George and the principles of the people of New England, had no difficulty in electing for the latter.

The state of affairs became daily more critical. Collisions had frequently taken place at Boston between the people and the officers of the customs,[1] and two regiments of soldiers were held in quarters in Halifax ready to embark for Boston the moment the Governor deemed their presence necessary. Meanwhile the latter, acting on instructions from England, had required the Assembly to rescind the resolutions of the preceding session, on which their letter to the other colonies had been founded. They refused to comply with his request, and were dissolved. The troops were now ordered to the town in aid of the civil power.

Nothing daunted by these threatening measures, a town's meeting was called on the 12th of September, and the Governor petitioned to convene a General Assembly. He replied that he had dissolved the last in accordance with instructions, and that he had no power to convoke another without his Ma-

---

[1] *Popular History of the United States.*

jesty's permission. On receiving this answer, the townspeople immediately took the bold course of deciding to hold a provincial Convention, to be held on the 22d of the same month. This gathering, composed of deputies representing Boston and the other towns of the province, laid no claim to legislative authority, and appears to have confined its deliberations to the consideration of the constitutional measures to be taken for obtaining redress of their grievances. It recommended the people to respect the civil power, and declared its readiness to assist the magistrates in maintaining the public peace. The Convention closed its sittings on the 29th of September, on which day the two regiments of soldiers arrived from Halifax. They landed under cover of a number of ships of war, and, with much parade, marched through the town to the Common. The Selectmen of Boston were required to provide them with quarters, and on their refusal to do so they were accommodated in the State House, in front of which were placed two field-pieces, while sentinels challenged all who came and went. The soldiers appear to have given great offence to the good people of Boston, especially by the performance of military music on the " sabbath day." This first division of troops was soon followed by transports from Cork, bringing reinforcements.

Though for a time everything went on quietly, there was no lack of signs of the coming storm. Each successive act of the Government tended only to deepen the detestation of tyranny among the colonists, while France, ever watchful to pay off old scores on her hereditary enemy, did her best, by secret agents and insidious advances, to kindle the growing heat into a flame. The non-importation movement, in spite of difficulties and conflicting interests, grew stronger and stronger as the time approached (January 1, 1769) for its enactments to become operative.

Such was the condition of things in America when Parliament met, and in the early part of February entered upon the consideration of colonial affairs. An address was presented to the King from both Houses of Parliament, in which they signified their approval of the measures already taken for the maintenance of the Royal authority in the colonies, expressed their willingness to support any further steps that might be deemed necessary to enforce them, and recommended the infliction of exemplary and condign punishment on those who had set the law at defiance. Nor was this all: the address went on to advise the revival of an obsolete statute of Henry VIII. for trying in England treasons committed beyond the seas, and the issuing a special commission for that purpose, if found needful. Although this unwise address was opposed by a considerable number of the more enlightened members of both Houses, conspicuous among whom were Burke and Colonel Barré in the Commons, it was carried by large majorities. That part of the ministerial programme relating to the obnoxious statute of Henry VIII. was, in particular, extremely repugnant to the friends of liberty in Great Britain, while in

149 THE OLD STATE-HOUSE, BOSTON (1748), AS RESTORED IN 1881.

America its effect was to estrange and embitter many of the calmer minds whose attachment and loyalty to the mother-country had hitherto remained beyond question.

This act of folly was no sooner committed than it had its inevitable effect. When the news of it reached America the General Assembly of Virginia was sitting. It at once took up the cause. An address was drawn up for presentation to the King, in which it was declared that any trial for treason, or misprision of treason, or for any crime committed by a person residing in a colony, should take place before the Court of that colony; that the sole right of taxation was vested in the provincial Assemblies; and that it was the right of the colonies to act together in regard to petitions for the redress of grievances. This bold step on the part of the Assembly brought about the usual result: it was dissolved by the Governor. The members thereupon adjourned to a private house, and passed non-importation resolutions. The example set by Virginia was ere long followed by Carolina, Maryland, Delaware, and New York.

The convocation of the Assembly of Massachusetts having been delayed to the utmost limit permissible by the charter, it was summoned to meet on the 31st of May, 1769. A committee immediately waited on the Governor, and represented to him the impossibility of conducting the business of the House with the proper freedom while the town was invested by sea and land, and while the State House was occupied by soldiers. The Governor, having no authority over the military or naval forces, replied that he could not help them; but when the Assembly refused to proceed with their deliberations, he decided to transfer them to Cambridge. They had no sooner got to work than trouble began. The Governor demanded funds for the payment of the troops; the Assembly fell back on the natural and constitutional rights of the people to conduct their civic business without the presence of an armed force; and finally declined to make the provision required. In consequence of this refusal the Assembly was prorogued until the 10th of January.

Thus in every possible way the irritation was kept up, and the people more and more thrown upon their own resources. Their determination to encourage colonial manufactures and to use no imported goods soon had a most important effect upon British trade. The value of the merchandise exported to America in 1769 was £744,000 less than in the preceding year, while the revenues arising from the American duties decreased from £110,000 in 1767 to £30,000 in 1769. English merchants and manufacturers became seriously alarmed, and immediately petitions began to flow into Parliament for a repeal of the obnoxious taxes.

In the meantime another change of Ministry took place, Lord North succeeding the Duke of Grafton in the Premiership. That noble lord possessed all the obstinacy of his predecessors, and more than their share of narrow-mindedness. One of his first acts was to attempt a compromise with the American colonies, by introducing a Bill to abrogate the duties on glass, paper, and painters' colours, while retaining that on tea. This, he declared, would be continued, "for the purpose of saving the national honour."[1] It was in vain that the friends of America contended for the repeal of the whole of the duties, insisting that their partial abolition left matters, so far as the Americans were concerned, exactly where they were, seeing that their objection was not to the amount of the duty, but to the claim of Parliament to impose it. Their contention was one of principle, not of money. But opposition was useless; an amendment to include the tea-duty in the Act of Repeal was negatived by 402 to 142, and the Bill, as introduced, received the Royal assent in April.

In most of the colonies this conciliatory Act was received as such; and though some advised that the non-importation resolutions should continue in force until the duty was taken off tea also, the majority did not agree to that way of looking at things. In Boston, unfortunately, a most regrettable affair had occurred on the very day on which the Minister brought forward his pacificatory measure: a collision took place between some young men and the military, with the result that several civilians lost their lives. This tended greatly to embitter popular feeling, and so to make the people of Massachusetts less inclined to accept the compromise. They determined to drink no tea upon which a duty had to be paid, and in consequence the merchants were not allowed to land their goods. Thus the spirit of re-

---

[1] *History of the United States.*

sistance was kept alive in the North, and it was further exasperated by the restrictions placed on

LORD NORTH.

colonial commerce by the new Board of Admiralty, and by the offensive way in which officers of the Navy too often enforced the revenue laws.

One man in particular made himself obnoxious by his insolent and foolish behaviour, and in the end did not a little to hasten on the crisis. He was the commander of the armed schooner *Gaspee*, stationed off Rhode Island, and, not satisfied with overhauling vessels suspected of carrying contraband goods, he was in the habit of further annoying the colonists by compelling their vessels to salute his flag. One evening in the early part of June, 1772, a packet, with passengers on board, passed him with flying colours, and, refusing to lower them, had a shot sent after her. As that was taken no notice of, the commander gave chase. The packet ran as close into land as possible, in order to try to get the *Gaspee* into shoal water. The ruse succeeded, and the schooner went aground a few miles below Providence. During the night she was attacked by a body of men in whale-boats, who forced the commander with his crew ashore, and then set fire to the vessel. Although a large reward was offered for the discovery of the persons concerned in this daring act, the offenders remained unpunished.

Other causes of irritation were not long wanting, nor—it must be added—were the people of Massachusetts slow to take offence. Possibly, too, they may have strained points of grievance. But, in the main, it must be acknowledged that they manifested uncommon forbearance in the face of incessant provocation. They were a high-spirited people, inheriting from their fathers more than a common share of the British love of freedom; they found themselves face to face with a governing class avid of dominion, and so greedy of the spoils of office that they cared little whence the money was obtained so long as they could handle it; it was the same class whose narrowness and intolerance had driven their progenitors forth from their English homes into the wilderness. Confronted with the same illiberal spirit, with the same brutal methods of governing, they would have proved themselves less than men if they had failed to resist; and not only they, but the whole world to-day, has cause to rejoice in the bold and determined stand they took.

One matter that further agitated the public mind was the granting of larger stipends to the colonial judges out of the American revenue. Hitherto they had been paid somewhat parsimoniously out of funds voted by the Assembly of Massachusetts, and it was only just that they should receive a more generous treatment ; but coming at the time it did, when every act of the home Administration was suspiciously scanned, the transaction had, to the excited minds of the people, the appearance of an attempt to purchase the subserviency of the judges, and naturally caused alarm.

This regulation took place in the early part of 1772, and after watching its operation for some time, the people of Boston presented a petition to Mr. Hutchinson, who, in 1770, had succeeded Sir Francis Bernard as Governor, making complaint of the new arrangement, and asking him to summon the Assembly. On his refusal to do so, the people called a meeting, and appointed a committee to consider and report what ought to be done to safeguard the common rights and liberties. The committee went very fully into the subject, and in their report they denied the right of Parliament to frame laws for the colonies in any shape or form. Making a full declaration of the rights of the colonists, they shewed how those rights had been persistently violated, not only in the Declaratory Act of 1766, wherein Parliament had claimed the right of imposing laws on them without their consent, and on the strength of that assumed right had subjected them to taxation; but in the subsequent appointment of new officers to take charge of the collection of those taxes. All these acts they denounced as " unauthorised by their charter and unknown to their constitution"; and ended by affirming that the Ministry, by the new ordinance touching the stipends of judges and other officers of the Crown, had in view the completion of that system of slavery which the House of Commons had inaugurated by assuming the right to levy taxes upon them without their consent.

This report met the views of the people of Boston, and they ordered it to be printed and distributed in the province. It was accompanied by a stirring appeal to the burgesses to stand up for their rights, and not allow them to be filched from them through their negligence or indifference.

These doings took place in the autumn of 1772, and when, in the following January, the Assembly met, the Governor still further agitated the troubled waters by affirming what the people denied—the supreme authority of the King and Parliament in the making of laws. The Assembly thereupon, by way of reply to his unwise address, boldly affirmed their adhesion to all the resolutions promulgated by the inhabitants of Boston, although a little later they " climbed down " somewhat.

To these were added other causes of irritation—many of them petty enough—which it is needless to recount. All tended to widen the breach between the two countries; although, up to the beginning of 1773, there appears to have been no thought—except it were in the minds of a few—of pushing matters to a complete rupture with the mother-country. But, unfortunately, Lord North and his colleagues had not the wisdom to hold their hands and let matters quiet down, but must go to further chafing of an old sore.

Curiously enough, by this fatal act, the two growing dominions of the English—the one in the East and the one in the West—were brought into momentary conjunction. The East India Company had had a series of bad years, due in part, we are told, " to the refusal of the Americans to import tea from England,"[1] and had seventeen million pounds of tea lying unsalable in their warehouses. The Government had to come to the Company's help with a loan of a million and a half to save them from bankruptcy; at the same time passing a Regulating Act for the better control of the Company's affairs. Under the circumstances it was decided to allow them to send to America as much of the tea as they liked free of duty, so far as England was concerned, but upon which a duty of threepence a

---

[1] *Popular History of the United States.*

pound would have to be paid in America. The directors, apprehending trouble from the proposal, suggested that they should be allowed to pay the import duty into England, which was sixpence a pound, and land the tea free in America; but this Lord North refused—" probably at the King's direction," says Bryant.[1] It was George III.'s notion that " there must be one tax to keep up the right."

Several ships were loaded with tea, and consigned to merchants in different colonial ports. " Information of these consignments began to arrive in America in September," says Bryant, from whose account I chiefly transcribe this episode. Public opinion everywhere was against having anything to do with the ships' cargoes, and it was decided before they arrived to send them back whence they came. In most cases they were so despatched; but, in Boston, Governor Hutchinson refused to grant a permit for the return of the ships. They lay, therefore, with their cargoes at the wharf awaiting the issue of the dispute. A town's meeting soon decided the matter.

The first of the tea-ships had arrived on the 28th of November, and two others soon followed. They were anchored near together, so that one guard might serve for all. At the town's meeting Samuel Adams moved that the tea should not be landed, and that no duty should be paid on it. This resolution was unanimously adopted, and those responsible for the tea were made acquainted therewith. Not only were the ships carefully watched, but riders were appointed to carry the news post-haste to the inland

[1] *Popular History of the United States.*

towns in case of any attempt being made to land it by force. Naturally the people of the town and the surrounding country were thrown into a state of great excitement by the tension of affairs. How was the matter to end? On the one hand there was the committee appointed by the town, which would not permit the landing of the tea; on the other hand the Governor, who refused to give the necessary pass to enable the ships to return to London. It was evident that such a state of things could not continue—someone or something must give way.

Another meeting was held (December 16th), and, after the position of things had been stated and discussed, Samuel Adams got up and said, " This meeting can do nothing more to save the country." Immediately the gathering dispersed, and an immense throng proceeded to the wharf where the ships lay. Arrived there, a number of armed men, disguised like Mohawk Indians, took possession of the ships. Hoisting-tackle was rigged up, hatches knocked off, the chests of tea were quickly brought on deck, split open, and their contents thrown into the water. The business was despatched with celerity, " without noise or disorder," most of the men of the town standing on the shore watching what was going on. Then, as soon as the work was over, every box of tea destroyed, the sentinels were withdrawn, and everybody went quietly to his home. It was then getting towards dawn. During their night's work the depredators had broken open and dispersed the contents of three hundred and forty-two chests of tea, valued at £18,000 sterling. In none of the other ports to which tea was consigned was violence proceeded to. In most cases, as already said, the ships were compelled to return; but in Charlestown, though the tea was, after considerable opposition, allowed on shore, it was immediately locked up in damp cellars, and, in the end, became unfit for use.

The news of these proceedings reached England while Parliament was sitting; it naturally caused great excitement, and among the supporters of the Ministry roused feelings of bitter hostility. It was resolved to make Boston feel that Parliament had the power to revenge and punish. The method of retaliation adopted consisted in bringing in a Bill " to discontinue the landing and discharging, lading and shipping of goods, wines, and merchandise at Boston, or the harbour thereof," until Boston manifested a spirit of " peace and obedience," and, further, until the East India Company and others had been indemnified for the losses they had sustained in the riots. This Bill was introduced on the 14th of March, 1774, and received the Royal assent on the 31st of the same month.

It did not pass, however, without much opposition. " Keep your hands out of the pockets of the Americans," cried Barré, " and they will be obedient subjects." " I never knew anything," said Burke, " that has given me more heartfelt sorrow than the present measure. I wish to see a new regulation and plan of legislation in that country, not founded upon your laws and statutes here, but grounded upon the vital principles of English liberty. In blocking up one port after another, you will draw a foreign force upon you, perhaps at a time when you little expect it."[1]

Warnings like these, however, uttered by some of the farthest-seeing men of the day, had so little effect that the Boston Port Bill was followed by another equally unwise. Barely had the latter become law than Lord North brought in a Bill " for the better regulating the government of the province of Massachusetts Bay." In other words, it was proposed to annul the charter of the colony. Despite alarming forecasts of what all this portended, a subservient Parliament quickly passed the Bill through both Houses, and Massachusetts was deprived of a constitution breathing " a spirit of liberty superior to anything of former or present times."[2] By this Act the General Assembly of the province was deprived of the power of electing the Council, that privilege being now vested in the Crown, and giving the King, or the Governor acting for him, the authority to appoint judges, magistrates, and sheriffs. The summoning of juries was placed in the hands of the sheriffs, and no town meeting could be held without the consent of the Governor.

The colonists looked upon this act of annulling their charter as the most serious that had yet been committed. They regarded that document as " a compact between them and the King," and held that the breaking of that bond of union set the people free from their allegiance.

But even this was not thought enough to break

[1] *Parliamentary Debates.*   [2] *Ibid.*

the back of opposition and bring the burgesses of Massachusetts into a proper state of subjection. Accordingly another Act of Parliament was procured by the Ministry, providing that, if any person were charged with murder, or with any other capital offence, committed whilst acting as, or giving aid to, a magistrate in Massachusetts, the Governor should have power to send the accused for trial to Nova Scotia or to England. Earnest voices were raised against the fatuity of these measures, Dunning, amongst the rest, declaring the policy that was being pursued to be " war, severe revenge, and hatred against our own subjects." But all was in vain; it was as though the whole of the Ministry was afflicted with the growing madness of the King. How mad, how unjust it all was, may be seen by noting the different measure that was meted out to Canada, where the colonists were favoured by the re-establishment of the laws of France and of the Catholic religion.

When the news reached Boston of the passing of the Port Bill, it naturally caused the utmost indignation. This was on the 10th of May, 1774, and a few days later a meeting was called to consider what should be done in the matter. Meanwhile General Gage, Commander-in-Chief in the colonies, had arrived as Governor of the province. His presence, however, did not turn the burgesses from their purpose. They resolved, " That it is the opinion of this town, that if the other colonies will come to a joint resolution to stop all importation from and exportation to Great Britain and every part of the

West Indies till the Bill be repealed, it will prove the salvation of America and her liberties; and that the impolicy, injustice, inhumanity, and cruelty of the Act exceed all our powers of expression; we therefore leave it to others, and appeal to God and the world."

The people of Boston were not long left in doubt as to how far they would receive the sympathy and support of the other colonies. Meetings were immediately held in many of the leading towns, and from the resolutions passed it was clear that they might rely upon the hearty co-operation and support of the different provinces. At the near-lying ports the Bostonians were offered the use of the wharves and warehouses to carry on their trade, the people generously refusing to profit by the misfortunes of their neighbours. Subscriptions were also raised in aid of the sufferers, and in every way Boston, which was held to be fighting in the common cause, was strengthened and sustained.

The provincial Assembly of Massachusetts met soon after the arrival of General Gage, but it was almost immediately adjourned until the 7th of June, when it was to meet at Salem. By that date the Boston folk had been assured of the full support and co-operation of their compatriots throughout the colonies, and were in consequence encouraged to act with an increase rather than a diminution of vigour. When the Assembly met, therefore, the question of holding a Congress of all the colonies at Philadelphia on the 5th of September, which had been suggested by the burgesses of Virginia, was discussed and agreed to. Five members were appointed to attend it, and a sum of money voted for their expenses. The Assembly of Virginia had been dissolved for deciding to hold the 1st of June, the day on which the Boston Port Act was to come into force, as a day of humiliation and prayer. The Massachusetts Assembly was treated to the same punitive measure when the Governor learned what they were about.

All through the early part of the year the country was in a ferment, and every successive Act of the Government seemed designed purposely to augment it. Barely was the day past which all had agreed to observe as one for humbling themselves before God, in order to avert the horror of civil war, than copies of the Act of Parliament subverting the constitution of Massachusetts, and commissions from the King to those who were to compose the new Council, arrived in Boston, and deepened the confusion, if not the irritation. The result was almost a total suspension of civil government. The people refused to acknowledge the judges, and juries declined to act. General Gage made a vain attempt to call in the aid of religion; but in his exasperation he made matters worse. Moreover, he was all the time strengthening his military resources, and evidently looking to the sword as the ultimate arbiter in the questions at issue. He seemed to be encouraged in this view by the action of the Governor of North Carolina, who, in a trouble that had arisen in that province, had successfully quashed opposition by military force. The narrow isthmus or neck of land joining Boston to the mainland was occupied by a body of troops on the pretext of preventing desertion; but to the Americans the step was only too evidently designed to cut off the communications between town and country, and possibly in the end to compel the people of the town to unconditional surrender. Nothing short of a miracle of wisdom was calculated to preserve the peace, and General Gage certainly did not possess that uncommon endowment. His next act precipitated matters almost beyond recall. He threw up fortifications on Boston Neck, and on the 1st of September sent a party of soldiers across the river Charles to remove a quantity of powder which had been stored in the arsenal at Charlestown, a small place opposite Boston. The news of this transaction spread like wildfire through the surrounding country, and caused a large number of farmers and others, many of them armed, to assemble at Cambridge; and it was with difficulty that they were dissuaded from proceeding to Boston to demand the return of the powder, which did not belong to the army.

In consequence of this affair, the report got abroad that the troops were firing upon Boston, with the result that thousands of men hastily armed and put themselves *en route* for what was now known as the martyr city. It was not until they had arrived within a few miles of the town that they were made aware of their mistake. In this superheated condition of the popular mind an assembly of delegates from the several towns and districts of the county of Suffolk, of which Boston is the capital, was held to consider what course should be taken in the existing crisis. In itself the gathering would have been of very minor importance but for the fact that the series of resolutions which it formulated and passed were accepted by the Congress, which had in the meantime met at Philadelphia.

According to these resolutions, no obedience was due to the late Acts of Parliament, the royally appointed justices were unconstitutional officers, those persons who had accepted seats at the Council-board on the King's *mandamus* were guilty of a violation of the duty they owed to their country, and the Act establishing the Roman Catholic religion in Quebec was a danger to the Protestant faith and to the civil rights and liberties of America. The resolutions finished by recommending the inhabitants to " acquaint themselves with the art of war," and, for that purpose, to appear under arms at least once a week.

The approval by the Philadelphia Congress of the Suffolk resolutions, and their recommendation to their brethren to persevere " in the same firm and temperate conduct " until conviction be carried " to the British nation of the unwise, unjust, and ruinous policy of the present Administration," was virtually an act of rebellion against the mother-country; although that the Congress did not so regard it is evidenced by the fact that they made representations to General Gage, desiring him to forbear from such irritating acts as would " prevent the endeavour of Congress to restore a good understanding with the parent State."

All the colonies were represented at the Congress

except Georgia, and that province was so much at one with the others that the gathering has since been known as the First Continental Congress. All the delegates were authorised to give their adhesion to any measures the majority decided to adopt. Their deliberations were carried on with closed doors, and only such of their proceedings as they saw fit were made public. Amongst the latter was a declaration of rights—the boldest, and, perhaps, the clearest and most distinctly expressed, that was ever set forth by any people, at any age of the world. They based their rights not merely on their charters, and on the principles of the British Constitution, but on " the immutable laws of nature." As the first of those rights they named life, liberty, and property, and they denied the right of anyone to dispose of these without their consent.

When the dispute first broke out between the colonies and the mother-country, the contention of the former was that there should be no taxation without representation. But with the progress of the quarrel the ideas of the colonists had gradually enlarged and developed, acquiring at the same time an amount of consistency which they had not hitherto possessed. The result is shown in their declaration of rights, which claims not merely that representation shall go with taxation, but that there shall be no legislation without representation. The foundation of English liberty, they held, and of all free government, was a right in the people to participate in their legislative councils, and that as the colonists were not, and, from various causes, could not be, represented in Parliament, they were entitled to a free and exclusive power of legislation in their several provincial Assemblies.

They recognised the legislative competency of Parliament only so far as regarded external commerce; and it is curious to note that while they drew up a petition to the King and prepared an address to the English people, they totally ignored Parliament. In their appeal to the people, they bade them beware lest, in supporting the Government in their attempt to oppress the American colonies, they were not forging chains for themselves. The warning was neglected, and it was only long after, when the country was driven almost to the point of revolution, that the English forced from their rulers a modicum of the right which the Americans won by one firm and determined stand.

The petition to the King was couched in the most loyal and respectful tone, and leaves no doubt in the minds of those who read it that the Congress were sincere in their desire for an amicable settlement of the questions at issue and a restoration of the condition of things which had obtained at the close of the last war.

Having completed its deliberations, the Congress closed its sittings on the 26th of October, not, however, before recommending the convocation of a similar assembly in the month of May following, unless in the meantime their grievances had been fully redressed. But, unfortunately, before that time arrived affairs had reached such a pass that there was no longer any possibility of reconciliation.

CHAPTER IX.

INDEPENDENCE OF THE UNITED STATES.

THE year 1775 opened very gloomily both for England and the colonies. At Boston, the focus and radiating point of the opposition to Parliamentary tyranny, the suffering in consequence of the closing of the port was very great. But not only was all trade at a standstill, there was practically an end of all government too; and it was only by the natural orderliness of the New England people—their instinctive obedience to the unwritten law of human society—that absolute anarchy was avoided. The newly appointed Commissioners of Customs, and the Council got together under the new Act for the government of Massachusetts, were regarded, and treated, with such hostility that in many cases they had to relinquish all pretence of carrying on their functions. Writs had been issued in the autumn for holding an Assembly at Salem, but General Gage appears almost immediately to have "repented him" of his decision, and by a second proclamation endeavoured to stop the elections. The burgesses, however, treated the latter proclamation as illegal, and went on with the selection of their deputies. On the appointed day (October 5th) they assembled at Salem, and, being ignored by the Governor, adjourned to Concord, a town twenty miles from Boston, and then, having chosen Mr. Hancock President, proceeded to appoint a committee to wait on the Governor and place before him the grievances of the province. They in particular complained of the fortification of Boston Neck, and begged him to desist from the work. All that Gage could do in answer to these remonstrances was to tell them that they, by assembling, were acting in contravention of their own charter.

Notwithstanding this warning, the Assembly, utterly unmoved from their purpose, continued their deliberations, and, adjourning to Cambridge on the 17th of October, there proceeded to take the most serious step upon which they had yet ventured, resolving to purchase military stores, and to enlist a number of "minute men," so designated because of their undertaking to be ready for action at a moment's notice. These, and the militia of the province, were placed under the orders of a Committee of Safety, general officers also being appointed in case of need. On the 27th the Assembly adjourned for a month. The Governor, by proclamation, denounced that body as an illegal gathering, and forbade the people to pay any attention to its resolutions and requisitions; vainly, however, the colonists regarding it as their only constituted authority, and obeying its mandates with the utmost alacrity. On their re-meeting the Assembly proceeded to still further lengths, deciding to have a force of twelve thousand men in readiness for any emergency, and appointing a certain number of the militia to act as minute men. They also made arrangements with the neighbouring provinces to have levies ready to act with them, should the need arise, and resolved, in case General Gage moved out of Boston, to oppose him with their whole force.

While such was the state of affairs in New England, the other provinces meanwhile eagerly watching the progress of events, with every desire to help when help should be needed, the outlook in England was not much better. Although there appears to have been a large section of the people opposed to the proceedings against America, they were powerless to make any effective protest. Their petitions were ignored, and the influence of those who raised their voices in Parliament in admonition or warning overwhelmed by the dead weight of unreasoning members. Chatham's eloquence was in vain in the Lords, Burke's in the Commons; and an address to the King in favour of coercive measures was adopted by large majorities in both Houses. In these debates the supporters of the Ministry were most contemptuous in their allusions to the colonists, referring to them as an undisciplined mob, incapable of organisation, and totally unfit to meet a body of regular troops. One braggart colonel went so far as to affirm that he would march through the whole of America with five regiments. Such was too much the sort of talk to which the Government of the day gave heed, and on which they based their measures.

One of the first acts of the new year was the putting in commission of thirty men-of-war and frigates to cover the American coasts and prevent the colonists from being supplied with foreign goods. Such was the Government's answer to Lord Chatham's attempt at conciliation. With his broader view, he saw that the "cancelling a piece of parchment" would not "win back America." It was necessary to "respect her fears and her resentments"; and his Bill, providing for mutual concessions on both sides, since it guarded the rights of the colonies, received the qualified approval of Franklin. But it failed to meet the views of the House of Lords, and was thrown out. Another attempt at conciliation was more successful—in Parliament. It might, too, have gone far to meet the need on the other side of the ocean if it had but come sooner. But, arriving as it did, it proved an untimely and inauspicious birth. It took the form of a resolution, brought forward by Lord North himself, in which he proposed that Parliament should forbear to tax any colony that would of its own accord provide for the cost of defence and civil government within its own confines. Unfortunately, it left too large a margin of doubtful questions to be accepted as a settlement now; moreover, in the course of the debate upon his proposal, North showed how little worthy he was of his high position, or of the trust that ought to be reposable in a statesman who has the destinies of people in his keeping. His "conciliatory proposition," in short, was designed not to benefit, but to breed discord amongst the colonies. "If one consents, a link in the great chain is broken," said he. The origin of his proposal appears to have been the fact that New York had not been so unanimous in accepting the decisions of the Philadelphia

THE EARL OF CHATHAM.

Congress as the other colonies, and the Prime Minister thought that if that colony alone accepted his conciliatory measure, the South would be cut off from the North, from which division much might happen. Both Burke and Colonel Barré, as well as others, spoke strongly against the resolution, but it was carried by large majorities in both Houses, and in due course found its way to the colonial Governors.

This measure was followed by a Bill to restrain the trade of New England to Great Britain and her colonies, and " to prohibit such provinces and colonies from carrying on any fishery on the banks of Newfoundland, or other places . . . under certain conditions, and for a time limited." Lord North justified the Bill on the ground that " as the Americans had refused to trade with this kingdom, it was but just we should not allow them to trade with any other nation." He proposed, however, in his generosity, to exempt certain persons from these regulations if their behaviour satisfied the Governors, and upon their " acknowledgment of the rights of Parliament." It is difficult to write with patience of such paltry measures, the meanness of which are hardly equalled by their cruelty. One can only wonder if these lordships of Ministers and their partisans ever thought of doing to others as they would be done by.

However, let us hasten to get to the end of this miserable chapter of England's folly—the darkest and most dismal of her history. This Bill received the Royal assent on the 30th of March, and, notwithstanding the fact that petitions were flowing in from all parts of the country, representing the ruin that the measures against the colonies were producing in England, and praying for a termination of the contest, Lord North introduced a Bill to serve the Southern colonies in the same way as he had already served the Northern ones in the matter of restraining their trade. Like its predecessor, it speedily became law.

Meanwhile the colonists were as active as ever. On the 1st of February the Assembly of Massachusetts had met at Cambridge; but that town being but four miles from Boston, they were somewhat apprehensive of a surprise visit from General Gage, and therefore decided to remove their deliberations once more to Concord. Those deliberations had mainly to do with their defensive position — the making of firearms and bayonets, and the purchase of powder, artillery, provisions, etc., so as to be ready in case the worst happened. The military stores acquired were to be deposited at Worcester and Concord.

The Governor soon had scent of what was going on, and was almost at his wits' end to know what to do for the best. However, he deemed it well to make sure of such military apparatus or stores as were within his reach.' An expedition for this purpose to Salem, though unsuccessful, gave umbrage to the people, and roused them to fresh activity and vigilance. Their watchfulness was soon rewarded with intelligence of another attempt of the kind. Having learned of the provincial stores at Concord, he determined to seize them, and on the night of the 18th of April, embarked eight hundred of his best troops, grenadiers and light infantry, at Boston Neck, whence they sailed up the Charles River for some distance, and then landed and proceeded on their way to Concord. Lieutenant-Colonel Smith and Major Pitcairn were in command, and they had not gone far before they were aware, from the ringing of bells and the firing of musketry, that their movements had been observed, and that the country was being everywhere aroused.

Reaching Lexington between four and five o'clock in the morning, Major Pitcairn, who was in advance with the light infantry, was there met by a small body of militia. They were standing near the road, and had, it is said, no intention of attacking so large a force as were opposed to them. However, they were there in hostile array, and Major Pitcairn, riding forward, bid them disperse. As they did not do so at once, he drew his sword and fired a pistol. This his detachment appear to have taken as a signal to fire, and did so. Several of the militia fell, the rest dispersed; but the firing was continued, and, on observing this, some of the retreating Americans returned a few shots. Eight colonists were killed in this preliminary encounter.

Pitcairn's detachment being now joined by the main body of the troops, they all proceeded, without further molestation, to Concord. There they were met by another body of militia; they retreated, however, over the bridge, which was held by the light infantry, while the remainder of the troops advanced into the town and destroyed the artillery and stores which had brought them thither. In the meanwhile the provincial militia had been reinforced, and the British troops, as they were about to leave the town, were menaced by the Americans; shots were exchanged, and a sharp skirmish ensued, a number of men falling on either side.

FORTIFYING BUNKER HILL.
(From a design by F. O. Darley.)

At noon the British, having buried their dead, began their march back to Boston; but news had spread of the commencement of hostilities, and blood having been shed, the wildest passions were roused. Armed men hastened to the scene, and, taking advantage of every cover that offered along the road, fired upon the retreating troops, harassing them incessantly until they reached Lexington. Here they were reinforced by nine hundred men under Earl Percy, who, having two field-pieces with him, was able to keep the Americans in check until the troops generally had taken some refreshment. But they had no sooner resumed their march than the provincials renewed their attack, which they kept up almost without intermission until the Royal troops, greatly exhausted, reached Charlestown Neck. This they did about sunset, having lost, during that memorable day, seventy-three men, besides having one hundred and seventy-four wounded. The American loss was forty-nine killed, thirty-five wounded, besides several missing.

Lord Chatham, in the debates in Parliament on the colonies, had warned the Ministry that "the first drop of blood shed in a civil and unnatural war would be *immedicabile vulnus.*"[1] That blood had now been shed, that wound inflicted, and though the time came when Englishmen would have given almost anything to repair the injury, it could not be done.

The battle of Lexington, as it is called, was the signal for war—a long and, for Englishmen, dis-

[1] *Speeches of the Earl of Chatham.*

mally painful war, in which, though there were many acts of noble daring and much wasted heroism, hardly a streak is visible of anything of which a Briton may be truly proud. It is not intended here to go over the record; it has nothing to do with the building of the Empire. The men who worked the business in America were destroyers, whom God forbid England should ever see the like of at the helm of State again.

Suffice it to say that almost immediately after the Lexington affair, colonial militia and volunteers blockaded the British garrison in Boston, preventing its being provisioned, and cutting off foraging parties. Gradually the Americans proceeded to bolder measures, and, making a dash in the night, fortified themselves on Bunker's Hill, an elevation from which they could cannonade the town. Surprised by the audacity of the movement, General Gage sent a body of troops to dislodge the provincials; he found, however, that it was no light matter —found, in fact, that he had to deal with men who were fully able to cope with regular troops—men, indeed, of splendid grit and courage. The British finally succeeded, but their success was achieved at such an enormous sacrifice of life, that General Gage was constrained to confine himself to defensive operations.

Early in July, General Washington, who had been appointed Commander-in-Chief of the American forces by the Congress which met in May, continued the blockade of Boston, the army in which had been greatly reinforced. The Congress had not yet relinquished all hopes of a peaceful settlement, though they despatched forces into Canada, commanded by Generals Montgomery and Arnold, in order, if possible, to induce that province to join with them against the British Government. The Canadians, however, wisely refused to be drawn into the quarrel, and Montgomery having been killed, and Arnold defeated in an attack he made upon Quebec, the invasion came to nought.

From a military point of view Lord North's blunders were as bad as those he had committed in other respects. At first no addition was made to the peace establishment, the impression being that the force on foot would be amply sufficient to reduce the colonies to obedience. Disappointed by their formidable resistance, he increased his expenditure and his armaments till they reached a scale of unprecedented magnitude. But all was in vain; everything went against him. Even his employment of German mercenaries was a sore grievance to the Americans; it proved, indeed, the extra straw upon the camel's back, and completed the alienation of the colonists. They resolved to separate themselves wholly from the mother-country, and on the 4th of July, 1776, Congress published their Declaration of the Independence of the United States.

When this bold step was taken the new Republic was destitute alike of money, ships, and allies; its army was a raw militia, badly armed and clothed, whilst its officers were for the most part wholly unacquainted with scientific warfare. Moreover, though the extent of its territory was enormous, its population was scanty, numbering little more than two millions and a half.

Against it was arrayed a nation, the richest and most powerful in the world, with a reputation for prowess as wide as the seas. The contest seemed almost hopeless. It would have been hopeless but for two things: on the one side there was an unjust cause, on the other side right, and the enthusiasm of right, which in the end carries everything before it.

Another disadvantage, besides that of an unjust cause, attended Britain at this crisis. She had not a single friend either to help or to sympathise with her. Every Court in Europe was soon on the side of the Americans, not because they had such lofty aspirations for freedom, but because they were jealous and envious, and wished ill to the moody and too often truculent old giant. They aided and encouraged the colonists in their resistance; under the guise of an armed association for the protection of maritime rights they supplied them with military stores, assisted them with able and experienced officers, gave their privateers shelter in their ports, and then, when their underhand practices could no longer be concealed, threw off the mask, openly espoused the cause of the revolted colonies, and did their mightiest utterly to overwhelm and undo the object of their hatred and their fear.

Conciliatory measures were at a late hour introduced by Lord North, conceding everything for which the colonists had contended, and they speedily passed both Houses; but before intelligence of this altered policy could be received in America, France had recognised the independence of the United States, and concluded a defensive alliance with them (February, 1778). There had long been many in Britain who favoured such a measure; it was, however, vehemently opposed by the Earl of Chatham, who regarded it as a dismemberment of the Empire; but while addressing the Lords he was struck down in a fit, and died in a few days. Although there had been some inconsistencies in Chatham's views regarding America, he was ever the generous friend of the colonies and the warm advocate of their liberties. While the nation deplored his loss, it did not the less vigorously prepare to meet the dangers which threatened it on every side. War was declared against France, and a fleet of thirty sail, commanded by Admiral Keppel, sent to cruise in the Channel. Keppel met and engaged a French armament of thirty-two sail off Ushant, under Count D'Orvilliers; but being inefficiently supported by Sir Hugh Palliser, his second in command, he was unable to make the most of the slight advantage he gained. The fact is, the canker at the seat of power had affected the services.

Thus far, of the Continental powers, France alone had openly taken part in the American struggle; but the intimate relations betwixt that country and Spain led to a general belief that the latter would not long remain a passive spectator of events. The truth of the suspicion was soon manifest; after a shallow pretence at mediation, the Court of Madrid threw off all disguise, and in June, 1779, openly pre-

ENGAGEMENT OFF USHANT, JULY 27, 1778, BETWEEN THE BRITISH FLEET UNDER ADMIRAL KEPPEL, AND THE FRENCH FLEET UNDER D'ORVILLIERS.

(From a print after a drawing by an officer on board the *Victory*.)

pared for hostilities. One of Spain's main objects in becoming a party to the war being the reduction of Gibraltar, that fortress was laid siege to during the summer. For a time the united fleets of France and Spain rode triumphant in the Channel, and even threatened Plymouth, but beyond the capture of the *Ardent* man-of-war, which fell by accident in the way of the combined forces, they accomplished nothing. While the coalesced Bourbons thus menaced England, Sir George Rodney ably maintained England's maritime renown abroad. He captured off Cape St. Vincent four Spanish ships of the line, under Don Juan de Langara, drove two others on shore, and set fire to a third; thence proceeding to America, he on three several occasions encountered the French fleet under De Guichen, and though he failed to obtain a decisive success, he prevented Washington from receiving naval aid in his meditated attack on New York.

Meanwhile England's perils increased with her exertions to overcome her enemies. A quarrel over the right of searching neutral vessels united Russia, Denmark, and Sweden in the Armed Neutrality league against Britain; nearly all the other states of Europe joining the confederacy, including Holland. The conduct of that Government had for some time given cause for suspicion, and on proof being obtained of its having entered into a treaty with the United States, war was declared (December, 1780), and operations at once commenced against its South American colonies. Admiral Rodney captured the Island of St. Eustatius, with two hundred and fifty

ATTACK ON GIBRALTAR BY SPANISH FLOATING BATTERIES, 1781.
(Redrawn from the *British Naval Chronicle*.)

ships and other booty, estimated at £3,000,000 sterling. Thirty Dutch West Indiamen and a 60-gun ship were also made prizes of, while the colonies of Essequibo and Demerara quietly capitulated. These successes were shortly after followed by the defeat of a Dutch fleet, under Zoutman, on the Dogger Bank, by Sir Hyde Parker.

But while the British held their own at sea, matters went from bad to worse in America. In those waters Sir Samuel Hood was reduced to inactivity by the superior force of the Count de Grasse. The French Admiral cautiously refrained from hazarding a general engagement, but went to the aid of Washington, who was gradually maturing his tactics for bringing the war to an end by a decisive blow. The result was so highly prejudicial to the British arms that Lord Cornwallis was compelled to capitulate with his whole force at Yorktown (October, 1781). This was the second army that had been obliged to surrender to the Americans, and the disaster led to a general feeling in England that any further protraction of the contest would be hopeless. The Government seemed at first resolved to continue the war at all costs, but being unable to command a majority in Parliament, they were forced to resign. A new Ministry, headed by the Marquis of Rockingham and Mr. Fox, commenced negotiations for peace, though without in the meantime relaxing their efforts to carry on the war; but before there had been time for any marked developments arising out of the change, the Cabinet was broken up by the death of the Marquis.

The brief life of this Ministry was signalised by two notable triumphs of the British arms—two victories which at that dark hour saved England's prestige. One was the decisive victory gained by Admiral Rodney over the French fleet under the Count de Grasse in the West Indies on the 12th of April, 1782. Rodney had arrived in those waters in December, forcing his way from England in five weeks. Shortly after reaching St. Lucia he had intelligence of the French fleet under De Grasse having sailed with a large body of troops on board for Cape François, where he was to be joined by a strong Spanish armament for a combined attack on Jamaica. Rodney at once started in pursuit, and came in sight of the fleet abreast of Domenica. An indecisive skirmish took place on the 9th of April, but on the 12th he was fortunate enough to be able to come to close quarters with his antagonist, and to gain a brilliant victory. The battle lasted from seven in the morning till sunset, and resulted in the capture of seven ships of the line and two frigates. Among the number was the *Ville de Paris*, of 112 guns, with Count de Grasse himself on board. This is said to have been the only first-rate man-of-war which up to that date had ever been taken and carried into port. In consequence of the varying nature of the wind, Rodney was enabled to break through the enemy's lines, and so deliver his attack on both sides at once, a manœuvre which was then for the first time tried and successfully executed. This victory not only saved Jamaica and ruined the naval power of France and Spain, but placed Great Britain on a

ENGAGEMENT ON THE DOGGER BANK, AUGUST 5, 1781, BETWEEN THE BRITISH SQUADRON UNDER VICE-ADMIRAL PARKER, AND THE DUTCH SQUADRON UNDER REAR-ADMIRAL ZOUTMAN.

very different footing in the negotiations for peace which had already commenced.

It only needed the splendid victory of General Elliott at Gibraltar (September 13th) to give a finishing blow to the war. On that day a grand attack was made upon the fortress by the combined French and Spanish forces. The cannonade and bombardment from the floating batteries was tremendous; but the Governor, by a well-directed and impetuous discharge of red-hot shot, set fire to the besieging flotilla, the vessels of which blew up one after another, amid a scene of terror and confusion past description. Not a vestige was left on the following day of the formidable preparations that had been made for carrying on this celebrated siege, which had now lasted three years.

The changes of Ministry had protracted the negotiations for peace; but the Earl of Shelburne, who succeeded the Marquis of Rockingham, was, notwithstanding his reluctance, obliged to yield to the demands of Parliament, and the independence of the United States was recognised by the signature of preliminaries at Versailles on the 30th of November, 1782. The honour of concluding this important arrangement is due to Dr. Franklin, who did as much, perhaps, as anyone by his quiet wisdom to bring about this momentous result. Peace with France and Spain, and then with Holland, soon followed; and thus came to an end one of the most disastrous of modern wars, so far as Britain was directly concerned. Indirectly, however, it was fraught with great gain.

Apart from the fact that the loss of the American provinces taught the nation a lesson of wisdom

COUNT DE GRASSE DELIVERING HIS SWORD TO ADMIRAL RODNEY.

which it has never since ceased to remember in its dealings with the colonies, the new start which England made immediately after the termination of the war was evidence of the fact that she had benefited by the loss of those transatlantic possessions. American commerce with England, instead of being destroyed by the War of Independence, began to increase with enormous rapidity the moment friendly relations were re-established. British trade, indeed, was never more prosperous than during the period that immediately succeeded the severing of the colonies. Its progress was accelerated by the sudden decline of the trade of Holland, the greater part whereof passed into the hands of the English. In the three years from 1771 to 1773 the exports to the colonies averaged £3,064,843. This was greater than the preceding years. In 1784 they had already risen to £3,397,500.

Nor was this the whole of the British gain. America had long been a source of expense to the mother-country. Two wars had been waged on her account, the cost of which amounted to upwards of two hundred and forty millions of money, and the expense of her civil government, from the accession of the Brunswick family to the year 1788, is estimated by Sir John Sinclair at forty millions more.[1] In return for these pecuniary sacrifices, Great Britain had the doubtful profit of some navigation and mercantile monopolies that cramped the energies and warped the good feeling of both countries.

During the years just passed in review, England, in every part of the world except one, had been a loser. In America, besides the thirteen colonies,

[1] *History of the Public Revenue of the British Empire.*

she had been obliged to relinquish the fertile province of Florida; so, in the West Indies, in Europe,

ADMIRAL RODNEY.

and on the coast of Africa, the fruits of victories in former wars had by consent to be lopped off. In India alone nothing had been lost. There, indeed, under the firm and resolute government of a man of genius equal to Clive himself, the dominions and power of Britain had been greatly augmented.

Warren Hastings had first gone to India in 1750 as a clerk. After years of service in that capacity chance brought him in contact with Clive, when that "heaven-born general" appeared in the Hugli to settle matters with Surajah Dowlah, and, on the restoration of peace, he was sent as the Company's agent to Moorshedabad. There he remained until 1761, when he was brought back to Calcutta as Member of the Council. Three years later he returned to England, but with so moderate a fortune that, in four years' time, he was glad to accept the position of Member of the Council of Madras. There he applied himself so vigorously to business, and was the means of effecting so many improvements, that the Court of Directors determined to place him at the head of affairs in Bengal. He removed thither in the early part of 1772. Nothing of any particular importance had taken place there since Clive's departure, beyond the famine of 1770, which is said to have swept away a third of the inhabitants of that province. There had been a great lack of administrative ability, combined with much oppression of the natives, however. Hastings was therefore chosen Governor, with express instructions to carry out an important reform and innovation; in short, the directors had resolved " to stand forth as diwán, and to take upon themselves, by the agency of their own servants, the entire care and administration of the revenues," and it devolved upon the new Governor to make the change. In the execution of this reform, Hastings transferred the exchequer from Moorshedabad to Calcutta, and appointed European

GENERAL ELLIOTT.

officers, under the title of collectors, to superintend the collection of the revenue and to preside in the civil courts. It was an important step towards the complete reorganisation of the administration of the Company's dominions, and Hastings would, no doubt, have carried his reforms still further but for the pressure of more urgent affairs.

When Clive returned to England, and had to face the storm of abuse which his reforms in Bengal had called forth, his exposures of the misgovernment that still went on caused Lord North to interfere, and, in 1773, a Regulating Act was passed by which the affairs of the Company were brought more under the supervision and control of Parliament.

Some improvements in the administration of the country were now introduced (1774). The power of the three conflicting presidencies were concentrated in the Governor-General and Council of Bengal, and a court of judicature was established. Under the Act Warren Hastings was appointed the first Governor-General, a post which he continued to hold until the spring of 1785. In his domestic policy he was greatly hampered by Francis, who was one of the Council appointed by Parliament; but so far as regards the external relations with Oudh, with the Mahrattas, and with Hyder Ali, he was generally able to compel assent to his own measures.

Hearing that the French were intriguing with the Mahrattas, Hastings sent an army against them, at first under Colonel Leslie, but afterwards under Colonel Goddard, who succeeded in leading it across the peninsula from sea to sea, and in conquering the rich province of Guzerat almost without a blow. Another officer, Captain Popham, worthy of co-operating with Goddard, had taken the field at the

RAISING THE SIEGE OF GIBRALTAR.
(From an old print.)

beginning of the year (1780) against the Mahratta foes of the Rana of Gohud, who ruled over a hill country between Oudh and the territories of the Mahratta chief Scindia, had driven them out of her dominions, pursued them to their own territory, and taken their fortress of Lahar by assault. This act was followed by one of singular daring; the rock-fortress of Gwalior, one of the strongest in India, defended at that time by a numerous garrison, and regarded as the key of Hindustan, being taken by escalade. These brilliant successes atoned in some measure for the disgrace of the convention of Wargaum, where the Mahrattas dictated terms to the British forces; they also taught the natives to regard nothing as impossible to the pluck and perseverance of the invaders.

But, notwithstanding the Mahrattas had been humbled, they were still able to give trouble by the aid they lent to Hyder Ali, who, with his son Tippoo, proved one of the most formidable foes the British had to deal with in India. Hyder Ali was a soldier of fortune who had raised himself by his abilities to the throne of Mysore. Under the influence of the French at Pondicherry, he had conceived the idea of driving the British out of Hindustan, and in pursuance of this object entered the Carnatic with an overwhelming force, which comprised four hundred French and other European adventurers. The Government of Madras was totally unprepared for the event, and the resources at its command were frittered away by the folly and incapacity of the Council. Nor did the military officers manifest any more ability than the civil authorities. A force under Colonel Baillie was in part cut up in cold blood, in part subjected to a horrible captivity, through the fault of that officer; while another division of the Madras army, under Sir Hector Munro, that might have gone to his aid, remained abjectly aloof within striking distance, then, upon hearing of Baillie's catastrophe, abandoned everything—tents, baggage, artillery, all—and fled to Madras.

BENJAMIN FRANKLIN.

But for the energy and resourcefulness of Warren Hastings at this juncture all would have been lost in the Carnatic and the Northern Circars. In order to raise the money necessary to meet the crisis he committed himself to some acts that will hardly bear justification; but every other consideration gave way before the paramount duty of saving British India. The money was obtained; the incompetent Governor of Madras was recalled, and Sir Eyre Coote, who had done such splendid service in the Carnatic twenty years before, was invited to assume command. The aspect of affairs soon improved when he appeared on the scene. Falling upon Hyder's army—seven thousand men against eighty thousand—at Porto Novo, he totally defeated it (July 1, 1781). Two more defeats—one on the 27th of August, and another on the 27th of September—satisfied Hyder Ali that "the defeat of many Baillies would not destroy these English," and recovered the Carnatic.

Intelligence having come to hand in June of the outbreak of war between Great Britain and Holland, all the Dutch factories and settlements along the coasts were taken (1781), Negapatam alone calling for bombardment before it consented to surrender. Lord Macartney, the new Governor of Madras, followed up these achievements by a successful attack upon Trincomalee, in the Island of Ceylon, a town and port which the Dutch had jealously guarded for more than a hundred years, but which succumbed to the British arms on the 11th of January, 1782. This success, however, was counterbalanced by the defeat of Colonel Braithwait, with a detachment of eighteen thousand natives and one hundred British troops, which was surprised and almost cut to pieces on the left bank of the Cauvery, by an overwhelming force under Tippoo Sahib, assisted by a European contingent of four hundred men commanded by French officers.

A series of engagements took place between Admiral Hughes and Suffrein, the French Admiral in the Eastern seas; but, though fought with great determination, they were invariably indecisive. The latter, however, succeeded in recapturing the weakly garrisoned fortress of Trincomalee. The operations of the British on land were enormous in their extent, embracing the two sides of the vast triangle of India, from the mouths of the Ganges to the Gulf of Cambay, while inland they nearly traversed the base of the triangle; and though many errors of judgment were committed, and numberless jealousies and other ignoble vices displayed, yet, on the whole, the record of achievements was highly creditable to the valour and perseverance of the British.

After the death of Hyder Ali and the restoration of peace between France and England, Tippoo Sultan was induced to listen to terms of accommodation, and the war was brought to a close (March 11, 1784) by a humiliating treaty with the old " Tiger," as the son of Hyder Ali was appropriately named by the natives. Nevertheless, though both parties were bound to restore all they had gained during the war, the result was not unfavourable compared with the outcome of the struggle in America.

Meanwhile, Parliament having now the time to devote to peaceful development, the affairs of India again came up for consideration. In November, 1783, Mr. Fox introduced a Bill for further regulating the affairs of the Company. His idea was to vest the entire administration of the civil and commercial affairs of India in a board of seven commissioners, nominated by the Bill, and irremovable by the Crown, except on an address from either House of Parliament. It was thought, however, that the effect of such a board would be to create a power which would rival that of the King. Whether it would or not, George III. took a dislike to it, and when it had passed the Commons he intimated to his obedient peers that he wished it to be thrown out, and out it went accordingly.

As the Coalition Cabinet had staked its existence on this measure, it resigned, and a Ministry was got together under the auspices of the younger Pitt. A new Parliament established that statesman in such plenitude of power that a fresh Bill was prepared for the institution of a board to check and superintend the civil and military government and revenue of the Company's territories. It transferred to the Crown the power which Mr. Fox's Bill proposed to entrust to Parliamentary commissioners; to the Crown also was given the sole right of appointing the commander-in-chief of the Indian forces. The Court of Directors preserved in appearance the political and commercial powers of the Company, although those powers were in reality delegated to a committee of three elected members of that body, to whom all the more important administrative functions were transferred by the Act. The President of the Board of Control became in effect Secretary of State for India, and the person chiefly responsible to Parliament for the administration of the affairs of that dependency. Thus an important step was taken towards that absorption of India into the British

WARREN HASTINGS.

Empire which was to be definitely accomplished some seventy years later.

This change in the government of India was followed by the impeachment of Warren Hastings, whose trial was protracted over several years, and was made the occasion for an intolerable deal of forensic verbosity. It ended in the acquittal of the ex-Governor-General, at least of wilful error. In short, it came to be recognised by nearly all, that, notwithstanding the many undoubted faults of his administration, Hastings had, on the whole, during a period of unexampled trial and stress, done so much for the maintenance of British rule in the East, that it would have savoured of ingratitude to inflict punishment upon him beyond what he had already received at the bar of public opinion, which almost universally condemned his acts.

Warren Hastings was succeeded in the governorship by Lord Cornwallis, who was also Commander-in-Chief of the forces in India. He found the country in a state of peace, and began his tenure of office with the intention and hope of being able to devote both his time and his energies to administrative reforms and improvements. But he soon found himself involved in a war with Tippoo Sultan, which ended in the old Tiger of Mysore being compelled to agree, in his capital of Seringapatam, to a treaty whereby he ceded one half of his dominions to the British and their allies, and to pay three crores and thirty lacs of rupees [1] towards the expenses of the war. Thus, notwithstanding virtuous resolutions to the contrary, the territories of the Company were greatly increased during the governorship of Lord Cornwallis. Many noteworthy reforms and improve-

[1] Nearly £3,500,000 sterling.

ments, both in the military and in the civil establishments, were also effected; but his first administration was chiefly marked by the permanent settlement of the land revenue.

CHAPTER X.

AN AGE OF DEVELOPMENT AND REVOLUTION.

IT is worthy of note that, while England was playing such a losing game in America, and in the East as well as in the West was fighting for very life single-handed against the world, she never lost heart or hope. Her foes thought that, after the severance of that noble limb, for which she had fought so strenuously, her resources would be curtailed and her energies crippled forever. Vain wish! Though mangled and bleeding from the furious contest, her momentary weakness was but the syncope of the Titan. The irrepressible vitality of the people, throwing itself with renewed vigour into every form of industry and commerce, soon set the nation to rights again.

But how much peace and wise counsels were then needed is shown by the condition of the Navy at the time of the peace of 1783. The confederated navies of the Bourbons greatly outnumbered that of Britain. Exclusive of the Dutch fleet of twenty-five sail of the line, the combined forces of France and Spain amounted to a hundred and forty sail of battleships; whereas the entire strength of this country, fit for service, did not exceed a hundred sail of the line; while of these many were undermanned, unclean, and in a rotten state from having been long employed on foreign stations. Nor were the land forces in a much better condition than the naval. Add to this the impoverished state of the country, with a national debt, funded and unfunded, of upwards of two hundred and fifty millions, requiring little short of nine and a half millions to pay the annual interest thereon, and, as it is alleged, a population greatly decreased by the war,[1] and it will be readily conceived how much the nation needed time to rest and to set its house in order.

There were also furious discontents to be reckoned with, some smouldering, some in open revolt, and an ignorance among the labouring classes that was appalling. But there were not wanting evidences of a nobler spirit that was arising, and that was destined to have an important influence upon the future " of this noble monarchy," as the elder Pitt described it. The growing change was due in part to the effect that had been produced upon the national conscience by such men as Wesley, Whitefield, and others of their spiritual force and stamp. Even the irresponsive nerves of a laggard Church began to show some signs of life, albeit rather of the material than of the spiritual sort.

Howard had already (1773) begun his self-imposed task of bringing about a reform in the management of prisoners, visiting most of the gaols in England,

[1] *Annual Register*, xxvi., 152.

and bringing the results of his inquiries before the House of Commons in 1774. He subsequently continued his investigations by visits to many of the Continental prisons, and by his unwearied exertions was the means of greatly ameliorating the conditions of prison life.

The first premonitory movements for the abolition of the slave trade also had their beginnings about this time, under the advocacy of Clarkson, Wilberforce, and others. Those ideas, as we have seen, had their inception among the Quakers of Pennsylvania, or more properly among their Moravian fellow-colonists ; and they doubtless acquired an added impulse from the agitation of the general question of liberty and the natural rights of man set on foot by the American colonies. When the newly established Republic was discussing its Constitution, some of the members of the Convention were in favour of then and there extending to the slaves the charter of freedom; but, on the ground that the question was one for each separate State to decide for itself, the opportune moment was allowed to slip by unimproved. Washington was then all powerful, and a warm friend of emancipation. Possibly, had he stood up for the negro, he might have had him too participate in the declaration of rights. But it is not to be expected that a man can be great all round and at all times. Still, if Washington had been equal to the occasion, what a misery and a stain he would have spared his country, and how much added glory, too, he would have given to perhaps the noblest Constitution in the world!

The country appeared almost ripe for the experiment. There were many friends of freedom to the slave among the planters, and societies in favour of

GENERAL WASHINGTON.

abolition were in existence throughout the Southern States. But all that was soon ended by an industrial invention. When the Constitution of the

United States was adopted it was not known that the cultivation of cotton could be made profitable in the Southern States. The implement for cleaning cotton, known as the "roller-gin," could only clean half a dozen pounds a day by slave labour. But Eli Whitney, a New England schoolmaster, residing in Georgia, seeing the imperfection of the machine, set his wits to work and invented what is called the saw-gin, by which the cotton was pulled through parallel wires with openings too narrow to permit the seeds to pass. By this simple contrivance one slave was enabled to clean a thousand pounds of cotton a day. What an effect this had upon the cotton trade may be gathered from the fact that the exports increased from a hundred and eighty-nine thousand pounds in 1791 to twenty-one millions in 1801; and in three more years they doubled.[1] The result of this sudden expansion of the cotton industry was to make the negro slave a far more valuable chattel than he had hitherto been; indeed, it rendered him indispensable to the planter, and thenceforward there was no more talk of abolition in the cotton-growing States.

From the commercial point of view, the influence of this contrivance, combined with a series of remarkable inventions made in England, which had prepared the way for it, has been almost too great for any formal estimation. Indeed, industrially, there is nothing more striking during the earlier half of the reign of George III. than the number of wonderful mechanical appliances that

[1] M'Culloch, *Statistical Account of the British Empire.*

gave an impulse to manufacturing activity, and enabled England to outdo all other countries in the race of competition.

In 1764, James Watt, a native of Greenock, began his wonderful improvements in the application of steam power which have rendered his name famous. A few years later, James Hargreaves, an ingenious carpenter of Blackburn, invented the spinning-jenny, by which he was able to spin with several spindles at once. It was subsequently carried to such perfection that a child could work no fewer than from eighty to a hundred and twenty spindles! Suspecting that he employed machinery, his neighbours broke into his dwelling and destroyed his machine; and on the repetition of this kind of persecution Hargreaves removed, in 1768, to Nottingham, where he set up business as a manufacturer.

The spinning-jenny could only be applied to the spinning of cotton for weft, being unable to give to the yarn that degree of fineness and strength requisite in the longitudinal thread or warp. This deficiency was soon after supplied by the introduction of the spinning-frame, which spins a vast number of threads of any degree of fineness and hardness, leaving the operator merely to feed the machine with cotton and to join the threads when they happen to break. The invention of this marvellous machine is usually ascribed to Richard Arkwright, a native of Preston. But Mr. Baines, in his *History of the Cotton Manufacture*, shows that the credit of being the original discoverer is due to John Wyatt, who, thirty years previously, had attempted to spin by the same method—that is, by rollers. Either from the imperfection of his machinery, the want of capital, or the necessary skill, however, Wyatt was obliged to relinquish his undertaking; so that the merit of rendering this important invention a practical success undoubtedly belongs to Arkwright. He took out his first patent for spinning by rollers in 1769; but, having made several additional discoveries and improvements in the processes of carding, roving, and spinning, he obtained a fresh patent for the whole in 1775, and thus completed a system of machinery of the most ingenious and complicated nature.

These inventions were followed by the contrivance of the mule-jenny—so called from its being a compound of the spinning-jenny and the spinning-frame. It was the invention of Samuel Crompton of Bolton. The mule shared in the odium excited among the Lancashire hand-loom weavers against machinery, and for a time Crompton was obliged to conceal his invention. Various improvements were made from time to time on the mule, but the original principle, as devised by Crompton, remained the same. The sum of £5000, voted to him by Parliament in 1812, was almost all the remuneration he received for an invention which contributed so largely to the development of British manufactures.

Somewhat later a still further advance was made by the introduction of the power-loom, the invention of Edmund Cartwright, a clergyman of Kent. His first power-loom was brought into action in 1785, and effected the same economy of labour in weaving which the jennies had brought about in spinning.

Although much opposed both by manufacturers and workmen, the power-loom made its way, and in a developed and improved form is still in universal use.

Another notable invention of this period was that of the processes of puddling and rolling iron. This was the achievement of Henry Cort, who commenced work at Gosport, Hampshire, erected ironworks, and studied with great success methods of improving the manufacture of iron. Having been brought to ruin through the conduct of a partner, Government came to his aid (1794) with a pension of £200 a year.

By these and other labour-saving inventions and discoveries an enormous impulse was given to manufactures and industry of every kind. At the same time vastly increased facilities were being given for the interchange of commerce by the construction of roads and canals. Up to near the close of last century the roads of the three kingdoms were for the most part simply execrable. Arthur Young says many of them were to be shunned as cautious people shun the devil. So late as 1763 there was only one coach a month from Edinburgh to London; and it took from twelve to fourteen days to perform the journey. But the beginning of better things commenced when, in 1767, the engineering genius of Brindley connected Manchester and Liverpool by means of a canal which crossed the Irwell on a lofty aqueduct. The success of the undertaking led to the construction of water-ways in every direction, and to their utilisation by every branch of industry. At the same time attention began to be turned very strenuously to the improvement of roads, and in the interval between 1784 and 1792 there were three hundred and two Acts of Parliament passed in relation to the construction of roads and bridges. Sixty-four other Acts were obtained in the same period for the formation of canals, harbours, etc.

Not only did manufactures and commerce benefit by these improvements, but agriculture likewise. The increased volume of trade also had its effect upon the methods of agriculture, which were greatly improved. Then, in consequence of the vast augmentation of individual and national wealth, and the general prosperity of the working classes, there resulted a rapid increase in population.

In other directions also the mind finds relief from the turmoil and strife of politics and the resounding tread of armed men. During the continuance of the work of discord and destruction, some useful results for progress and civilisation were being achieved. About the time when the American quarrel was becoming acute, Admiral Byron, the grandfather of the poet, began that series of maritime explorations which was ere long to result in the foundation of colonies as great as those England had lost. He had previously sailed in Anson's famous expedition, when he suffered shipwreck in the *Wager*, and returned to write a very interesting story of his adventures. It was thought that he would be a suitable man to make explorations in the Pacific; he was therefore given the *Dolphin* and the *Tamar*, and despatched on a voyage of discovery; but, though he circumnavigated the globe, he succeeded in adding very little to the world's geographical knowledge, beyond discovering some of the most northerly islands of the group known as the Low Archipelago, to which he gave the name of St. George's Islands. He had previously taken possession of the Falkland Islands for Great Britain. Spain claimed a prior right to them, but finally ceded them to England in 1770.

Byron's run round the world was the quickest then on record, and it was, on the whole, the least noteworthy. Much more satisfactory were the voyages of Captains Wallis and Carteret in the *Dolphin* and the *Swallow* (1766-69). Carteret had been Byron's lieutenant in his circumnavigation. Now, in the *Swallow*, after separating from Wallis and the *Dolphin*, he showed the true exploring instinct by zig-zagging and cruising to and fro in the Pacific. On the 2d of July, 1776, he discovered Pitcairn's Island, famous in connection with the mutineers of the *Bounty*, and in the same year completed Dampier's discovery by showing that St. George's Bay in New Britain was really a channel dividing the island into two, New Britain and New Ireland. After making many other discoveries, and naming the islands of Sandwich, Byron, and New Hanover, and several others, Carteret returned to England by way of the Philippines, Java, and the Cape of Good Hope, thus concluding one of the most successful exploring expeditions since Dampier's time (1769).

Wallis had returned the previous year, having discovered, or revisited, a number of islands, including that of Tahiti, first discovered by the Spaniard Quiros.

The year before Carteret's return saw the departure of the greatest of modern navigators on his first voyage of discovery. Captain Cook, then simply lieutenant, and forty years of age, was the son of an agricultural labourer, who, having served his apprenticeship as a sailor, joined the Royal Navy to avoid being pressed, and, in 1759, was appointed master of the *Mercury*, in which, during the naval operations in the St. Lawrence, he was employed in surveying the channel of the river and in piloting the vessels of the fleet. So well did he do the work that he was reported to Lord Colville, who appointed him master of his own ship, the *Northumberland*. After spending some time in Newfoundland, where he held the position of marine surveyor of the coast of that island and of Labrador, he returned to England.

About this time it was decided to send an expedition to the Pacific to observe the transit of Venus, and Cook was appointed to take the command in the *Endeavour*. He was accompanied by Mr. (afterwards Sir Joseph) Banks and Dr. Solander. The *Endeavour* reached Tahiti in April, 1769, and the transit having been successfully observed, six months on the homeward voyage were spent on the coast of New Zealand, which was for the "first time sailed round, examined, and charted with some approach to accuracy."[1] Proceeding thence to Australia, or New Holland, as it was then called, Cook sighted the southern point of that island-continent on the 18th of April, 1770. On the 21st he descried ascending smoke, and concluded that the country was

[1] *National Dictionary of Biography.*

inhabited. On the 13th of May natives were seen. The same day a landing was effected, and the whole coast, from the 38th to the 10th degree of south

CAPTAIN COOK.

latitude, taken possession of in the name of George III. From a supposed resemblance to the coast of Wales, Cook gave the country the name of New

South Wales. Passing then between Australia and New Guinea, he proved them conclusively to be different islands.

THE "ENDEAVOUR" OFF TAHITI.

The first port in the larger island—the largest island in the world—that Captain Cook entered was Botany Bay (April, 1770). Thence he sailed to the north, passing Port Jackson, which, from its narrow entrance, he supposed to be merely a boat harbour, and named it after the sailor then on the look-out at the masthead. Eighteen years later that port was to become the site of the first British settlement in the Southern seas, and to form the nucleus of the colony of New South Wales. After a voyage of nearly three years the *Endeavour* reached England about the middle of 1771.

In the following year Cook commanded a second expedition, the main object of which was to verify the reports of a great southern continent. It consisted of two ships, the *Resolution*, of 460 tons, of which Captain Cook had the command, and the *Adventure*, of 330 tons, under Captain Furneaux. In order to settle the question of the supposed Antarctic continent the ships were kept for months along the edge of the ice. At length they were separated owing to the prevalence of fogs, and the *Resolution* arrived alone in New Zealand. After exploring the New Hebrides and discovering New Caledonia, Cook reached home in July, 1775. His exploration of the Southern Pacific was so thorough that he left but little for future explorers to do, and the maps of that region remain practically as he left them.

A year later Captain Cook started out on his third expedition, its object being to ascertain the possibility of a north-west passage. He sailed in the *Resolution*, and was accompanied by Captain Clarke in the *Discovery*. After exploring the western coast of North America until stopped by the ice, and discovering Nootka Sound, afterwards the cause of a famous dispute with Spain, he turned south and discovered the Sandwich Islands, and anchored in Karakakoa Bay on the 17th of January, 1779. They were well received by the natives, and remained in the harbour until the 4th of February, when the ships put to sea. In consequence, however, of the

Resolution having sprung her mainmast in bad weather, they returned to their former anchorage. For some unexplained reason the demeanour of the natives now changed; insolent thefts were committed, and when Captain Cook went on shore with an escort of marines, intending to bring off the king as a friendly hostage, the islanders interfered and would not let him go, although he was quite willing to do so. As the natives began to arm, Captain Cook, anxious to avoid bloodshed, returned to the boats. On reaching the shore, the marines and the men in the boats fired on the crowd of natives. Cook commanded them to stop firing, and called out for the boats to close in. Only one obeyed, and in the struggle to get into it several of the marines were killed. Captain Cook, who was left alone on the shore, in trying to reach the boat, was struck from behind and stunned. While thus powerless, and on his knees, another native stabbed him with a dagger. Others now joined in the attack, and what with clubs and knives he was soon a lifeless corpse. While this was taking place the in-shore boat was thrown into such a state of confusion by the marines struggling to get into it that it could render the captain no assistance. The other boat, which might have gone to his help, remained passively looking on, and finally returned on board without so much as attempting to rescue the captain's body from the savages. Some portion of his remains only were afterwards secured.

Thus ended (February 14, 1779) the career of one of the most notable of England's seamen, none the

THE DEATH OF CAPTAIN COOK.

less worthy of a high niche in the temple of fame because his achievements were of peace. His discoveries caused almost as great a sensation in Europe as had previously those of Columbus, and before his death was known, M. Turgot, the Minister of Louis XVI., had issued an order to the French cruisers not to molest the famous navigator should they fall in with him on his homeward voyage, since he was a " benefactor of all nations." In consequence of these explorations the islands of the Pacific were soon as well known as those of the West Indies, and their productions as much sought after. Nor was it long before the viking race of these islands was founding trading stations and settling colonies at a hundred points in those far-off seas. It was as though a new world had been thrown open for the growth and expansion of the British people. Cook himself had suggested the expediency of forming a settlement on the coast of New South Wales, and within ten years of his death the first unpromising nucleus of the swarming millions that now people the various islands of Australasia set sail from England.

Here, again, we see the influence of the revolted colonies. It had been the inhuman custom to get rid of the cost and inconvenience of criminals by selling them into slavery in the plantations. This had been going on since the year 1717, the price per head averaging about £20, and the number of offenders thus disposed of being about two thousand a year. The separation of the unlucky thirteen colonies put an end to this unrighteous system, and for a time Government was at its wits' end to know what to do with the convicts that were crowding its gaols. One proposal put forward was to send them to the coast of Africa, and set them loose among the natives—black sheep among black men; another was to build huge penitentiaries for their reception. It happened, however, that the public mind had only recently been stirred by John Howard's descriptions of the abominations of prison-life, and the general conscience was too much awake to allow of either of these methods to be adopted. The one was abandoned primarily on account of the unhealthiness of the climate of the west coast of Africa, the other by reason of its hopelessness as a means of reclaiming offenders.

At this juncture the favourable account given by Captain Cook of New South Wales determined the Government to attempt the formation of a penal settlement at Botany Bay (so named by Sir Joseph Banks). Accordingly in the year 1784, an Act was passed empowering his Majesty in Council to appoint a place beyond the seas whither offenders might be transported; and by two orders in Council, dated the 20th of December, 1786, the eastern coast of Australia and the adjacent islands was fixed upon as the places of banishment.[1]

The first batch of criminals was sent out in the spring of the following year, under the command of Captain Arthur Phillips, R. N., who was to be Governor of the penal settlement. A small fleet, consisting of the frigate *Sirius* and an armed tender,

[1] Martin, *The British Colonies.*

together with three store-ships and six transports, carrying 565 male and 192 female convicts, besides the necessary guard of marines, with the wives and children of many of the latter. Setting sail about the middle of May, the expedition reached Botany Bay in January, 1788, after a voyage of upwards of eight months. Four weeks, however, had been spent at the Cape of Good Hope.

On examination Captain Phillips found Botany Bay so ill adapted for a settlement that he resolved to examine another inlet, to which Captain Cook had given the name of Broken Bay, and see if it offered a better site. On his way thither he tarried to look into the " boat harbour," which Cook, in his ignorance of its true character, had designated such, and called Port Jackson. To his astonishment he " found himself in a haven in which the whole of the British Navy might securely ride at anchor, navigable for vessels of any burden fifteen miles from its mouth, indented with numerous coves, and sheltered from every wind."[1]

To this more promising situation the fleet was at once removed, and on the 26th of January, 1788, the British flag was hoisted on the shores of Sydney Cove, which soon began to echo to the stroke of the woodman's axe and to other sounds of human and humanising labour. The ground, which was but thinly wooded, was quickly cleared, tents were pitched, stores and live stock landed, and the little colony, numbering 1030 souls, provisionally planted. This done, the Governor's first care was to give

[1] Martin.

every encouragement to cultivation, so that the settlement might as soon as possible produce its own food. Farms were laid out, and, to encourage the others, a few of the more trustworthy convicts were set at liberty and given grants of land, so that they began life afresh in the new colony as free settlers.

THE "SIRIUS" AND "SUPPLY" IN JACKSON'S BAY.

In February, Lieutenant King sailed in the tender *Supply* for Norfolk Island, an islet of about twelve square miles in extent, six hundred miles east of New South Wales, where, in accordance with Captain Phillips's instructions, it was proposed to form a settlement for the cultivation of the flax plant, which Captain Cook had found growing there in great profusion, as well as the famous pine named after the island. In addition to provisions for six months, the *Supply* carried a surgeon, three marines, two persons supposed to have a knowledge of the process of dressing flax, nine male and six female convicts, with the necessary tools, implements, and so forth. Great difficulty was experienced in landing the little colony, the coast being very precipitous, and five lives were lost in the operation. However, the climate was found to be healthy and the soil productive, and so the settlement started with every prospect of success.

Meanwhile, at Sydney Cove the inevitable difficulties attending such an enterprise were encountered. Scurvy broke out, idleness was rampant among the convicts, and, to add to other annoyances, the natives became troublesome. This evil was augmented by the bad conduct of many of the convicts, who, when they could get a chance, would wander away into the woods, and, if they met the aborigines, too often behave very ill to them. There was a notion among these settlers-against-their-will that China lay but a little way to the north of Port Jackson, and they were forever making off in order to escape to that celestial land. At one time there are said to have been no fewer than forty persons absent on that wild-goose quest. Many of these men died of famine in the woods, while others were killed by the natives, and, not improbably, eaten.

To other griefs was presently added the prospect of famine. That danger was, however, ere long warded off for the time being by the arrival of the *Sirius* with a four months' supply of flour from the

Cape. But, other difficulties arising, it was deemed advisable to send a large number of the colonists to Norfolk Island, from which the accounts continued favourable. Accordingly, in the month of February, 1790, upwards of two hundred convicts, together with two companies of marines, were sent thither in the *Sirius* and the *Supply*. A serious disaster attended this unfortunate expedition, the *Sirius* being wrecked on a reef just off the island, and all the provisions she carried with her lost. Happily no lives were sacrificed, all on board being dragged on shore by means of a grating.

Martin gives an interesting account of the way in which the population of Norfolk Island, thus greatly augmented without a corresponding increase of the food-supply, was preserved from starvation. Just when everybody thought they were on the eve of perishing of hunger an enormous flight of aquatic birds alighted on the island to lay their eggs. " Owing to the length of their pinions, these birds take wing with difficulty; and their numbers were so great that for two months the settlers caught at least from two thousand to three thousand every night, and also procured an incalculable quantity of eggs." No wonder these timely visitors were hailed as " the birds of Providence."

No such winged food-supply came to the aid of the settlers at Sydney Cove, however, when, in the early part of 1790, in consequence of the non-arrival of the long-looked-for ships with provisions from England, the ration issued from the public store to each man for seven days was, $2\frac{1}{2}$ lbs. of flour, 2 lbs. of rice, and 2 lbs. of pork. Every exertion was made to eke out these miserable doles by hunting and fishing, and some amelioration of the condition of the people was thus effected. This state of things lasted from April till towards the end of June, when the *Justinia* arrived from England with a large supply of provisions.

During these trials, as indeed throughout the entire period of his governorship, which was brought to a close through declining health at the end of 1792, the conduct of Captain Phillips was such as one would expect from a true man. "He gave up," says Martin, "three hundredweight of flour which was his private property, declaring that, although it was not in his power to remove the want felt by the convicts, they might at least know that it was equally experienced even at the Government House; and to this resolution he rigidly adhered." Along with the supplies, or at least a few days afterwards, arrived another large accession of convicts, whose numbers, however, had been terribly reduced by sickness on the voyage.

After this all anxiety respecting provision supplies was obviated by the adoption of a more methodical system. Other improvements were likewise introduced, and a brighter and more stable aspect was given to things by the laying out of the lines for a regular town, and the commencement of various public buildings. The non-commissioned officers and privates of the marines were encouraged to become settlers by grants of land; and as a few unforced colonists arrived from time to time, the settlement began gradually to assume the appearance of a place of some life and importance. Towards the end of 1791 another large consignment of convicts arrived in ten vessels convoyed by H.M.S. *Gorgon*, of whom about twenty per cent. died on their way out. Thus began the first British colony started under Government auspices and at the expense of the executive, and it was done to get rid of an incumbrance.

The great mistake of the governing classes up to this period was that they rarely did anything for the toiling and producing millions, whose inexhaustible energies and quenchless vitality made empire possible; and even when they were obliged to do something for them, it was done badly, and with a grudging, stepmotherly hand. Anything in the way of repression, curtailment of rights, or squeezing for revenue, that they did willingly and with much natural ease; but anything more they had not yet risen to the nobility to do. An historian of the time has well observed, the happiness and real well-being of the people was a thing not then thought of. As a small instance in point, it may be mentioned that it never occurred to the members of the Privy Council, who were concerned in sending out the first clutch of jailbirds to New South Wales, to appoint a clergyman to go out with them. One was found to proceed with them at the last moment, albeit not through their instrumentality; and, if Mr. Martin is right, this clergyman had for several years to hold his services in the open air, and when a temporary place of worship was finally put up, it was at his own expense.

This is perhaps a minor matter, and may be attributed to forgetfulness; but in 1775 there was passed a repealing Act which exhibits all the ingrained self-seeking and injustice of the then governing classes. By the statute 31 Eliz. cap. 7, it was enacted that no labourers' cottages should be erected without laying four acres of ground to them. It had worked well for two centuries. But the Act was repealed; thus beginning the injurious policy by which, in the course of a little over half a century, the backbone of the country was driven from the land. No more perilous policy was ever inaugurated; and should the day come when Britain has to fight for dear life, as she has had to do many a time before, it may be found that men will not stake their lives for a land in which they have no inheritance save one of sentiment.

However, notwithstanding evidences like these of a narrow and selfish statesmanship, there were some signs of improvement during the peaceful years between the close of the American war and the outbreak of the upheaval following the French Revolution. One of these was Pitt's liberal and comprehensive measure for the government of Canada. While it copied some of the defects along with the excellences of the British Constitution, it avoided the cardinal error that gave rise to the American contest by leaving the Canadians to levy their own taxes. Another sign of the changing spirit was the treaty of commerce with France, framed on a more liberal principle than had theretofore been possible. Trade, however, was not destined long to benefit from it, for within two years of its enactment occurred the Revolution, which for many a year to come threw Europe into the condition of a disturbed ant-hill, and upset thrones like nine-pins.

It is curious to note, in connection with that social and political earthquake, how remorseless is the unsighted Nemesis, waiting on each event with its inevitable and passionless doom. France saw England in a death-grip with her revolted colonies, and, light of heart, went to the aid of suffering liberty—went to the aid of a people struggling for liberty, who, compared with her own sons, were as enfranchisement to degradation. Her sons fought nobly in that great cause, saw victory won, and the great achievement established. Then they returned home, to mark the contrast in unhappy France, and to sow the seeds of liberty and the rights of man there. In the homely phrase, Louis XVI., and still more Marie Antoinette, played with fire, and presently saw their own homestead in a blaze. It cannot be maintained, of course, that the French Revolution was entirely the outcome of the successful establishment of American independence—other causes had unquestionably been long at work; but there can be no doubt that it was a very powerful proximate cause and stimulus, and that the acts of the King and the Court, conceived in no spirit of righteousness, bore within themselves the seeds of their own punishment.

BOOK IV.

COMPLETING THE EDIFICE.

CHAPTER I.

A TITANIC CONTEST.

LOOKING at the process of empire-building with a sufficiently large perspective, one is struck with the points of resemblance it presents to the work of the polypiferous reef-builders. In each case the individual, whether coral-insect or man, following an innate instinct, takes its appropriate place in the industrial army, and with views no larger than its simple wants, surely and silently helps forward the united effort, each deftly fitting in its part and accomplishing its appointed task, each in its way as strong as the completed whole. The difference in the case of man is that his instincts are wider, his structure nobler, and that, notwithstanding his added power to know, and to aim at, better ends, he is not always allowed a latitude and verge commensurate with his needs. Others of the species cannot be satisfied with their own native and legitimate sphere, but with infinitely finite powers, must for ever be trying to modify, and in the attempt ever marring, the Divine plan; failing to observe, or forgetting, that all true impulse comes from within, and that the natural powers and instincts of the human mind are such as to fit the race to work harmoniously and with the nicest adjustment of the individual to the aggregate need. The world will learn in time, perhaps, that the greatest part, if not the whole duty of government, is to educate, to guide and direct from within, not to force, check, and restrain from without. But the history of mankind is little else but one long and wearying record of the application of the most brutal methods, of the stirring up of passion, prejudice, and hatred, of the attempt to enrich and aggrandise some at the expense of others—a chapter of blunders, injustice, and folly.

One cannot help being struck with these things as one reads how, when Pitt proposed his new treaty of commerce with France—one of the brightest streaks of light in the dismal chaos of politics that characterises George III.'s reign—one Member of Parliament expressed a fear lest such a *rapprochement* should have a pernicious influence upon the character of the English; as though that celestial race might lose something of its angelic quality by too close a contact with the French—a people every way as noble, every way as brave, and with a record as regards achievements in science and letters in all respects as great as that of the English. Not less surprising is it to find another statesman reproaching the author of the measure with the fact that he had risen to a higher view than his father, the elder Pitt, in that he had ceased to regard the French as the natural and hereditary enemies of the English. Another wise statesman, we read with an astonishment that almost takes away the breath, professed to believe, and was in the habit of hysterically propounding, that the British Constitution was so perfect that to touch it was to endanger its ruin; while the House of Commons was "as good as human nature would permit it to be," although the said House was at the time absolutely steeped in corruption. Even Pitt, with his larger view and deeper insight, could not leave the human polyps to do their work unhindered, but must be everlastingly interfering to preserve that figment of political chicane, the balance of power.

It was this blind policy that, in 1793, committed Great Britain to a war which, with a break of a few months, kept her people throbbing to the battle-drum and the sword until 1815, and besides costing the lives of thousands of her sons, drained the country of millions of treasure. In the end there was some reason for the expenditure; but in 1793 Great Britain was hurried into an unjustifiable contest through the ravings of Burke and men of his stamp—men who at a time when the ripest wisdom of the wisest was needed to guide the nation through as acute a crisis as the world ever saw could do no better than cry, "Be alarmists; diffuse terror!" and urge the world on to carnage in order to extirpate an opinion.

Up to that time the French Revolution, notwithstanding some excesses, had been beneficial. The body politic had fallen into such a corrupt state that it needed purifying, and the purification could not be effected by the innocuous draughts of coloured water with which obliging physicians amuse their deluded patients. A drastic remedy was necessary; and there was nothing thus far to show that the treatment had gone beyond the requirements of the disease. But the crowned heads of Europe, always intolerant of a free people, decided to interfere, and their interference drove a spirited people to acts which cast a shade over the glory of their achievement, and to which they would not have had recourse but for that intermeddling. The welter of carnage that followed was as much—if not more—the result of European diplomacy and tyranny, as of the French Revolution. The spectacle is one calculated to drive a philosopher to despair. Fortunately it is not the business of this record to trace its rise and progress—to do more, indeed, than refer briefly here and there to its course, as it touches the more vital interests of that Greater Britain, the expansion of which, like the work of the coral-insect, goes on much the same whether the surrounding elements be in a state of storm or calm. The earlier part of the contest was one of almost continued disaster and reverses to England. It was a war in which, as in the case of the American colonies, there was arrayed against us and our allies a nation in a state of the wildest enthusiasm—a nation which, standing alone, had defeated the confederated despotisms of Europe, transformed the dregs of cities into warriors and heroes, and wedded Victory like a bride to her banners.

Well had it been if England had withdrawn from the contest at the commencement of 1795. The object of the war was unattained and unattainable. The restoration of the Bourbons had become hopeless; the people were more than ever enamoured of their republican principles; had they now been allowed to settle down in peace with their new constitution the world might have been spared that delirium of glory which was, unfortunately, soon to follow, and the consequent deluge of blood. Already (in 1794) the Convention had caused to be printed and published a list of their triumphs. Among their conquests were enumerated the Austrian Netherlands and the seven United Provinces, exclusive of their acquisitions on the Rhine, in Spain, in Savoy, and in Italy. In seventeen months they had won twenty-seven pitched battles, besides no end of minor victories, in which they had slain eighty thousand of their enemies, taken over that number of prisoners, besides capturing an enormous quantity of cannon and other material of war. These losses had induced many powers to withdraw from the confederacy. At the end of 1795 England had for allies Russia, Naples, Sardinia, and the Pope. Prussia had had the meanness to take the British subsidy, and then, making peace with France, use the money for the destruction of Poland. All these powers were ready to sacrifice England at any moment, and turn their arms against her, as some of them ere long did. On land it had been one dismal chapter of disasters for the allies. England herself had suffered a miserable defeat in Holland,

THE "GLORIOUS FIRST OF JUNE," 1794.

against which, and the loss of so many allies, the destruction of the Toulon fleet, the acquisition of Corsica and Guadaloupe, and the naval victory of

Lord Howe, afforded but small compensation. The latter, nevertheless, was a brilliant affair, and sent London almost delirious with joy. It was fought in the Bay of Biscay on the 1st of June, 1794. The opposed fleets were fairly equal, the French numbering twenty-six ships against twenty-five on the side of the British. The battle began a few minutes before ten in the morning, and was practically over by noon, all concerted action being by that time at an end, and the afternoon being spent overhauling and taking possession of the disabled ships. Seven were captured, of which one, the *Vengeur*, went down almost immediately after being taken, hardly any of her crew, who had fought with signal bravery, being saved. In the captured ships alone the killed and wounded amounted to 1270, while the total British loss was 904.

Pitt would have ended the war, but he stood almost alone in the desire for peace. Immediately afterwards the character of the contest changed; the almost unchecked triumph of their arms on land, especially under the ascendant star of Napoleon Bonaparte, had created in the French an appetite for victory, coupled with unbounded dreams of conquest; there was no stopping now until that meteoric scourge had run his course. But, mad as the conflict was, it produced giants—giants on the part of the British to meet and contend against the giants born of the Revolution in France, and in the end they brought the country safe out of the Titanic struggle.

When, however, in return for all her subsidies and

BATTLE OF ST. VINCENT, JULY 14, 1797.
(After a drawing by Lieut. J. Brenton, R.N.)

sacrifices, England was finally not merely left alone in the struggle, but threatened with a coalition such as well-nigh proved her destruction during the American conflict, she again rose to the height of her imperial destiny, and in two great naval engagements inflicted irreparable disaster on her enemies. There was a plan to win possession of the Channel by a union of the French, Dutch, and Spanish fleets, and under their cover to land forces in Ireland to aid a projected rising. But when, in the month of February, 1797, the Spanish Admiral put to sea with twenty-seven sail of the line, he was met off Cape St. Vincent by Sir John Jervis with fifteen sail, and driven back to Cadiz with the loss of four of his finest vessels. The Spanish loss was six hundred killed and wounded, the British three hundred. The action is the more notable as being the first in which Nelson came prominently into notice. He was then commodore; and for the way in which he distinguished himself in the action, he received the honour of knighthood, Jervis himself being raised to the peerage.

The other victory, which was of almost more momentous importance, because won against men who really knew how to fight at sea, was that of Admiral Duncan over the Dutch, on the coast of Holland, off Camperdown, on the 11th of October. The design of Admiral de Winter was to protect a French force intended for Ireland. But Duncan was lying in wait for him, when his squadron should issue from the Texel, and after a fiercely contested engagement, in which the Dutch showed all their wonted prowess,

LORD NELSON, K.B.
(After a painting by A. W. Devis.)

it was all but annihilated. Eight ships, including that of the Admiral, the Vice-Admiral, and four frigates, were captured. Only three ships of the line escaped.

A noteworthy circumstance in connection with this battle is that the British seamen engaged in it manifested all their matchless qualities of coolness, courage, and daring, although but three months before they had been in open revolt, and were with difficulty brought to terms: another of the symptoms of that black time, when the rulers of the nation—men who should have been real men, and above, at least, some of the commoner weaknesses of ignoble minds—could not be just, could think of little beyond their own interests. Truth compels the avowal. The men revolted because of the needless severity of the discipline to which they were subjected, insufficiency of food, unequal distribution of prize money, and smallness of pay. In the scare of the moment a Bill was passed through both Houses in a day augmenting the pay alike of sailors and marines. This, and a little needful severity, reduced the men to reason. But it was long before all the evils of which they complained were remedied. As we know, Nelson himself complained of the treatment his heroes received at the hands, be it remembered, of noble lords and unhanged civil servants.

By these victories two of the Directory's schemes were brought to nought—one for overthrowing England's maritime supremacy, and, as auxiliary to it, a plan to support the proposed insurrection in Ireland. A still more daring project against British power was

THE BATTLE OF THE NILE, 1798.
(Based on an old engraving.)

conceived by Bonaparte, and approved by the Directory. It was, in the first place, to effect the conquest of Egypt, and thus to use that country as a base of operations against India. In July, 1798, Bonaparte landed in Egypt, which was quickly prostrate at his feet. But, on the 1st of August, the thirteen sail of the line and four frigates that had escorted the expedition from Toulon, of which Nelson had been in anxious search, were discovered in Aboukir Bay, near the mouth of the Nile. They lay close to the shore in a line protected by shoals, and guarded at either end by gunboats and batteries. Nelson, whose squadron numbered thirteen ships of the line and one frigate, decided on an immediate attack. With the eye of genius he saw that his chance was to thrust his ships between the French line and the shore. His flag-ship led the way, all the others following except the *Culloden*, which grounded in the operation. A tremendous and overwhelming fire was at once opened upon the French van, to which they could reply only at great disadvantage, Nelson's unexpected attack and startling manœuvre finding them altogether unprepared. " At twenty-eight minutes past six," wrote Nelson, " the sun in the horizon, the firing commenced. At five minutes past ten, when the *Orient* blew up, having burnt seventy minutes, the six van ships had surrendered." Three more sail of the line were subsequently captured, while two others and two frigates were destroyed. Only two sail of the line and two frigates escaped. Many of the French ships were much superior to the English, while the flag-ship, *L'Orient*, which carried a hundred and twenty guns, was regarded as equal to any two of the English. A more brilliant and decisive victory is not to be found in the annals of the British Navy, and the effect it produced throughout Europe was prodigious.

This crushing blow was followed, in 1801, by the defeat of the land army of Egypt by General Abercrombie, and the ejection of the French from the country three months later. Thus Bonaparte's insidious project of attacking British power in the East from this base was brought to grief; while, at the same time, Wellesley's military skill and rapidity of movement were shattering the plans of Tippoo Sultan, the ally by whose aid he had hoped to drive the English out of India.

Tippoo Sultan's appetite for war had not been satisfied by the beating he received at the hands of Lord Cornwallis. He was still brooding over schemes of revenge when emissaries from the French reached his court, and kindled the embers of his hope into a flame by offers of help from France. During the governorship of Sir John Shore, who had succeeded Lord Cornwallis, peace had reigned in India so far as concerned the dominions possessed or controlled by the British. In 1796 there had been an invasion by the fierce and warlike Afghans, who had so often devastated the peninsula. Crossing the mountains from Cabul and Candahar, they advanced to Lahore, and threatened Delhi. The fierce Rohillas, themselves of Afghan origin, were ready to join the invaders and take their revenge for the cruel war of conquest and extermination which had been waged against them by the Subahdar of Oude with the aid of Warren Hastings. British troops were ordered into the field, and preparations made to meet the invaders; but, fortunately, while Zemaun Shah was on his way from Lahore to Delhi, a rebellion, headed by his own brother, compelled him to retreat with all haste to Cabul. In the two following years there were rumours of a renewed advance of the Afghans, but nothing came of them, and Sir John Shore was enabled to carry on his administration in peace to the end.

But while there was no extension of British territory on the mainland during Shore's pacific administration, beyond the capture of the Dutch settlements, several important acquisitions were effected in the neighbouring seas, chiefly under the direction of Lord Hobart, Governor of Madras, aided by a squadron under Admiral Ranier. All the Dutch colonies in Ceylon and Malacca were reduced, and the valuable islands of Banda and Amboyna annexed. The same year (1795) the settlement of the United Provinces at the Cape of Good Hope was taken by an English fleet and held for the allies.

Two years later, namely in 1797, preparations were made for expeditions against Mauritius and the Spanish colony of Manila. A portion of the armament against the latter had already set sail for Penang, on the Strait of Malacca, which had been acquired by purchase by the Company some twelve years previously, and was now made the place of rendezvous ; but, on account of the suspicions roused by Tippoo Sultan and the Mahrattas, both enterprises were abandoned.

Fortunately, before the actual emergency arose, Sir John Shore, now Lord Teignmouth — who, though a capable administrator, and one under whose sway efforts were made for the moral and intellectual elevation of the people, was hardly the man to meet a crisis and direct warlike operations — had resigned his position, and was succeeded in the governor-generalship by the Earl of Mornington, afterwards Marquis Wellesley, who arrived at Madras in May, 1798. He had no sooner landed than he was made aware of the very critical state in which matters stood. Tippoo Sultan had put himself in communication not only with the French authorities in Mauritius, but with the Directory at Paris—inviting their assistance, and offering to enter into an offensive and defensive alliance with them. Nor was this all. When Lord Mornington reached the scene of his labours there were two French forces in the country, one in the pay of the Nizam of the Deccan, and another in that of the Peshwa. The former was got rid of by peaceable means, the Nizam preferring the protection of the British against his Mahratta foes to the overbearing insolence he had experienced from the French officers. The Peshwa, or Sindhia, who acted for him, was not to be dealt with so easily. He not only refused to disband his force, but declined to allow the British to settle matters in dispute betwixt him and the Nizam. Moreover, it was known that he was at this time in communication with Tippoo.

It was necessary, therefore, to proceed against the Mysorean potentate without any satisfactory arrangement being come to with the Mahrattas. There was reason to believe, too, that Sindhia was greatly inclined to throw in his lot with Tippoo, and that as soon as hostilities were commenced the French in the Mahratta territory would endeavour to join their forces with those of their countrymen in the service of Mysore, especially if, as was to be anticipated, a French armament, either from the Isle of France or from Europe, should effect a landing on the coast. That the latter was a contingency to be apprehended was evident when intelligence reached India of Bonaparte's expedition to Egypt. This was immediately afterwards confirmed by the interception of a letter from the Corsican adventurer to Tippoo, requesting him to send a confidential person to Suez or Cairo, to confer with him and concert measures for the " liberation " of India.

Although at the end of October Lord Mornington heard of the destruction of the French fleet at Aboukir Bay, it did not free him from the apprehension of a French armament. But nothing had appeared up to November, except a few recruits who had found their way to Seringapatam—the refuse of the gaols, it was said. Meanwhile, the British forces having been got into a condition of readiness, explanations were demanded from the Sultan. At first he temporised, then sent an insolent reply—after a delay of nearly a month. By that time, however, his patience exhausted, Lord Mornington had put his armies in motion, it having been ascertained that Tippoo had sent another embassy to the French, desiring them to hasten the equipment and despatch of a force to his aid. It seemed evident, therefore, that his procrastinations were for the purpose of gaining time.

A finer army than the one which was collected by General Harris, the Commander-in-Chief, at Vellore, in February, 1799, had not theretofore taken the field in India. It numbered upwards of twenty thousand men, of whom upwards of four thousand were Europeans, and between two and three thousand cavalry, and was supported by a strong park of artillery, forty pieces of which were heavy battering guns. Before proceeding far on his march General Harris was joined by the Nizam's contingent, consisting of a British detachment six thousand five hundred strong, about an equal number of the Nizam's infantry, and a large body of cavalry. This Deccan contingent was under the command of Colonel Wellesley, whose regiment—the 33d—formed part of the force, and who had arrived in India a year before his brother, the Governor-General, and had in the interval done much to improve the character and discipline of the army.

Nor did these constitute the whole of the forces that were put in motion to settle matters with his Sultanship of Mysore. A Bombay corps numbering upwards of six thousand men, sixteen hundred of them Europeans, was advancing from the Malabar coast under General Stuart; while a still further force, though of smaller dimensions, from the southern districts of the Carnatic and Mysore, under

Colonels Read and Brown, was designed to cooperate with the main army, and expedite the bringing up of supplies.

Instead of advancing to meet General Harris, Tippoo set out towards the Malabar coast, apparently with the intention of crushing Stuart's force before it got through the jungles that lay in his path; but, in place of inflicting, he suffered a severe defeat, and fled to Periapatam, hurrying thence with all speed to protect his capital. From there he advanced to meet the main army, and in two encounters was compelled to fall back with loss. He was pursued with vigour by the British, who, on the 5th of April, came in sight of Seringapatam. Since the last war Tippoo had greatly strengthened the defences of the city, and looked upon it as impregnable. He had, indeed, rendered it a formidable place, and as he was unwearied in his exertions to counteract the approaches of the besiegers, their task was no light one. However, the difficulty of the undertaking only increased the vigour with which the siege was pushed forward; and on the 4th of May, less than a month from the day when the army arrived within sight of the city, Seringapatam was finally taken by storm. Tippoo fell in the action (his corpse being subsequently found beneath an arch), and, along with several of his sons and a number of French officers, the victors captured booty in gold and jewels to the amount of about a million sterling, which, by order of the Governor-General and Council, was distributed among the army.

The empire which Hyder Ali had built up was

THE LAST EFFORT AND FALL OF TIPPOO SULTAN.
(From a painting by H. Singleton.)

now dismembered, parts of it being retained by the Company, a portion handed over to the Nizam, another portion reserved for the Peshwa, while a fourth and smaller portion was formed into a rajahship for a descendant of the ancient Hindu family which had reigned over Mysore until dispossessed by Hyder Ali. By this arrangement " the district of Canara, including the whole line of coast contiguous to the Company's possessions in Malabar and the Carnatic, the fortresses and posts at the heads of the different ghauts, or passes, which lead into Mysore, as well as the fortress of Seringapatam, were all committed to the English; the tracts of country bordering upon his dominions became the property of the Nizam of the Deccan; and Harponelly and various other provinces and districts were to be made over to the Mahrattas."[1]

The last clause, however, was never carried out, the Peshwa, or Sindhia on his behalf, refusing to treat with the Governor-General, and the territory intended for him being in consequence divided between the Nizam of the Deccan and the English.

The prince raised to the throne of Mysore was Maharajah Krishna Oudawer, a chief of six years old. The territory ceded to him yielded thirteen lacs of pagodas, a revenue greater than that of the ancient rajahship of Mysore. It was completely engirdled by the districts and fortresses which were annexed by the British, and held by their troops. By the treaty of investiture, the overlordship of the country was entirely in the hands of the English, the Maha-

[1] *History of British India.*

rajah being, in fact, a mere puppet, bound to pay an annual tribute and to seek the advice of the Governor-General and Council at every turn. The residence chosen for him and his court was the ancient city of Mysore.

The territory which thus, by the overthrow of Tippoo, fell to the lot of the Company exceeded in extent twenty thousand square miles, and was capable, when reduced to order and tranquillity, of yielding an enormous revenue. It was, however, some little time before complete tranquillity was restored. Much trouble was given, amongst others, by a Mahratta freebooter named Doondiah, who, in the Mysorean service, and after the downfall of Tippoo, had collected a band of several thousand men, and with them ravaged the district between Mysore and the sea. It became the duty of Colonel Wellesley, as administrator of the conquered territory, to rid the country of this pest, which he did very effectually the following year, falling upon his camp in the chief's absence, taking all his baggage and artillery, and driving " the bulk of his troops, at least five thousand in number, into the Malpoorba, where they were drowned."[1] Before the end of the summer, the remainder of Doondiah's force was come up with and annihilated, with him at the head. The whole of the country formerly under the sway of Tippoo was now so orderly and peaceful that it contributed very materially to the success of the operations against the Mahrattas which were soon rendered necessary.

[1] Yonge, *The Life of Wellington*.

As we have seen, the great Mahratta chief Sindhia had rejected all offers of friendship on the part of the English, and had reduced the Peshwa, the nominal head of the confederacy, to a state of helpless subjection. Not satisfied with the power he thus exercised, Sindhia, in combination with other Mahratta chiefs, now drove him out of Poona, his capital. That unlucky potentate, escaping to the court, took refuge in Bassein, where he entered into negotiations with the English; and by a treaty made in December, 1802, the Indian Government agreed, on condition of the Peshwa submitting to British suzerainty, to restore his authority.

The moment was a favourable one to put an end to the Mahratta confederacy, which was too restless and too formidable for safety, and it was resolved to take advantage of the opportunity. The Mahratta territory was at this time divided amongst five principal chieftains, all suspicious and distrustful of each other, and as often as not warring amongst themselves. The two most powerful of these leaders were Sindhia, whose territory included the great central city of Hindustan and the seat of the Mogul, Delhi, besides Agra and other strongly fortified towns, and Rao Holkar, whose dominions were contiguous to those of Sindhia on the south and east. Only a year or two before these two had been enemies, and in the autumn of 1802 Holkar had inflicted a severe defeat on the combined forces of the Peshwa and Sindhia. But, apprehensive of the growing power of the British, these two were now in alliance, and, like the misguided Tippoo, entertained the hope of being able, with French aid, utterly to overwhelm the gradually all-conquering race.

The crisis was the more threatening to the English because, by the Treaty of Amiens, Pondicherry and their other factories had been restored to the French; and the officers who were sent out to resume operations there made no secret of the design of their Government to use that city, during the continuance of peace, as a centre of intrigue from which to undermine British influence, and on the first fresh outbreak of war to reopen the contest for Oriental dominion.

Immediately after the ratification of the Treaty of Bassein, which took place in February, 1803, General Stuart, who had succeeded Harris, was ordered to advance with the Madras army into the Mahratta territory with a view to reinstating the Peshwa; and Wellesley, who had been raised to the rank of major-general, was given a force consisting of eight thousand infantry and two thousand cavalry, with which he was to advance upon Poona. Starting from Seringapatam, he crossed the Mahratta frontier on the 21st of March, and calculated that he should be able to accomplish the six hundred miles before him by the 23d of April. But on the night of the 18th, when sixty miles distant from Poona, he received intelligence that a lieutenant of Holkar's was pushing with all haste to the capital, intending to burn it before the arrival of the British. Leaving his infantry to follow, Wellesley advanced with one or two detachments of native cavalry, described by himself as "about equal to Cossacks"; and so

splendidly did they second the zeal and energy of
their commander that they accomplished the distance in thirty-two hours, entering Poona at noon
on the 20th. This " surprising march," as Wellesley called it, saved the city from destruction.

SERINGAPATAM.

The march was not the only surprising thing about
this advance. General Wellesley's previous experience in the Mahratta country, during the pursuit of
Doondiah, had made him so thoroughly acquainted
with the people, and had given the various chiefs so
great a respect for his military capacity, as well as
for his just dealings, that not a hand was raised
against him. It was a sign of the changed conduct

which was being gradually introduced into the government of the country, and of the higher class of men which was being employed in its administration, when Major Malcolm, the political agent who accompanied the expedition, could write: "The confidence and respect of every class in the provinces south of the Kistna is in a very great degree personal to Major-General Wellesley; and to the admiration which the Mahratta chiefs entertain for that officer's character, and the firm reliance which the inhabitants place on his justice and protection, the extraordinary success which has hitherto attended the progress of the march must be principally attributed."

As the result of this successful operation the Peshwa was enabled the following month to re-enter his capital, while to Wellesley was given "the general direction and control of all the military and political affairs of the British Government in the territories of the Nizam, of the Peshwa, and of the Mahratta states and chiefs." In pursuance of the authority thus invested in him, Wellesley required Sindhia to retire to the north of the Nerbudda, which empties into the Gulf of Cambay. This course was demanded of him as an evidence of the honesty of his intentions, and as he failed to comply, war was declared (August 6, 1803). Acting with his usual celerity, Wellesley at once put his army in motion, and on the 11th captured Ahmadnagur, one of the strongest of the Mahratta fortresses. Ten days later he crossed the Godavery, and, sooner than he was aware, found himself in the vicinity of Sindhia and Bhoonsla, the Rajah of Berar. Unfortunately, before he had learned their immediate whereabouts, he had been forced to detach Colonel Stevenson with a division of his army to proceed by one route, whilst he himself advanced by another and more direct road. On the 23d of September he suddenly found that the whole of the combined forces of the Rajah and Sindhia were immediately in front of him, at the village of Assaye. The enemy's numbers were so much superior to his own that it was necessary so to dispose of his little army as not to be open to attack on every side. Taking advantage, therefore, of the junction of two rivers, the Kistna and the Juah, at Peepulquon, a little above Assaye, he took up a position between the two streams, and having one on each flank, he was secure from the enemy's cavalry. Yet, even with this advantage, the odds were enormous. Sindhia's army is said to have been as seven to one of the British; he had, moreover, two hundred and fifty guns as against twenty opposed to him, and they were admirably served by French artillerymen. Nor did Wellesley wait for the attack, but moved at once against the enemy's lines. He was met by a tremendous cannonade, against which his poor equipment of guns was powerless. At one moment such a gap was made in the British right that a body of Mahratta cavalry endeavoured to charge through it; but some English cavalry in the third line met these with such a determined onslaught that they were speedily driven back. In order to stop the terrible execution that was being done by the artillery, Wellesley ordered the infantry to charge with the bayonet. But his steady, resolute advance had already struck such terror into the Mahrattas that they could not be kept cool enough to meet the British line of steel, and they broke and fled. One body of them re-formed, and looked like doing execution, but a charge of British cavalry, under Lieutenant-Colonel Maxwell, soon put them to flight again. The action terminated with an attack, led by Wellesley in person, on the village of Assaye,

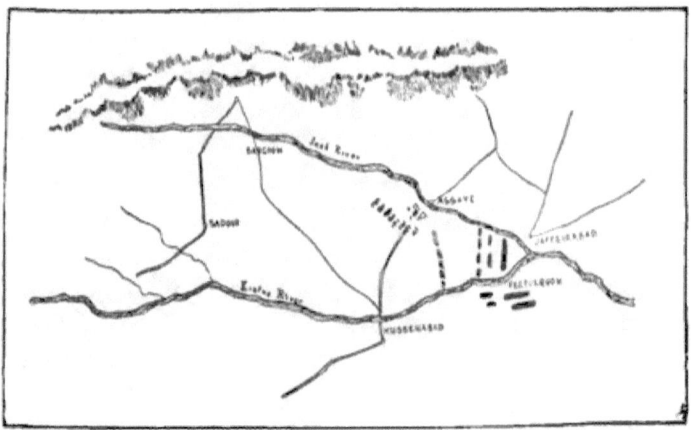

PLAN OF THE FIELD OF ASSAYE.

which was not cleared without a desperate fight. The victory was dearly bought, more than a fourth of the army being put *hors de combat*, but it did more, perhaps, than any previous battle to impress the natives with the dauntless and invincible character of the people who had won and were still winning dominion over them. It has been said that " all the fighting that had hitherto taken place in

India was child's play in comparison with that at Assaye," and it is probably not far from the truth. Joining his forces now to those of Stevenson, Wellesley followed up his success by the capture of the fortresses of Burhampoor and Asserghur, the last of Sindhia's possessions in the Deccan.

While these operations were going on under General Wellesley, General Lake, in command of a portion of the Bengal army, was acting against the Mahrattas with equal vigour in the North. It is needless to follow his movements in detail. On the 4th of September he had taken Alighur, one of the strongest fortresses in India, and the headquarters of Perron, the Frenchman who had had the drilling and organisation of Sindhia's army, and his chief military depot, and compelled that adventurer to retire from the Mahratta service. This action was followed a few days later by another in the neighbourhood of Delhi, which placed that ancient capital of the Grand Moguls in his power, together with the living representative of that great dynasty, poor, blind old Shah Alum, who regarded Lake as a deliverer, and, in lieu of anything better, gave him a number of very high-sounding, though equally empty, Oriental titles. Marching from Delhi to Agra, General Lake laid siege to that place on the 4th of October, and took it on the 17th. While this operation was going on, Sindhia had despatched seventeen disciplined battalions and upwards of four hundred horse to the capital in the hope of regaining possession of it. Lake now hastened in search of this force, and coming upon it on the 1st of November, at the village of Laswari, attacked with his cavalry alone, but was obliged to draw off until his infantry arrived, when the battle was resumed. The Mahrattas fought in splendid style, disputing for a time every foot of the ground, " and only giving way when the bayonets were at their breasts, and their own captured guns were turned against them." These troops bore the name of the " Invincibles of the Deccan," and, with the exception of some two thousand who surrendered, were annihilated. They " were considered," says Major Thorn,[1] "as the flower of Sindhia's army, which altogether had made immense and rapid strides towards the point of perfection of European troops. Throughout this eventful Mahratta war every conflict gave evidence of this improvement, which was attributable to the connection of the natives with the French, whose energies, address, and abilities were exerted to the utmost in exasperating the chiefs against the English, and in forming their subjects into hardy and disciplined soldiers, with the view of thereby overthrowing our dominion in the East."

Thanks to Wellesley and Lake, this army, which had given the Governor-General such just cause of alarm, was, before the end of the year, utterly broken up, and a formidable danger to British supremacy destroyed.

Towards the end of November Sindhia seemed anxious to come to terms, and asked for a truce, which was granted. His ally, the Rajah of Berar, however, still kept the field, and it was more than

[1] *Memoirs of the War*, etc.

suspected that Sindhia only opened negotiations in order to gain time to bring up more troops. Determined to bring matters to a crisis, Wellesley, on the 25th of November, joined Stevenson, who was close in the rear of the Berar army, and the next day found himself face to face with the united forces of Bhoonsla and Sindhia. The battle was short and decisive. The Mahrattas advanced with some spirit, but their attempt was not so stubborn as before, and when one effort after another had been repulsed, they began to give way with disorder, which was soon converted into a rout by the onslaught of the British cavalry. With this victory, and the capture of the fortress of Gawilghur, which followed shortly after, the war was brought to a close.

Of course, these successful operations meant further accessions of territory to the conquerors. Berar, Beroach, and other districts of great importance politically, as well as commercially, were ceded to the Company; and, what was of equal importance, by the treaties signed by the Mahratta chiefs, they were bound to refer their disputes to the mediation and decision of the Governor-General of India. Not the smallest advantage derived from these conquests was the fact that they " went far to secure the navigation of all those immense lines of coast from the mouths of the Ganges to the mouths of the Indus, and to cut off all the turbulent Mahrattas from any communication with the sea, or with the French and other transmarine enemies of the British Government." [1]

[1] *History of British India.*

CHAPTER II.

A STRUGGLE FOR EXISTENCE.

SEVERE as had been the struggle during the first part of the great war, it was destined to be still more terrible from the termination of the short-lived peace until the battle of Waterloo. During that momentous period, indeed, the conflict assumed almost the proportions of one of those cataclysmic upheavals when, in consequence of some inharmonious condition in the workings of nature, the elements dash themselves together in chaotic battle, and appear as though, in their blind fury, they would rend the very foundations of the universe asunder. The demon of disorder and ruin, suddenly breaking loose, spread devastation and carnage on every hand; anarchy reigned supreme; and for a time it seemed that all the fairest and most promising conquests of time must go down in the general riot of confusion and slaughter. But amidst it all, even in the darkest hour of turmoil, there was working that nobler human instinct, that diviner impulse which, most potent perhaps in the humblest, still makes for peace and orderly ways and the steady progress of the ages. As long as human nature remains sane, and abides by the divinely implanted laws of its being, that must ever be the case. The current may be checked or turned aside, the human mind may be brutalised or degraded; but wherever and whenever it gets a chance for normal growth and development, especially if aided by true education, it will fall into the ordered ways that are as natural to it as the comb and the cell and honey-making to the bee. If those monarchs and their satellites could only be brought to see how little they make and how much they mar with all their anxious striving, and so could be induced to withhold their hands a little, what a happy and prosperous world it would be, and how much nearer they might come to what some of them assume themselves to be—half divine!

One cannot help having some such reflections as these when one looks on the more than twenty years of war that deluged Europe with blood at the end of the last and beginning of the present century, and all because the principalities and powers would not let the French people order their affairs as they liked; albeit, they did no more than take a bold leap for a more normal condition of life. But it could not be allowed; they must be beaten back into the less natural state. The result was those two decades of butchery; then more upheavals and more wars; and, after all, a settlement on the very lines the country had chosen for itself in the first instance, but was not permitted to pursue. It is amazing to think of the enormous quantity of blood spilt and treasure wasted, and so little gained. And the astonishment grows when we consider that King George's Ministers allowed themselves to be hurried into a renewal of hostilities mainly by the hectoring words of a braggart. It was like the conduct of schoolboys on the opposite sides of a ditch. "You can't fight us single-handed!" cried the First Consul. "Oh, can't we, though?" comes back from the other side. "Just you wait and see!" And immediately the arena is cleared for action, and the contest begins.

There were, of course, other causes of grievance besides Bonaparte's idle gasconade. As a matter of fact the peace of Amiens was a hollow one; its terms were never consummated, and perhaps could not be. Both combatants knew how treacherous was the truce, and so remained with lance in rest, ready at any moment to renew the contest. France complained of the non-evacuation of Malta; England replied that the surrender of the island to the Knights of St. John of Jerusalem had been rendered impracticable through the conduct of France and Spain in destroying the independence of the order by the sequestration of its revenues. Still more serious grounds of suspicion and mistrust existed between the two nations. Bonaparte, raised to power by his military genius, felt that he could only maintain his position by dazzling the people with brilliant exploits in the field. Drunk with the glory of arms himself, and surrounded by men who were equally intoxicated, he could see no way to greatness except through conquest; and so, aspiring to universal dominion, must needs go to meet his inevitable doom, and fall, as he had risen, by the sword. Busied unceasingly with projects of aggrandisement, in forming secret alliances, in fitting out expeditions hostile to England, in annexing territory, and in sending out exploratory expeditions to Egypt, and even to this country, he continually increased the jealousy and distrust of Britain. Moreover, another cause of irritation was the fact, or the report, that his consuls in England occupied themselves taking soundings and plans of harbours, and in general acting as spies. None of these causes of annoyance, however, seem to have had so much to do with the fresh outbreak of hostilities as Bonaparte's coarse brag.

This thoroughly roused the British blood, which never wants much chafing for a fight. The press helped to work up the heat by depicting in odious colours the character and personal history of the First Consul, while he on his part was not backward in giving food for mordant pens by his petulance and want of dignity. Add to this that a powerful war faction existed, made up chiefly of those who benefit by war, which had from the first deprecated the peace of Amiens as dangerous and inglorious, and seized every opportunity to aggravate the differences, and, if possible, produce a rupture between the two countries, and it will be seen that the materials were not wanting for a second Punic war —a war of the first sea-power against the first land-power. In this instance, however, it was not the land-power, but the sea-power that was destined to triumph.

In the first years of the war England swept the seas of her enemy, and took possession of her colonies; while France seized Hanover, notwithstanding the paltry declaration of George III. that he was at war as King of England only, not as German Elector. Contrary to international usage, but on the pretext that French ships had been captured prior to the declaration of war, Bonaparte arrested all the English in France, and detained them as prisoners. The threat of an invasion was revived, and while French troops for that purpose were collected in Brittany and Holland, hundreds of thousands of volunteers were enrolled to meet the storm in England. These commotions naturally occasioned widespread interruption to trade and commerce, as well as much personal suffering. The termination of the first year of the war was marked by the assumption of the imperial dignity by Napoleon, who became, in May, 1804, Emperor of the French. The same month witnessed the return to power of Mr. Pitt. Addington had sought his auxiliary aid; but, acting in accordance with his rule of "not accepting any subaltern situation," Pitt declined co-partnership. Nothing short of the premiership would satisfy his ambition; and, in this case, to will was to achieve. He had at first given his support to the Ministry; but, thinking it was time to resume the direction of affairs, he joined the opposition of Fox and Lord Grenville, thus compelling Addington to resign. His Ministry was popular in the country, but without strength in Parliament; and it was still further enfeebled by his attempt to screen the delinquencies of Lord Melville, who was charged with, and ultimately found guilty of, scandalous misconduct, including peculation, while First Lord of the Admiralty (1786 to 1800).

It hardly needed these difficulties and distractions at home on top of the disastrous turn of affairs abroad to make the outlook sufficiently black. In order to avert the storm of invasion alleged to be threatening England, the Government had succeeded in forming a new coalition on the Continent; but it was badly planned, while its conduct was worse managed than any previous confederacy against France. The co-operation of Russia was secured; but without the aid of Prussia there was little chance of success, and Austria hurried into hostilities before she knew whether the Court of Berlin would be hostile or neutral in the struggle. The result was terrific. With his masterly strategy Napoleon contrived the destruction of the Austrian battalions ere he quitted the Tuileries, and with the rapidity of a thunderbolt he executed the annihilation he had planned. By the surrender of Ulm the armies of Austria were ruined without a battle; her capital was taken without resistance; and scarcely had the remnant of the Austrian forces joined the Russians in Moravia ere she was compelled to hazard an engagement which laid her prostrate at the feet of the demoniac Corsican. The battle of Austerlitz (December 2, 1805) utterly quenched the spirit of the allies, and was followed at the close of the year by the Treaty of Presburg.

As a set-off to these brilliant exploits, however,

THE BATTLE OF TRAFALGAR, 1805.
(From the painting by C. Stanfield.)

Napoleon had witnessed the defeat of his last hopes against England. From his camp at Boulogne he had scanned the Channel and the shores of the devoted island that was, as he thought, soon to become his prey. It was his plan, with his own and the Spanish fleet, to crush the British squadrons that protected the Channel ports before the fleet that was watching the Spanish armament could come to their support, and then to carry his army across in the innumerable gunboats which he had got together for the purpose. There was, however, a genius at work supreme as his own, setting his schemes at naught, and once more the threatened danger of invasion was warded off from this island. Admiral Villeneuve, with the combined French and Spanish fleets, had drawn Nelson away to the West Indies, and then suddenly returning to Cadiz, thought to join the squadron at Brest, and so carry out Napoleon's design upon England. But Nelson was after him like his fate, and now brought him to a final reckoning. The ships of the enemy numbered thirty-three sail, all of the line. The British fleet consisted of twenty-seven ships of the line, mostly of the largest rate. About noon, off Cape Trafalgar, on the ever-memorable 21st of October, 1805, the contest began. Nelson had run up the signal—since become a national motto—"England expects every man to do his duty"; and with that for their battle-word, the British bore down, under Nelson and Collingwood, and at the first onset succeeded in piercing the enemy's line. The conflict now became furious, and continued so for a couple of hours; but by the

THE DEATH OF NELSON.
(After the painting by Ernest Slingeneyer.)

end of that time nineteen of the enemy's ships had struck, including the French Admiral's and two other flag-ships. The loss of the combined fleets was enormous; the Spanish Admiral, Guarina, was mortally wounded; and Villeneuve, soon after, unable to survive the disgrace of his defeat, put an end to his life. The loss of the British in killed and wounded was 1589, and, including the hero of the day, cast a shade over this brilliant naval achievement.

Austerlitz is said to have killed Pitt. He died within a month of the Treaty of Presburg, sighing over the fate of his country—a country that mourned, but did not miss him—a country whose destiny was in other hands than his; for though statesmen may imagine that everything depends on them, infinitely more depends on the heart-soundness of the nation as a whole. If that be right, nothing much can go wrong. Even when, to Pitt's dying eyes, everything looked so dark—and it was dark—the shuttle of life was flying fast to and fro, weaving the web of national character broad and strong, mingling, too, amid the warp and weft the giant figures of men—giants in mind—who were to lead the van and give the time and tune of the march—the march towards greater things than Pitt and his set had ever dreamed of.

Internally, the whole period was one of the greatest depression, and, politically, worse than stagnation. The first splendid outburst of the Revolution had fired the noblest minds with an enthusiasm as of a new day-dawn. Naturally calm and conservative

WILLIAM PITT.

intellects like Wordsworth hailed it as the first sign of a social regeneration—a reawakening of mankind to nobler issues. Others, however, who saw nothing in the prevalence of such ideas but the downfall of their own class and their own privileges, were wrought to a white heat of fury at the prospect. The result was a reign of repression in Great Britain the like of which had not been witnessed for generations. The Habeas Corpus Act was suspended. It became sedition to attend a public meeting, high treason to talk of reform; scores of innocent and well-meaning men were sent into penal servitude for criticisms of political abuses as just as they were natural. One man was condemned to fourteen years' transportation for lending a book. For upwards of twenty years the boldest man in Parliament dare hardly breathe the word reform. The time was, indeed, one of almost unutterable darkness; and it was in some respects the darker because the new industrial era that was in its dawn found the workers, alike through their ignorance and their poverty, unprepared for the change. Again and again, in consequence of bad harvests, famine was rife, and bread riots the consequence; and the workers, unable to see far, attributed their sufferings to the new machinery that was in every direction throwing industry into new channels, bringing bankruptcy and ruin to those who were dependent on handicrafts which were now being set aside by the new industry. One cannot wonder much that the time came when they went about burning and destroying to get rid of the instruments of their suffering; they were only imitating their betters, who were equally running amuck against hated innovations. A wise country that was benefiting so enormously from the change would have spared a little from its growing wealth to enable these men to tide over the period of transition. But all the rulers of Britain could do was to put them down with the strong hand, while they were spending millions to bolster up tottering thrones that had, perhaps, been just as well in the dust.

It is enough to make one blush for shame to read that the Government of a country, nominally free, and boasting its liberties, should make war to put down new ideas—fresh forms of machinery for government, in fact—whilst it had no pity on the misguided men who wished to do the same thing at home—abolish the new ideas and the new machines that, for the time being, were effecting their ruin. But it was all in keeping with the debased ideals of the time. Democratic excesses must be punished, while the crimes of Cabinets were witnessed unmoved. Sympathy was felt for the death of a monarch, but none for the extinction of a nation. Louis XVI. was bewept to the length of hysteria; for murdered Poland there was not so much as a tear, though its only crime was the establishment of a free constitutional monarchy.

But even in this dark and depressing picture there are points of breaking light. The closing years of the century were marked by several noteworthy inventions and discoveries. Gas was successfully employed as an illuminant by Bolton and Watt in their works near Birmingham in 1798, to become in a few years' time the light of the streets. The lifeboat was invented the same year by William Wouldhave, of South Shields, though the credit of it was appropriated by Greathead, a boat-builder. Greathead received a gratuity of £1200 from the Government, and honours from many crowned heads, but died a drunkard and a pauper. Wouldhave went to his grave unrecognised save by a few. Another important improvement, albeit not in the arts of peace, was in the discovery of the methods by which gun-barrels could be bored out of a solid piece of steel. More noteworthy, as being for nobler ends, were the experiments made in the first year of the nineteenth century in regard to the application of steam to the propulsion of vessels. In July of that year trials took place on the Thames for working a barge by means of a steam-engine. They were considered highly satisfactory by the experts, the craft answering the helm quickly, and making her way against a strong current " at the rate of two miles and a half an hour,"[1] but on the whole the trials appear to have attracted little attention.

These were not, of course, the first experiments of the kind. As early as 1736 an Englishman, named Jonathan Hulls, had patented a method of propelling vessels with steam by means of a stern wheel. Other experiments followed; but the real precursor of the paddle-wheel steamer was built in 1788 by Patrick Miller of Dalswinton, on Dalswinton Loch, Dumfriesshire. This vessel, which was a double, or twin-boat, measured twenty-five feet in length by

[1] *Annual Register.*

seven in breadth, and was fitted by two paddle-wheels, one before and one behind the engine. The speed attained was about five miles an hour. The following year a larger boat was built and successfully tried on the Forth and Clyde Canal. In 1801 Lord Dundas employed William Symington of Edinburgh, who had constructed the machinery for Winter's steamboat, to build a steamboat for use on the Forth and Clyde Canal. This vessel, which was launched in 1802, had one paddle-wheel near the stern, and was driven by a direct-acting horizontal engine with a connecting-rod and crank. It was seen by Robert Fulton, an American engineer, who, in 1807, employed the famous firm of Bolton & Watt to construct an engine upon the same principle, and this he fitted into a steamer called the *Clermont*, a hundred and thirty feet long, which plied successfully on the Hudson River. A number of vessels propelled by steam were soon plying in American waters. About the same time steam navigation was making steady progress in England; but the first passenger steamer to run in Great Britain was the *Comet*, a vessel designed and built in 1812 by Henry Bell and John Wood, of Port Glasgow. Thus was the good worker-animal man industriously toiling away building and making and improving, while his law-makers and governors were as busily destroying.

As no market of any special importance was closed against Great Britain by the outbreak of the war, English commerce continued to increase after its commencement. When Holland was overrun by the

French, and forced into hostilities against England, the shipping interest was benefited by the acquisition of a part of the carrying trade of the United Provinces. The largest share of the trade, however, was transferred to neutrals, the Americans, Danes, and Swedes being the chief gainers. Being mainly a Continental, not a naval or mercantile war, the impulse previously given to commerce and manufacturing industry by the numerous mechanical inventions and improvements continued unabated to the peace of Amiens. During the period from 1793 to 1802 the official values of the cargoes exported more than doubled, and the amount of tonnage employed in the export trade increased in nearly an equal ratio. But while trade and industry continued to thrive, agriculture suffered. From 1793 to 1802 there were only three good harvests. Thus the war had a bad effect on agriculture, partly through the withdrawal of labourers, and partly through the rise in the rate of interest, which prevented the application of capital to improvements.

This continued increase of trade is one of the most remarkable features of the period, and affords a striking proof of the effective manner in which the Navy saw to the police of the sea. Nor was it a light task, with thousands of ships ploughing all the seas, and carrying cargoes of enormous value. An instance in point is worth noting. Captain Dance, who, in February, 1804, was acting as commodore to a rich homeward-bound East India fleet, was set upon by a French squadron under Admiral Linois at the entrance to the Strait of Malacca. Linois had a line-of-battle ship, three frigates, and a brig; and, as the British merchant-fleet had no battle-ship to protect them, he thought he had got a sure catch. But in those stirring times of war the Company's ships were generally provided with a few guns, and it not unfrequently happened that they were in charge of men who had both the knowledge and the will to use them. Dance was such a one, and when the Frenchman made his swoop, he found that he had a tartar to deal with. After an hour's fighting, he hauled his wind and stood away to the eastward, he and all his squadron, under every rag that they could set. Dance made signal to give chase; but, after pursuing the Frenchmen for a couple of hours, he decided that in his case prudence was a better card than valour. And so he bore up for England, and brought his chickens all safely home to roost. For this sturdy bit of derring-do the Company voted Dance and his officers rewards to the amount of £50,000. No wonder: the fleet thus safeguarded was reputed to be worth £8,000,000 sterling.

The increased volume of commerce, and the general activity in shipping, caused a vast improvement to be effected in the ports and harbours of the kingdom. These resulted partly from the extension of canal navigation already referred to, but more directly from the vast increase of shipping and commerce. It was only after the termination of the American war, and the loss of the transatlantic colonies, that the commerce of the river Thames began rapidly to increase. At the commencement of the eighteenth century, in the year 1700, exclusive of the coasting trade, the imports of the Thames amounted to £4,875,538, the exports to £5,387,787. By the middle of the century (1750) the imports had increased to £5,540,564, and the exports to £8,415,218. So that in fifty years the imports and exports together had increased to the extent of £3,692,456 only. But in the six years from 1790 to 1796 the trade of the port of London had, despite the war, increased more than three times the amount of its advance during the first half of the century. Thus, in 1790, the imports and exports combined amounted to £22,992,095, while in 1796 they reached the total of £33,282,046, showing an increase of upwards of £10,000,000 sterling. As showing the enormous development that had accrued to the trade of the Thames, it may be said that in 1796 the total exports and imports of the other ports of England amounted to but little over one-half the trade of the port of London.[1]

The accommodation in the river for this vast augmentation of traffic became altogether inadequate, all that magnificent series of docks that are now the pride of London and the admiration of the world being as yet things of the future. The cargoes of the thirteen thousand vessels that arrived annually in the Thames had to be landed at what were called the legal quays, twenty in number, extending from the Tower to London Bridge; or, if these were insufficient, at the sufferance-wharfs on the opposite side of the river. It was only the smaller craft that could approach the quays, all the

[1] £17,476,953.

larger vessels being obliged to deliver their cargoes by means of lighters. The American ships, and those in the West India trade, employed lighters, while the East India ships discharged their cargoes into decked hoys belonging to the Company. The delay in the delivery of cargoes, in consequence of this system, was frequently very great; while at particular seasons of the year, when the Pool was crowded with shipping, the confusion was beyond description. Innumerable opportunities were thus afforded for pillage, fraud, and embezzlement. The revenue suffered, and individuals were subjected to immense losses from depredation and the exposure of their property on the wharfs.

In consequence of these evils and inconveniences, a Parliamentary committee was appointed in 1796 to devise plans for the better accommodation of the shipping and general trade of the river. No legislation, however, followed the appointment of this committee. But the subject was again brought before Parliament in 1799, when an Act was passed for the construction of the West India Dock. In the course of a year or two the London and East India Docks followed, the first being opened and the second begun in the early part of 1805. Other improvements effected about the same time, and to a similar end, were the formation of the Commercial Road, to facilitate communication with the docks, and the establishment of the Thames police, who soon put an end to the greater part of the dishonest practices that had been the bane of the Thames trade.

About the same time (1805) the Grand Junction Canal, the project of Brindley to join the ports of Hull, Liverpool, Bristol, and London, was completed by the opening of the tunnel, two miles in length, through Blisworth Hill, near Northampton, the metropolis being thus brought into direct water-communication with the north and west.

Other events indicate the trend which the national will and the national conscience was taking. A trifling increase was given to the pay of the seamen who had been the means of winning such victories for England; though, to the general shame, it must be said that, while successful commanders were ennobled and feed largely from the public purse, these noble fellows, when no longer able to work or fight, were only given the freedom of the streets—to beg and die in. The abolition of the African slave trade, after years of agitation, was finally effected in August, 1807, and so—thanks to the perseverance of William Wilberforce and his friends—one more disgrace effaced from the escutcheon of England's honour. The same month Mr. Whitbread, a Quaker, brought forward in the House of Commons a comprehensive measure for encouraging industry and relieving the poor. From the returns made up in 1830 it appeared that, out of a population in England and Wales of a little under 9,000,000, no fewer than 1,234,000 were participators in parochial relief; that is, nearly one-seventh of the people were indebted to the other six, wholly, or in part, for support. Mr. Whitbread's aim was to elevate the character of the industrial classes, "to give them

WILLIAM WILBERFORCE.

consequence in their own eyes, to excite them to acquire property by tasting its sweets, to render dependent poverty degrading in their estimation, and at all times less desirable than independent industry." For the attainment of these ends he proposed a scheme of national education by the establishment of parochial schools. The Bill is noteworthy as being the first proposal for a comprehensive system of national education; and it was finally thrown out by the Lords in the month of August. It seems, however, to have done some good by calling attention to the subject of education, and, four years later, the National Society, for the education of the poor in the principles of the Established Church, was instituted.

Meanwhile the Emperor of the French, despairing of conquering England by the sword, had resolved to dry up the sources of her wealth, which he affirmed had been the bribe and mainstay of all the coalitions that had been formed against him. Dictator of Continental Europe, he sought to exclude British commerce from every port and place to which his power and influence extended. He began with his Berlin Decree, by which he declared the British Isles to be in a state of blockade; all British subjects found in countries occupied by the French to be prisoners of war, all English property to be lawful prize, and all vessels touching at England, or a British colony, not admissible to any harbour under the control of France. This decree was followed by others in 1807, enforcing with great strictness what has been called his "Continental System."

BATTLE OF COPENHAGEN, 1801.

To counteract these decrees, orders in council were issued by the British Government, and the effect of both was the destruction of neutral commerce. The war, in short, had assumed such an acrimonious character that the rights of nations were no longer regarded by either belligerent. England commenced her infractions of international law by a piratical attack on four Spanish men-of-war, laden with treasure, in 1804, and filled the cup of her baseness by the bombardment of Copenhagen and the seizure of the Danish fleet in 1809. Nothing could justify such deeds, and it is but right to say that the better conscience at large condemned them. As yet, however, the people had but little chance to make their opinions felt in Parliament. Hence justice continued to be outraged; the peaceful pursuits of commerce were impeded on every side, while the benefits arising from the mutual intercourse of nations were almost wholly suspended—and all this simply because of the unreasoning hatred of two governments.

But notwithstanding the fact that France had now, under the sway of her imperial master, reached the meridian of her powers, that despot could not succeed in establishing his Continental System. In spite of his vast efforts to stop it, British commerce continued to push its ramifications and profit from its secret supporters in every direction. One man might resolve; but the interests of every nation, of every individual, were opposed to him. British energy, indeed, was hardly ever so triumphant; smuggling rarely so lucrative a game. The obscurest creeks and tiniest coves were made use of;

and the darkest nights were not too dark for the carrying on of their trade by men who were as resolute as the Dictator himself, and more fearless. Heligoland, which had been taken from Denmark in 1807, became the great depot of English manufactures, and from thence they found their way all over the Continent, despite fines, confiscations, and burnings at Hamburg and Antwerp. A noteworthy fact connected with this secret trade was that many English merchants sent goods to their Continental agents in Hamburg and elsewhere without invoice or written document of any kind; yet payment came back in due course with the exactitude and regularity of an open and legitimately ordered trade.

This anti-commercial crusade was in the highest degree suicidal, and proved in the end the ruin of the inaugurator. It led to the introduction of French troops into the Peninsula, at first on the pretext of excluding British commerce from Portugal, then on the plea of " infusing youth into the decrepid Spanish monarchy." Into the war that tore up the two sister kingdoms until the end came it is not necessary to enter. Napoleon left the conduct of his affairs there to his generals, little thinking it was in that region the most dangerous enemy to his power was at work. But notwithstanding the way in which Wellesley was checking the career of his arms, Napoleon affected to treat the war in the Peninsula with indifference, representing the lengthened hostilities there as a politic means of enfeebling British power. In an address to the *Corps Législatif* in June, 1811, he remarked that " when England shall be exhausted—when at last she shall have felt the evil which, for twenty years, she has with so much cruelty poured upon the Continent, when half her families shall be in mourning—then shall a peal of thunder put an end to the affairs of the Peninsula."

But in the mysterious decrees of Providence it was otherwise determined. Within a year of the utterance of this grandiloquent speech, Napoleon had cast the die of his fate. He had embarked upon the campaign against Russia, partly to punish Alexander for his failure to carry out with sufficient stringency his Continental System. By the Treaty of Tilsit the Tzar had agreed to shut his ports against England; but it was perhaps more than he could do to put an end to British trade with his people. Its importance to his empire was too great to be readily stamped out. Many of the nobility of Russia derived a large portion of their income from the sale of products of which Great Britain was the principal market; their connection, therefore, with the mercantile interest of England was so intimate and vital that it meant ruin to put an end to it. On this account English goods had never been committed to the flames in the country of the Tzar, and British colonial produce was freely admitted into the Russian ports in neutral vessels. This laxity in regard to the Continental System on the part of Alexander, however, together with other causes of offence, gave great umbrage to his Imperial Majesty of France, and he resolved to inflict condign punishment on his " brother " of Russia.

Meanwhile, however, the policy of despair on the part of Napoleon had had the effect of stirring up a fratricidal war between the United States and England—a war which put back for years the feelings of confidence and amity which had been growing up between the two countries. Fortunately, after continuing for nearly two years, the British Government saw the unwisdom of it, and concluded an honourable peace.

With what lightness of heart Napoleon's punitive expedition to Russia was undertaken, and with what results, everybody knows. The world has hardly witnessed another such catastrophe—so fitting, so dramatically complete. When he went forth on his momentous campaign—the wielder, as may be said, of a thunderbolt of half a million shafts —kings and princes who held their power at his nod met him with fawning courtesy, while the people stood and gazed upon him as though he were a god: in his intoxication he felt himself to be almost a god. Crossing the Russian frontier in June, he found the people no longer regarding him as a divinity, but as a Dagon or Moloch; and they heaped his path with fitting tribute—a wasted country, devoid of supplies, and an enemy lurking everywhere, but rarely to be got at in tangible shape. Pushing his legions rapidly forward, he finally came to death-grips with his foes, defeated them at bloody Borodino, drove them everywhere from his path, and came at last to Moscow, to find it a mass of seething flames. The shock of this climax was so great that the demigod was like one confounded; he had lost that power of rapid initiative which had been the marvel of the world; he could not make up his mind what to do, and so lost precious time. However, he came at last to see that it would be madness to attempt to pursue a flying enemy through a country that had been rendered a desert; stay where he was he could not; and to go back was hardly less desperate. All the horrors of that winter's retreat will never be known. The season was uncommonly severe, and swarms of mounted Cossacks incessantly harassed the invaders, adding the sword to the deadly trio of cold, famine, and disease. Of the half million who entered only about twenty-five thousand left Russia. With this miserable remnant the Moloch of blood reached France.

So opportune a moment had not before presented itself for groaning Europe to free itself, and the nations rose almost to a man. Napoleon met the fresh coalition that was formed against him by another conscription, and confronted the allies with an army of three hundred and fifty thousand men, defeating them at Lutzen, Bautzen, and Dresden. The last, however, was so dearly bought a victory that the victor, outnumbered, was obliged to fall back on Leipzig. There he was completely hemmed in, and in the great "Battle of Nations," fought on the 16th, 18th, and 19th of October, 1813, he suffered a crushing defeat. Compelled to retreat to Paris, he again met the allied hosts with a new army in the early part of 1814. But numbers were against him; while the enemy he had despised was advancing rapidly from the South. On the 30th of March

A STRUGGLE FOR EXISTENCE. 291

the allies captured the fortifications of Paris, and on the 31st the Tzar and Wellington entered the city.

Then followed abdication, and the transmogrification of the great Jupiter Tonans of Europe in to the little Jupiter of Elba, where he reigned for ten months; then the landing at Fréjus (March 1, 1815), and the triumphal march on Paris, a large part of the army flocking to his banners, while Bourbon the Eighteenth and Pusillanimous fled incontinent to Ghent. The allied sovereigns were in conference at Vienna, trying to make up accounts, when the news of these sudden "excursions and alarms" broke in, like a lighted fuse, upon their counsels, causing them to throw down the pen and again take up the sword. The confederated armies once more marched towards the French frontier, and Napoleon advanced into Belgium to meet them. On the 16th of June he defeated Blücher at Ligny, while Ney held the British in check at Quatre-Bras.

Wellington fell back upon Waterloo, eleven miles south of Brussels. With little more than sixty thousand men, only some twenty-four thousand of whom were British, he prepared to contest the advance of the trained legions of France, in numbers nearly if not quite equal to his own. The field of battle he had selected was a low ridge over two miles in length, which commands the two roads to Brussels by which the enemy must reach the capital, if they reached it at all. Along this ridge the British were deployed in two lines, while fourteen thousand men were kept as a reserve. Six thousand more men were in advance, holding the important posts of Hougomont, a country house on the right, La Haye Sainte, a farm-house in the centre of the British position, and Papelotte, La Haye, and Smohain, on the left.

Around Hougomont and La Haye Sainte, both of which were turned into temporary fortresses, the main tide of battle rolled throughout the day. Against these posts Napoleon hurled his battalions in vain fury hour after hour. Again and again, amidst a murderous fire, they reached and even pierced the very enclosures of Hougomont, in some cases met in hand-to-hand conflict, but again and again were driven back. In the case of La Haye Sainte the orchard was taken after a fierce and deadly contest, but even then the buildings held out for several hours, until, through lack of ammunition, the commander was obliged to withdraw his force, a detachment of the German legion, and fall back on the main British line.

But there was no withdrawing from Hougomont. For seven long hours that brave garrison sustained assault after assault, and the last was no nearer success than the first. Once the number of assailants was so overpowering, and their attack so fierce, that they burst open the gate of the courtyard, and forced an entrance. But the barrier was speedily closed again, and none of those who entered went out alive.

The attack on these positions had begun about half-past eleven. Two hours later, Napoleon launched his first attack on Wellington's main line. His serried columns of infantry, flanked by cavalry,

THE LAST CHARGE AT WATERLOO.
(From an engraving after the picture by Luke Clennell.)

rushed forward with ringing cries of "Vive l'Empereur!" but ere they topped the ridge they were met by a withering fire from the English, followed by an impetuous charge with the bayonet that sent them headlong down the slope again—this by the British alone, a division of Belgian-Dutch troops with which they had been strengthened decamping at the moment of crisis.

The sight must have been a revelation to his French Imperial Majesty, who, in all his campaigning, had never before met the stout red line of British infantry; and who, ere the battle began, had mocked at Soult when he affirmed of the English, "they will die rather than quit the ground on which they stand." Charge after charge was hurled against that dauntless line of British valour, every man a hero, to recoil before its steady blaze of fire and its glittering edge of steel.

At length—almost, we may imagine, in despair, for Blücher's Prussians were now making their presence felt on the French right and rear—at length the forlorn genius of battle brought up his reserve, the infantry of the Guard, with its brigade of cavalry, all as yet fresh and eager for battle, and sent them in two columns against the British right and centre. That on the right advanced first, and, unchecked by the murderous fire of the artillery, gained the summit of the ridge. On its approach the British Guards, who had been lying down in a line four deep behind the ridge, sprang to their feet at Wellington's word of command, poured in a volley and charged. Surprised at the onset, and shattered by the fire, the heavy French column reeled before the terrific onslaught with the bayonet, and fell back in confusion.

The left column fared no better than the right. Advancing from the south-east corner of Hougomont against the same part of the British line, it was met by a withering fire on its left flank from the light brigade, followed by an equally destructive volley from the Guards in front. An impetuous charge with the bayonet completed their discomfiture. Never since its formation had the Imperial Guard been thus broken. Napoleon made a supreme effort to rally them, but it was too late. Wellington, perceiving that by this time Blücher was advancing in force on Planchenoit, ordered the entire British line to advance. There was nothing to check its forward movement. The battle was won, and the brave Prussians soon converted the defeat into a disastrous rout. Such was the great "battle of the West," that terminated the struggle in which for well-nigh a generation Britain had fought, not merely for empire, but for very existence.

CHAPTER III.

FROM WAR TO PEACE.

The battle of Waterloo marked the end of a period. Although the Bourbon monarchy was restored—for a time—in France, and most of the other thrones were re-established on their ancient foundations, it was soon manifest how great a change had come over the face of Europe. People had been awakened, as it were, to a new life by the tocsin of war, and were set a-thinking and working in new channels. The monarchs might form their Holy Alliances to keep down the people and check reform, but they could not stop the ferment of new ideas.

In short, during the after-throes of the Revolution the nineteenth century had been born, that century of marvels, the full effect and meaning of which has not yet been developed. The effect upon Britain of the re-awakening was nothing less than a resurgence of national life, a requickening of national energy. It was soon visible in every department of activity, in every form of thought. In the realm of literature it was marked by an efflorescence, the like of which, for spontaneity and wealth, had not been matched since the time of Elizabeth. It burst forth in turbulence, and, to some extent, in rebellion; but ere its full tide was spent it had broken into a thousand streams and fructifying rills, yielding beauty and delight, and a general kindling of thought, the full influence and significance of which we have not yet, perhaps, completely realised.

Much of this, of course, was the work of years, and was slow to appear, the first visible effect of the war being one of seeming exhaustion. But this was more apparent than real; the fact being that the sudden peace threw the social machine out of gear, and the rulers of the country had not the wisdom and moderation to ease matters, and so put it right. Indeed, the spectacle of abject class selfishness seeking its own ends, and those alone, which was now seen, even at such a crisis, is one that it would be hard to parallel. The labouring classes, as is almost invariably the case, had been the worst sufferers by the war. Not only had they to suffer from the dearness of the necessaries of life, but it was they who had been called upon to supply the enormous demand for the human stuff for the shambles. Even France did not drain herself to the same extent as Great Britain, which, during these years of dynastic warraying, had to yield more than one in ten of her able-bodied population to the man-mashing machine.[1]

Yet what do we see? When the country was thrown into the direst distress through the burden

[1] Lord Liverpool in Parliament, March, 1804.

of debt and taxation, when, through the overstocking of the world's markets with her manufactured goods, the mills and factories were brought to a standstill; when, in consequence of bad harvests, scarcity was so gripping the people that they were not able to procure enough food for their children,—at such a time it was that a land-owning Parliament chose to prohibit the importation of foreign corn until wheat had reached famine prices.[1] This Act of statutory starvation was passed in the year 1815, the year of the country's deliverance from the Napoleonic incubus—a deliverance which had been won as much by the courage and stamina of the working population, by their sinews and spirit in work and in war, as by any other class; yet, destitute of all feeling of recognition, without generosity, without justice, the governing classes at once proceeded to penalise those who had so nobly helped to bring England through the crisis of her fate, and to make her strong and great.

One would have thought that the common danger, the common need, would have united all, brought rich and poor closer together, and eliminated some of that degrading selfishness which is too apt to become all-absorbing during a prolonged and prosperous peace. But we see nothing of that larger nobility amongst those whose motto, we are told, used to be *noblesse oblige*. Like the Bourbons, they learn nothing, and forget nothing. The effect of the war upon the British people, as a whole, appears to have been to toughen the national character, and

[1] Green.

in some respects to deepen the moral consciousness. But the ethical leaven was slow to take effect upon a class so entrenched in privilege, so buttressed round and about by corruption, that it was afraid of the dishonest tenure by which it held power becoming known, and sent a Member of Parliament to the Tower for daring to describe the House of Commons as a " part of our fellow-subjects collected together by means which it is not necessary to describe." [1]

The people continued for long years debarred from all participation in political affairs; and it was with the utmost difficulty that any sort of concession could be wrung from the governing classes on behalf of the multitude of the nation—that large body that produces all, makes all, and by whose industry the whole is sustained. Legislation continued to be all for a class. We look in vain in the statute-book even for any mention of a suitable recompense for the men who through that long fateful day at Waterloo withstood the legions of France— those common men, who, as Soult said, would, and did, stand to be cut to pieces, but could not be conquered. Is it not an astonishing thing that, while commanders were rewarded with titles and estates, these men received nothing but the freedom to beg their bread? During the foregoing hundred years they and their fathers had stood stronger than walls of masonry, hurling back the enemy on a thousand fields of death—at Blenheim, Malplaquet, Quebec, Assaye, Salamanca, Talavera, at St. Vin-

[1] Sir Francis Burdett.

cent, Aboukir, Trafalgar; and while a delighted country huzzaed and illuminated, it, or those who legislated for it, did nothing in recognition of the services of these heroes.[1]

Nay, they even robbed them the while. During the period from 1710 to 1797 upwards of three million acres of land were enclosed and added to the estates of those who had already broad acres enough. The lands thus taken were for the most part the commons upon which the peasantry had pastured their flocks and herds, and sustained their common weal for ages. Of the area thus absorbed, some 330,000 acres were enclosed during the reigns of Anne and the first two Georges; the remainder, 2,804,197 acres in all (representing upwards of 1500 Acts), constituting a suggestive cantle of the legislative works of George the Third's Parliaments from 1760 to 1797, during the longer portion of which time the people were contributing so largely of their blood and treasure to build up and protect the Empire.

It was, perhaps, well that these lands, or some of them, at least, should be enclosed and subjected to proper cultivation; but it was an act of gross spoliation for a land-owning Parliament to appropriate them to the uses of its class to the detriment of those who were doing as much for the country as themselves. But even this, or much more, one could have overlooked if it had been purely the good of the common home they had sought—if

[1] It is true a public subscription produced nearly half a million for the widows and orphans of the men killed at Waterloo.

they had aimed at some sort of reward for those who had deserved well of their country. But to them never an acre was voted. It is hard to read the record of those years without tinglings of shame for the scant sense of justice or humanity possessed by the rulers of that day. So absorbed were they in their own interests that they could not give one generous thought to the workers—to the workers who had supplied the backbone of the army, who had tilled the fields and toiled in the factories to make the wealth with which England had carried on the war. It was nothing to them if they were pauperised by the laws which made them rich; it was nothing to them that the masses, sunken in poverty and ignorance, were driven into crime. They were always ready, these classes, to build gaols, to hang, and transport, and ride down with their dragoons anything that looked like open defiance of the laws; but to aid, instruct, uplift—what a desert the page of legislation is in these respects! Well was it that their reign was soon to come to an end, or England might ere long have seen an overthrow rivalling that of France.

It is necessary to say these things; for the building of the mighty Empire, upon which we boast that the sun never sets, was not the work of any one section of the community. It was not the work exclusively of English, or Irish, or Scotch, of Whig or Tory, patrician or plebeian, but of all combined; albeit, some may have brought better and more enduring qualities to the task than others. It is therefore with a sense of forlornness that one hopes the building may be for all time, seeing how eager one class has ever been to arrogate to itself all the honour, glory, and rewards of the work, forgetting the while to do even the commonest justice to those who, if they build small and without sound of trumpet, build strong and firm, willingly cementing the fabric with their blood and the blood of their children if the need arise.

How ceaseless and irrepressible was the activity of the common man during the drummings and paradings after the Little Corporal is seen in the industrial and commercial record of the time. Although during the second period of the war, trade underwent great vicissitudes, the volume of it steadily increased. The anti-commercial decrees of Napoleon checked all dealings with a considerable portion of the Continent, while the orders in council on England's part, and the non-intercourse acts and embargoes of the Americans put an end to mercantile relations with the United States. The glutting of these markets caused great speculative activity among merchants, and such commodities as silk, cotton, hemp, tallow, tobacco, etc., rose enormously in price. At the same time the price of agricultural produce went up enormously in consequence of the bad harvest of 1809. But while these things were telling against British trade in the northern hemisphere, new markets were being opened to the manufacturer and merchant by the emancipation of the Spanish colonies. Adventurers, however, rushed into these new channels with too much avidity, the result being for a time unfortunate. Some ruinous failures in 1810 and the following year were the consequence. A similar reaction occurred in 1815, as the result of the glut of British goods sent to the Continent on the overthrow of Napoleon and the downfall of his Commercial System.

Notwithstanding these unfavourable conditions, however, the commerce of the United Kingdom steadily increased in the second, as it had done in the first, period of the French war. The average official value of British exports in the nine years from 1793 to 1802 was £30,760,000, while the average in the ten years of the second war, from 1803 to 1812 inclusive, rose to £42,145,000. The tonnage that cleared outwards between 1803 and 1815 jumped from 2,019,382 tons in the former year to 2,759,720 tons in the latter; while the value of cargoes exported from Great Britain during the same period rose from thirty-one millions sterling in 1803 to nearly double that amount in 1815. Another curious and interesting fact connected with these years of war is that, notwithstanding the constant drain upon the able-bodied, the population of England and Wales alone is computed to have increased a million and a half in the ten years from 1805 to 1815.

It is astonishing to think that with a population of no more than fifteen millions, Great Britain should have been able to conduct a war extending over twenty-three years of hostilities against a warlike nation with twice its population—some of the time assisted by others—at an average yearly expenditure of upwards of forty-eight millions sterling, or a total of £1,111,214,731. The expenditure on the war of 1793 to 1802 was nearly double that of any preceding contest; and the expenditure of the war of 1803 to 1815 exceeded that of the first period in the ratio of more than three to one. The enormous expenditure of the latter period, however, was greatly increased by the accumulated interest on the previous expenditure. The depreciation of the currency also tended to enlarge the amount.

What England had won by the war—apart from securing a protracted peace—made but a poor show as against the enormous cost. She had added to her possessions by conquests at sea the island of Malta, the Dutch colonies of Ceylon and the Cape of Good Hope, the French colony of Mauritius, and several West India islands, including Tobago and St. Lucia. These at first sight appear small gains for so great an outlay; but some of them have proved of enormous advantage to the general interests of the Empire.

The most important of these acquisitions was undoubtedly that of the Cape of Good Hope. Settled originally by the Dutch in 1652, it was taken by the British, acting for the Prince of Orange, in 1795, and ruled by them in his name until the peace of 1802, when it was restored to Holland. In 1806, however, it was again seized for Great Britain by Sir David Baird, and has since remained an integral part of the Empire, having been finally ceded to England by the King of the Netherlands at the peace of 1815. At that time the limit of the colony was formed by the Great Fish River and the line of

CAPE OF GOOD HOPE.
(From an old print.)

the mountains south of Bushmanland to the Buffalo River and the Atlantic, and comprised a district of about a hundred and twenty thousand square miles —more than three times the area of England. Its population consisted of some twenty thousand white men, with their slaves, as abject and as cruelly treated a race as ever came under the dominion of Christian men. The story of their treatment by the Dutch colonists is revolting in the extreme. Not only would they, " in cold blood . . . destroy the bonds which nature has knit between husband and wife, and between parents and children," but, says Spurrman,[1] " I have known some colonists not only, for a trifling neglect, deliberately flay both the backs and limbs of their slaves by a peculiar, slow, lingering process, but even, outdoing the very tigers in their cruelty, throw pepper and salt over the wounds." The same writer goes on to say: " Many a time have I seen unhappy slaves, who, with the most dismal cries and lamentations, were suffering such punishments, during which they are used to cry, not so much for mercy as for a draught of water; but, so long as their blood is inflamed with the torture, it is said that great care must be taken to avoid allowing them drink of any kind, as experience has shown that in that case they would die in a few hours, and sometimes the very instant after they drank it. . . . There are many who hold them (these cruelties) in abomination, and fear lest the vengeance of Heaven should, for all these crimes, fall upon their land and their posterity."

[1] *Voyage to the Cape of Good Hope.*

The chief trouble of the new rulers, after the annexation, arose out of the determination of the British authorities to put a stop to slave-raiding, which was one of the pleasures and pastimes of the Boers, and to forbid the making of fresh captives. Laws also began to be enforced for improving the condition of those already in bondage. The Dutch resented such interference with what they considered their rights, and trouble and mischief was the result. Unfortunately, the conduct of the English was not always guided by wisdom, while their treatment of the natives was often little, if at all, better than that of the Dutch. Naturally, the Bushmen who were still free, and the Kaffirs, who abounded in large numbers in the eastern districts of the colony and its adjacent parts, gave a great deal of trouble. Those of them who had come in contact with the Christians had been both demoralised and exasperated by the treatment they had received at the white men's hands. The Kaffirs in particular, being a finer and more intelligent race than the Bushmen, caused themselves to be much dreaded.

"Some of them," we are told, "harassed the border colonists by frequent predatory incursions; but a considerable number lived quietly, engaged in cultivating the ground and herding their cattle, and these, together with another class who had entered the service of the colonists at their request, would gladly have pledged their allegiance to the British Crown had the privileges of British subjects been offered and duly explained to them in return. The chiefs were daily becoming more sensible of the advantages to be gained by civilisation, and entreated that missionaries should be sent for the instruction of their young people. Under these circumstances, there is little doubt a large body of Kaffirs might, by legalising their tenure of certain lands, and otherwise by judicious treatment, have been incorporated with and rendered useful members of the community. Others might have been bought out with far less expense than they could be driven out; and the really irreclaimable, when proved so, expelled with consent of the chief and council of the sub-tribes to which they belonged."[1]

Such wise and just counsels, however, do not appear to have entered into the thoughts of the British rulers of the colony. Too often in these cases the Governors, or those by whom they were chiefly supported, have been military men, and it is very difficult indeed for one brought up to the sword to refrain from using the sword as the arbiter in whatever disputes may arise. If all the troubles that have arisen in connection with England's colonising enterprises were carefully examined it would be found that a very large proportion of them had their origin in this cause alone. Barely had the colony of the Cape of Good Hope come into British hands ere we find this evil at work. In 1809 Colonel Collins, who had been employed as a commissioner for the settlement of the frontier, advised the expulsion of all Kaffirs from the colony, not excepting even those who had entered the service of farmers

[1] Martin, *The British Colonies*, vol. iv.

and others. This barbarous policy was adopted and in 1811 was put into execution. "A great commando," says Martin,[1] "comprising a large force of military and burgher militia, was assembled under Colonel Graham; and, though the Kaffirs earnestly pleaded the cruelty of including the innocent and the guilty in the same condemnation, all were expelled with unrelenting severity. No warning was given; but they were forced to abandon their crops of maize and millet, then nearly ripe, and so extensive that the troops were employed for many weeks in destroying their cultivations by trampling them down with large herds of cattle, and burning to the ground their huts and hamlets; and a much longer time elapsed before they succeeded in driving the whole of the people, to the number of twenty thousand souls, over the Great Fish River."

Of course, all this was not done without exciting evil passions, and bringing about barbarous retaliations; but it may be truly said that in this war of races, the superior, the more civilised people, displayed more aptitude in learning the wiles and the savage ways of the blacks than in teaching them the arts of civilisation. Great complaint was made of the cruelty with which the Dutch had pursued and made slaves of the Hottentots, as the Bushmen were called; but, with the exception that the English did not make slaves, they often showed little improvement on the methods of their fellow Christians. Cattle raids were allowed, and even given the sanction of Government, on the same plan that had

[1] *The British Colonies*, vol. iv.

previously been employed by the Boers for the acquisition of slaves. "A leader of one of their tribes, named Gaika, being at feud with the other chiefs, was, in 1817, made an ally by the Governor, Lord Charles Somerset; and it was agreed between them that Gaika and his people should have exclusive right of trade with the English, and should be aided in war against his rivals, on condition of their helping to punish those rivals for their misdeeds. One curious provision in this treaty was that, whenever cattle were stolen from the colony, the colonists should seize an equivalent number from the nearest and most convenient kraal, or village, of the Kaffirs, and that Gaika should make good the loss, if it fell upon his own tribe, by seizure from some of his neighbors."[1]

In the year 1818 Gaika was aided by a force of British and colonial troops against several allied tribes of Kaffirs. The war was carried on in the most ruthless manner, the natives being slaughtered in the villages, or in the woods whither they had fled for safety. Thirty thousand cattle were taken, of which nine thousand fell to the lot of Gaika, while the remainder was distributed among the colonists. Of course, this sort of thing led to reprisals by the Kaffirs, and in the end thousands of them were driven from their homes and a new province was added to Cape Colony. Thus the civilisation of Africa went on.

In spite of the mistaken policy pursued towards the natives, the colony made substantial progress.

[1] Bourne, *The Story of our Colonies.*

Although in 1807 the total population did not much exceed fifty-six thousand, by 1817 it had reached seventy-four thousand. The advance would have been still more marked but for the trouble occasioned by the Dutch, who manifested a sullen and determined opposition to any and every measure that was an innovation upon the ways to which they had been accustomed. In 1815 they broke out in open rebellion, and were with difficulty brought to terms.

During the long Napoleonic wars, England, as we have seen, captured most of the Dutch East India settlements, including Java and Amboyna. On the conclusion of peace, however, not only were these islands restored to their former owners, but the Dutch were put in possession of the keys both of the Strait of Malacca and the Strait of Sunda. To remedy these evils, Sir Stamford Raffles established the settlement and colony of Singapore, on the island of that name at the southern extremity of the Malay Peninsula, from which he routed a nest of pirates. Situated in the direct route to China, within a week's sail of that country, close to Siam, and "in the very seat of the Malayan empire," Singapore, under the direction of its able founder, in little more than three years grew from nothing into a thriving and important community, with a population of ten thousand souls, composed of all nations. Nor did its subsequent growth belie the promise of its remarkable start. Within a few years the number of its inhabitants had doubled and quadrupled, and it became the most important trading place in South-east Asia, its only competitor being Batavia, in Java. All the peoples of the surrounding countries brought thither the produce of their fields and their manufactures, to exchange them for Western and other commodities, thus making of it one of the most cosmopolitan cities in the world, rising within seventy years to a population of a hundred and sixty thousand.

While these things were going on in other parts of the British world, it had not been all plain sailing in India. When peace was made with Sindhia and the Rajah of Berar, Rao Holkar had been left in the field, and he, for a time, was enabled to support his Mahratta followers by ravages in the provinces of Malwa and Rajputana. These practices called for fresh operations in 1804, and they were protracted, with little credit to the Company or the British name, through the closing months of Governor Wellesley's term of office. The disastrous retreat of Colonel Monson through Central India gave a serious check to English prestige in that quarter, while the repeated failures of General Lake to reduce Bhartpur were little calculated to improve the record. Notwithstanding an enormous deal of marching, countermarching, and fighting, much of it brilliant enough in its way, Holkar was left still unconquered. This was no fault of Lake's. His quarry liked better to scour the country than to fight. He thus made the game a very extensive and an extremely harassing one; but, when it was nearly played out, the Commander-in-chief got the counter-check from home, and the freebooting Mahratta was allowed to triumph by the concession of a highly favourable treaty of peace. The directors had become tired of the long-protracted warfare, and sent out Lord Cornwallis to supersede the Marquis of Wellesley; but, dying ere he had been in the country three months, he was succeeded (in 1805) by Sir George Barlow, a civil servant of the Company. A more unfit person for the post at such a crisis it would be difficult to imagine. It may have been wise to come to a peaceful settlement with Holkar, but to allow that potentate and his ally, Sindhia, to make war upon the Rajput chiefs, who were nominally under British protection, was more disgraceful than the loss of many battles. During Barlow's administration also occurred the mutiny of Sepoys at Vellore—a mutiny occasioned by a peddling interference with the men's head-gear, which, though quickly suppressed, mainly through the presence of mind and spirit of one man,[1] gave a shock to the fabric of British dominion in India.

Fortunately, Sir George Barlow was succeeded by one of the wisest and most successful of Indian administrators in Lord Minto, who remained at the head of affairs from 1807 until 1813. Under his rule the acquisitions made by Lord Wellesley were reduced to order and consolidated, and friendly relations were established with the Sikhs of the Punjab, with Afghanistan and Persia, to each of which powers embassies were sent. The only military enterprises of any moment undertaken by Lord Minto were those which resulted in the occupation of the island of Mauritius, and the conquest of Java,

[1] Colonel Gillespie.

already referred to. During the last year of his rule an important modification of the Company's charter was effected by the throwing open of the trade to the East, that to China only remaining the monopoly of the Company.

Lord Minto was followed by the Marquis of Hastings, who, Commander-in-chief as well as Governor-General, soon found himself engaged in wars with the Gourkhas of Nepaul (who, after a bit of brave fighting, were reduced to submission, henceforth to contribute to the Indian army some of its hardiest soldiers), the Pindarees, and the Mahrattas, all of which were brought to a successful issue.

It was during the administration of Lord Hastings that the islands which had been wrested from the Dutch in the east of the Indian Ocean were restored to that power; but it was also during his term of office that the reduction of the whole of Ceylon—the Serendib of the *Arabian Nights*—was completed. Although the Governor of that possession was independent of the Governor-General of India, the Marquis of Hastings contributed not a little, by his advice and assistance, to the final achievement. Before the close of the eighteenth century the British had ejected the Dutch from all their maritime settlements in Ceylon. Roughly speaking, it may be said that, in the year 1800, the sovereignty of the island was divided between Great Britain and the king of Kandy, the latter holding possession of the mountainous interior, while the British were masters of the lowlands round the coast. During the next few years several unsuccessful attempts were made to subjugate the brave Kandyans, who, during the nearly three hundred years that different European nations had had a footing on the coast, had been able to maintain their independence, and would probably have continued to do so but for the dissensions among themselves. After a period marked by blunders innumerable, atrocious brutalities, and a general lack of wise command, an able Governor was at length appointed in the person of Sir Thomas Maitland. When, in 1805, the new ruler arrived, a civil war was and had for some time been raging in the interior. This he wisely left to take its course, confining himself to the protection of the districts in the hands of the British, and to improving those possessions as much as possible. Sir James Mackintosh, who paid a visit to Ceylon in 1810, gives high commendation to this officer. "It is impossible," he says, "for me to do justice to General Maitland's most excellent administration, which, I am convinced, never had an equal in India. By the cheerful decision of his character, and by his perfect knowledge of men, he has become universally popular amidst severe retrenchments. In an island where there was in one year a deficit of £700,000, he has reduced the expenses to the level of the revenue; and with his small army of five thousand men he has twice, in the same year, given effectual aid to the great Government of Madras, which has an army of seventy thousand men."[1]

It is to men like Maitland, wisely seconding the industry of the army of toilers and traders who are

[1] *Memoirs of the Life of the Right Hon. Sir James Mackintosh.*

never far to seek when there is work to be done, that Britain owes much of the successful building of her extensive Empire. His administration was marked by the endeavour to establish a system of government and jurisprudence suitable to the character and habits of the natives. In these efforts he was greatly indebted to the learning and industry of a man of singular genius in the Ceylon civil service. This was John D'Oyly, who, having made himself a perfect master of Cingalese, compiled a code of laws in that language. In order to become thus proficient in the tongue, laws, manners, and customs of the people, D'Oyly had for four years lived among them, assuming their dress, and conforming in every possible way to their habits and modes of life. Both the Governors and the governed were indebted to this talented and eccentric individual.

In 1812, Sir Thomas Maitland was succeeded in the governorship by Sir Robert Brownrigg, to whom an opportunity soon offered for subjugating the interior of the island to British rule. The king, after the successful termination of a war which he had conducted against his chief adigar, or minister, was seized with a lust of blood, and, not satisfied with victims among his own subjects, captured and horribly mutilated a number of British subjects who were trading in his country. This brutality could not be allowed to pass unpunished, and accordingly several divisions of troops were got ready, and, in the early days of 1815, they advanced against the Kandyan capital, one of them under General Brownrigg himself. The expedition was entirely successful; there was little fighting, the king was taken prisoner, and the army welcomed at the seat of government as a deliverer. On the 2d of March the British flag waved over the palace of Kandy in sign of the complete subjugation of the island. Thus one of the most interesting spots on the earth's surface, and one of the strangest people, became a part of the ever-broadening Empire, to benefit or suffer from the connection, according as the Anglo-Saxon people rise to or fall short of the height and vastness of their responsibility.

CHAPTER IV.

COLONIAL EXPANSION.

WHEN England entered upon the long peace of nearly forty years—broken only by the small bubble wars that do not count—she had already got her foot firmly established on the four extra-European continents. Notwithstanding the loss of the thirteen colonies, she still possessed in North America the two Canadas (Upper and Lower), Hudson's Bay Territory, Newfoundland, Nova Scotia, New Brunswick, and the Bermuda Islands; in the West Indies, the islands of Jamaica, Trinidad (wrested from Spain during the first Napoleonic war), Tobago (ceded to the British at the peace of Paris), Barbadoes, Grenada, St. Vincent, St. Lucia, St. Kitts, Nevis, Anguilla, Dominica, Montserrat, and the Bahamas; on the mainland, British Honduras (a little settlement of British blood and bone that, commencing as a nest of buccaneers and logwood-cutters, had held its own against the Spaniards since the middle of the seventeenth century) and Guiana; and, in the far south, Falkland Island and South Georgia. In Asia the British dominions stretched from Calcutta to Bombay, and from Madras to the foot of the Himalayas on the mainland, besides Penang and the Wellesley Province on the Malay Peninsula, the island of Ceylon, Mauritius (the latter taken from the French in 1810), and the Seychelles, a small archipelago between S. Lat. 3° 4' and 5° 35' and E. Long. 55° 15' and 56° (likewise ceded by the French in 1814). In Australasia, the infant colonies of Port Jackson, Norfolk Island, Tasmania (then Van Dieman's Land), which had begun to be used as a receptacle for convicts in 1803, and we may add New Zealand, where British vessels were already calling, and where gunpowder, rum, and the Bible had commenced to do the work of civilisation, the first missionaries having gone thither in 1814. Lastly, in Africa, the British flag was paramount in Cape Colony, Sierra Leone, and St. Helena, the lone island home and prison of the erewhile disturber Napoleon.

Now began a period of peaceful development and extension such as England had not enjoyed for the best part of a century—in short, since Walpole held the reins of state. How marvellously it told in the way of building up and organising the different parts of the Empire we shall presently see.

It is strange to note, but nevertheless true, that civilisation for the Australasian world had its centre and starting-point in that dumping-ground of British scoundrelism, Port Jackson. But even the outscourings of the English gaols of that time were not all refuse; for in that bad period it was as criminal to hold advanced political views as to forge a Bank of England note, or commit a highway robbery—far more criminal than to fill the purse by political corruption. Hence it not unfrequently happened that men of cultivated minds, men of high views, inspired by the noblest sentiments of humanity, were doomed to share the ignominy and degradation of the most vicious of the population.

Everything, however, serves its just ends; and many of the men impiously condemned by English tyranny lived to serve the ends of a higher justice and a nobler humanity in their enforced exile at the antipodes. It is significant of much when, years later, a local historian could write of men who had come out as criminals, but were then honoured citizens: "They form no uninteresting part of the population. . . . Some of them are reckoned among our most honourable tradesmen and merchants—among the most liberal supporters, too, of the benevolent institutions which adorn our land. Some of these institutions have been all but entirely founded, and are now mainly supported, by their means. In many cases they have, by their industry and perseverance, acquired considerable wealth; and in most instances the wealth thus obtained has been generously and honourably devoted to the public benefit, the real and substantial advancement of this land of their expatriation. . . . No sooner was wealth thus poured into their lap than they gave it back, spreading it through numerous channels, through each of which, as it flowed, it left blessings that even succeeding ages may enjoy."[1] The men who

---

[1] Braim, *History of New South Wales*.

thus became honoured citizens and benefactors of their country may have been "offenders" against iniquitous laws, but it is open to serious doubt whether, in the true sense, they were ever criminals. Judged by the higher standard of right, the judges who condemned them were the criminals.

The colony, however, had to pass through many years of darkness and difficulty before thus much could be said. The early Governors were either military or naval officers, used only to the despotism of the regiment or the quarter-deck, and little qualified for the task of government in the true sense. In the first years of the settlement they were, of course, nothing more than gaol-keepers; but the time came when, free settlers having increased, they were required to put the despot aside—at least, in dealing with free men. But some of them found it difficult to do that, and trouble was the result. One of the worst offenders in this respect was Captain Bligh, notorious as commander of the ship *Bounty*, the crew whereof was driven to mutiny by his behaviour. He, in consequence of his tyrannous conduct, was seized by the colonists, and ultimately sent to England. The immediate cause of this rebellious act was his unjust treatment of one of the foremost of the colonists, and the one who, in those early days, did the most for the colony. This was John Macarthur, who was the first to put Australia to the test as a wool-producing country. Importing a flock of sheep in 1797, he gradually improved the breed by careful selection, and by intermixing with Spanish merinos, of which, after great trouble and perseverance, he obtained some specimens, until he was able to commence the growth of wool on a large scale, thus founding an industry which in a very short time became the staple of Australia.

With Bligh's expulsion commenced an era of reform. General Macquarie, who was sent out to succeed him, was in every way a higher type of man. He ruled the colony from 1810 to 1821, and left his mark for good on every department of the public service. Up to this time there had been one dark blot on the colony which, so long as it remained, made all improvement impossible. This was the curse of rum. " Rum," we are told,[1] " supplied the place of coin. Land, houses, and property of every description, real and personal, were bought and paid for in rum. It is recorded of one of the officers of the 102d Regiment that, a hundred acres of land having been distributed in half-acre allotments as free grants amongst some soldiers of the regiment, he planted a hogshead of rum upon the ground, and bought the whole hundred acres with the contents of the hogshead. A moiety of this land a few years ago realised £20,000 at a sale in Sydney."

This evil, which had been battled against by both Bligh and his predecessor, was finally put an end to by Governor Macquarie, a marked improvement in the morals of the community being the immediate result. Schools were established under his auspices, and the children, who had hitherto grown up in " total ignorance, were taught to read and write,

[1] Therry, *Reminiscences of Thirty Years' Residence in New South Wales and Victoria.*

and instructed in useful handicrafts." He turned to account the various trained workmen and artisans, whose crimes or misfortunes had sent them to the colony, in the building of hospitals, churches, and other public edifices, and in the construction of roads and bridges, thus developing and extending the colony, besides usefully employing and rewarding men who were willing to put their hands honestly to the plough. Therry's sentence of eulogy on him is: " He found a garrison and a gaol, and left the broad and deep foundations of an empire." When Macquarie laid down the governorship in 1821, the population of New South Wales numbered close upon thirty thousand souls, of whom the great proportion were convicts. Many of these, however, were " emancipists," as they were called; that is, men who by their good conduct had been set free from restraint, and engaged in business or other occupations the same as ordinary settlers. Some of them were men not only of high character, but of great ability.

During these years of gradual growth exploration had gone on step by step with the development of the colony. Governor Phillip had done what he could to increase the geographical knowledge of the new country in which Providence had for a time cast his lot; but it was under his immediate successor that the two foremost heroes of Australian discovery commenced their work. These were Matthew Flinders and George Bass. The former was a midshipman, the latter a navy surgeon, when, in 1795, they began to turn their attention to exploration, employing all the time they could be spared from duty on shipboard in examining and surveying the adjacent coasts. At first they confined themselves to the neighbourhood of Sydney, all their sailings to and fro being done in a boat nine feet long, with the sole assistance of a boy. But as the quality of their work became known they were encouraged to proceed to greater distances, and allowed the use of larger craft. In this way they spent the years 1795 and 1796, and, sometimes together, sometimes alone, made voyages that added greatly to the geographical knowledge of those parts. In the following year, Bass, in charge of a whaleboat, proceeded to Cape Howe, and then, turning westward, sailed through the strait which now bears his name, thus proving Tasmania to be an island, and not, as until then thought, part of the Australian continent. On his return he found that Flinders had in the meantime discovered a number of islands to the north of Tasmania. Later in the year the two together sailed right round the island, bringing back a faithful record of its chief bays and inlets. This was their last exploit in common. Soon after his return from Sydney, Bass sailed for England, but never reached his destination, and was heard of no more.

Flinders's fate was, in the end, almost as sad. But in the meanwhile he had many years of work, and he made such good use of them that he left little for subsequent investigators to do in the way of charting the east, and a considerable portion of the north and south, coasts of Australia. In 1801 and

1802 he carefully explored the coast from Port Phillip to the Great Australian Bight, including Kangaroo Island and the adjacent gulfs, thus reveal-

CAPTAIN FLINDERS.

ing South Australia proper. Then, after refitting at Sydney, he made a similar careful survey of the Gulf of Carpentaria and adjacent parts in the north, but was obliged to return before his work was completed through the sickness of his crew. In 1803 he started upon another expedition, but the loss of both his vessels compelled him to return. This was only the beginning of misfortunes. Setting sail in September for England, to report his discoveries and seek aid for still further enterprises, he was obliged by the condition of his vessel to put in at Mauritius, where he was detained by the French Governor, and kept in captivity for nearly seven years. Nor was this the worst of his ill-luck. His charts were taken from him, and many of his most important discoveries claimed by the French explorer Baudin. Released at length, he reached England in 1810, to find his greatest achievements claimed by another, and himself forgotten. With failing health he set to work to put his journals in order for publication, and died the day that his book appeared, July 19, 1814. It is worth while recording, somewhat in detail, the exploits of men like Bass and Flinders; they, and such as they, are the men who put in the corner-stones of the Empire, while the smaller men follow after, building to their height, and according to the pattern they set.

The high terms of praise in which Bass and Flinders spoke of Sullivan's Cove, at the mouth of the Derwent to the south-east of Tasmania, led to a party of settlers being sent to that river under Lieutenant Bowen in 1803, and they were followed by another to Port Dalrymple the next year under Colonel Paterson. In the meanwhile Colonel Collins had been despatched from England with a number of convicts to form a settlement at Port Phillip; but, finding the place unsuitable from lack of water, he decided, at the end of three months (February, 1804), to remove to Tasmania, selecting for his station the site now occupied by the town of Hobart.

During the same year, George Town, on the James, was founded. Unfortunately, the newcomers and the natives almost immediately came into collision, and a war of extermination, known as the Black War, commenced, and did not cease until the aborigines were practically extinct.

As in the case of Port Jackson, the early days of the colony were darkened by the frequent scarcity of supplies and by the want of good government. The first settlers, too, were ill-fitted to struggle against the initial difficulties of a new country, and so the hardships of the position were increased. Bit by bit, however, things improved; although not to any great extent until, in 1813, the ports were thrown open to traders, and, six years later, free settlers were welcomed. Up to that time obstacles had been put in the way of such immigrants; but now, the embargo removed, British farmers and others began to take up land and make their influence felt for good.

After Bass and Flinders had finished their labours there was little done in the way of exploration for a number of years, and then it was by land rather than by sea that the work was resumed. For the first twenty-five years of its existence the colony of Sydney was confined within the Blue Mountains— that is, to a distance of fifty miles inland. In 1813 that barrier was passed, and the valley of the Fish

River and the Bathurst Plains were for the first time brought within the limits of civilisation. In the following year the town of Bathurst was founded by Governor Macquarie, and a road between the new settlement and Sydney constructed by convicts. Thence started other journeys of exploration, disclosing the rivers Lachlan, Macquarie, and Murrumbidgee, and revealing the nature of the country for long distances west of the mountains. One of the most painstaking of these early explorers was Oxley, who subsequently pushed his investigations so far north as to pass the present boundaries of New South Wales, discovering the Brisbane River, ere long to see grow up on its banks the capital of Queensland, the youngest of the Australian colonies.

But this feat took place during the governorship of Sir Thomas Brisbane, who followed closely in the footsteps of his predecessor, encouraging exploration, inviting the immigration of free settlers, and giving every possible stimulus to useful works generally. He was succeeded, in 1825, by Sir Ralph Darling, who remained at the head of the Government until 1831. During the " reigns " of these two Governors the character of the colony changed very materially. In 1821 the population had amounted to nearly thirty thousand, of whom the convicts constituted two-thirds. By 1828 they formed but half of the total of 36,589, so greatly had the number of free colonists increased. These gradually formulated a very strong public opinion in favour of some sort of constitutional government in place of the despotism of a governor of convicts. The result was that in 1823 a Legislative Council was appointed to assist the Governor in making laws for the colony. At the same time the powers of the Governor in regard to civil and criminal jurisdiction were restricted by the institution of a supreme court of justice. Trial by jury was also established, and, hardly less important as an instrument of civil right, the press was declared free from censorship.[1]

These concessions towards self-government and the public control of affairs would hardly have satisfied the constantly growing demands so long as they did if the Governor who succeeded Darling had not been in every way a man of exceptional character and ability. This was Sir Richard Bourke, who has been justly described as "the most statesman-like and liberal-minded" Governor "ever sent to the colony."[2] The development of New South Wales made enormous strides under his rule. It had been the policy of previous Governors to keep the colony as compact as possible within a certain radius round about Sydney. He took the opposite course, and encouraged settlers—squatters, as they were called—to go farther afield. His reason for this altered policy was set forth in a despatch to the Colonial Secretary. "The proprietors soon find," he wrote, "from the increase of their flocks and herds, that it becomes necessary to send their stock beyond the boundary of location, and to form what are termed 'new stations'; otherwise, the only alternative left to them would be to restrain the increase of their

---

[1] Coghlan, *Wealth and Progress of New South Wales.*
[2] Bourne, *The Story of our Colonies.*

stock or to find artificial food for it. The first of these courses would be a severe falling off in the supply of wool; and as to artificial food, from the uncertainty of the seasons and the light character of the soil, it would be quite impracticable. Besides,

SYDNEY IN ITS EARLY DAYS.

either course would seem to be a rejection of the bounties of Providence, that spreads, with a prodigal hand, its magnificent carpet of bright green sward over boundless plains, and clothes the depths of the valleys with abundant grass. Moreover, the restraint on dispersion would entail an expense in the management which could not profitably repay the Government."

In pursuance of this view, he had vast districts of the country surveyed and divided into lots, which were sold from time to time by public auction. Moreover, to encourage squatters to go farther and farther afield, he took every possible means to clear the outlying districts of bushrangers, and so make life and property secure. He introduced humaner methods, too, of treating the convicts, employing them as much as possible in ways that had less the appearance of punishment, and which at the same time were advantageous to the community. Thus there were fewer runaways from penal labour to turn into bushrangers.

Another way in which the Governor benefited the colony was by the introduction of the system of assisted immigration, the Imperial Government doubling the amount given by the colony for this purpose. Thus a useful class of settlers were taken out that could not otherwise have found their way thither, including women for wives. In short, there was no wise project for the improvement of the community which Governor Bourke did not readily adopt and do his best to make a success.

Nor did these measures exhaust the benefits he conferred upon the colony. Coghlan, in his *Wealth and Progress of New South Wales*, says: " Sir Richard Bourke may be said to have been the real founder of our free institutions, as under his rule the foundations of the Constitution we now enjoy were well and firmly laid, on the solid basis of full and equal rights to all, whatever their sect or belief, and whether emancipist or originally free." But the greatest achievement of his administration, the same writer goes on to say, " was the establishment of religious equality, and the breaking up of the monopoly of Government aid enjoyed by one communion."

Under Sir Richard Bourke's *régime* the work of exploration was continued, chiefly by Sir Thomas Mitchell. Besides examining the country as far north as the Liverpool Plains, he traced the Darling from its source to its junction with the Murray, and finally, crossing the latter river, and proceeding farther south, he found himself amidst " the beautiful expanse of mountains, valleys, and table-lands " to which he gave the name of Australia Felix. Continuing his explorations, he came at length to the coast, where, to his surprise, he saw the rude beginnings of two or three different settlements. One of them was at Portland Bay, whither, in 1834, an enterprising farmer of Launceston, Tasmania, named Henty, had transferred his family and belongings, and laid the foundations of a pastoral and agricultural station. The following year saw two other men pass over from Tasmania to the mainland and settle on the shores of Port Phillip; the first, John Batman, choosing a location near Geelong; and the second, John Pascoe Fawkner, passing to the innermost corner of the bay, and landing on the bank of the Yarra Yarra, where the humble domicile which he erected was destined to become the centre of the city of Melbourne.

Mitchell's description of the country he had traversed and of the beginnings of the settlement at

Port Phillip, attracted attention both in Sydney and at home, and led to an immediate flow of immigrants thither. In the course of a year it had acquired an English population of one hundred and seventy-seven, which numbers, by the month of April, 1837, had increased to four hundred and fifty. "In the previous month," says Bourne, "Sir Richard Bourke had visited the colony and superintended the laying out of the towns of Melbourne and Geelong." The land was sold by auction. One half-acre in Melbourne realised £80, more than double the usual price. Two years afterwards it resold for £5000. "In January, 1838, Melbourne consisted," says Martin,[1] "of a nucleus of huts, embowered in the forest foliage, and had much the appearance of an Indian village. Two wooden houses served the purpose of inns for the settlers who frequented the place. A small square wooden building, with an old ship's bell suspended from a tree, was used as a church or a chapel by the various religious denominations. Two or three so-called shops formed emporiums for the sale of every description of useful articles. The flesh of the kangaroo and varieties of wild fowl were abundantly used, for fresh mutton was still scarce, and beef seldom seen. A manuscript newspaper, established by Fawkner, one of the enterprising men to whom England is indebted for the formation of the settlement, was the organ of public opinion in the colony."

Such was the now stately and magnificent city of

[1] *The British Colonies.*

Melbourne what time our sovereign lady the Queen was beginning her auspicious reign. It started under better auspices than most of the other early settlements in Australia. One of the first offshoots from Sydney, after those to Tasmania, was the settlement of Moreton Bay, founded by Sir Thomas Brisbane in 1825. The river Brisbane, which empties into it from Darling Downs, had been explored two years previously by Oxley, who was sent out by the Government of New South Wales to choose a site for a new convict establishment. He reported in favour of Brisbane, and during the next few years many substantial buildings were put up by the convicts. The colony, however, made but slow progress, owing largely to the difficulties which for some time were thrown in the way of free colonisation.[1]

Meanwhile other settlements were either founded or attempted at different parts of the coast. About the time that the convict station was planted at Moreton Bay, Major Lockyer carried a party of convicts and soldiers to St. George's Sound, in Western Australia, and took formal possession of the country on behalf of the Crown, although the same thing had been previously done by Vancouver. It was thought the French had a design upon the Sound, and Lockyer's expedition was intended to frustrate it. The convicts were kept there until 1830–31, when they were taken back to Sydney. In the interim Captain Stirling had been sent out to examine the Swan River, and his report excited so

[1] Bourne, *The Story of our Colonies.*

much interest in England that it led to the starting of a free settlement on the banks of that river. Upwards of eight hundred emigrants went out in 1829, with all the necessary stock and utensils for a pastoral and agricultural colony. Eleven hundred more followed in 1830, they, too, with a good supply of live-stock. But the first years of the settlement were a record of misery, failure, and distress. The project was formed in a moment of enthusiasm, and carried out with an almost total lack of practical common sense. Men, women, and children were dumped down in a barren wilderness without any sort of preparation having been made for them, and in the midst of hostile savages. According to the aggrieved settlers, too, those in charge of the undertaking, naval and military officers in the main, showed the grossest selfishness, dividing among themselves the best land, and leaving that which was useless to the emigrants,[1] who had been induced to go out on the promise of generous grants. The result was as might have been expected. An indignant remonstrance on the way they had been treated, addressed by the emigrants to the Governor, shows how pitiful had been the lack of all forethought and organisation. "The entire material of the settlement," they wrote—"the official staff, settlers, property, and live-stock—were hurried out to an unknown wilderness before one acre was surveyed, before one building had been erected, before even a

[1] As a matter of fact, thousands of acres were assigned to or reserved for civil, naval, and military officers, and in many cases such grants were reserved for a considerable period.

guess had been formed as to the proper scene of their labours, before the slightest knowledge had been obtained of the soil, climate, products, or inhabitants. Nay, further, it was absolutely made a condition of the grants of land that the emigrant should bring his family, dependents, and property into the colony while in this state. The ghastly spectacle of the town-site of Clarence—its sole edifices crowded, buried, and neglected tombs; its only inhabitants corpses—the victims of disease, starvation, and despair; the sea-beach strewed with wrecks; the hills and borders of the rivers studded with deserted and half-finished buildings—bears witness to these consequences, and speaks of brave men, delicate females, and helpless children perishing by hundreds on a desert coast from want of food, of shelter, and even of water, and surrounded by armed hordes of angry savages." [1]

Nor was this the blackest of the picture, according to independent accounts. Some, who should have learned more self-control, became reckless, and took to the spirit casks; others gave way to despair; many died; those who could get away, with the wreck of their fortunes, to Hobart or Sydney, held themselves fortunate. It was a dismal state of things; but the tougher or sturdier sort, who had the patience and the fortitude to hold on, gradually found the prospects brightening. In time people got settled down somehow, and, having their task and their belongings fairly before them, began to put forth their energy. Other immigrants ar-

[1] *Parliamentary Emigration Papers* for 1849, 1850.

riving, fresh from home, tended to encourage the downcast and to revive the generally flagging spirits of the colony. After a while it was discovered that the country was less inhospitable than it had at first appeared; the climate was salubrious; better land, admirable for vegetables and fruit, was found by penetrating the forests, while sheep throve on its extensive pastures.

Thus some sort of order was steadily evolved out of chaos, and prosperity began to show its pleasing face. In the meantime, however, the free settlement had become a Crown colony, the town of Perth had been founded " on a well-chosen site by the side of the Swan River, and Freemantle was appointed as its port, at the entrance of the river into the Indian Ocean. The village of Albany, destined to become a town, was planted by St. George's Sound, on the southern coast, and other settlements were formed along the shore and here and there inland."[1]

Western Australia, however, remained for years the most backward of the antipodean colonies. Although upwards of nine hundred times the size of England, the settlement in 1834 contained only about 1600 British inhabitants, and there were under 1000 acres of land in cultivation. By 1842 the population had little more than doubled, although the number of sheep had grown from 3500 to upwards of 60,000, while the acres under cultivation had risen to 3364. It is pleasing to be able to record, amid all this backwardness, that the natives of this part of Australia were much better treated,

---

[1] Bourne, *The Story of our Colonies.*

and, in consequence, did less mischief, than in the other colonies. Martin[1] attributes this in part to the fact that the early settlers of Western Australia belonged largely to " the better classes of society," and in part to the circumstance that, being small in numbers, they were obliged to observe " caution and forebearance." There is, as we know, great virtue in necessity, and it was probably that need, rather than any superiority of class, that accounts for the better treatment of the natives.

South Australia, which, as regards its commencement, dates next after the Swan River settlement, owes its origin to a body of philanthropists with a leaning towards percentages derived from other people's exertions. Those parts of South Australia which were first subjected to the experiment of colonisation had been condemned in 1822 by Captain King, who, following Flinders, devoted some time to the exploration of that coast, as barren and unsuitable for settlement. But in the years 1829, 1830, Captain Sturt, famous for his inland explorations, descended the Murray to its outlet in Lake Victoria, and examined the ridges which divide that water from St. Vincent's Gulf, now the magnificent harbour of Adelaide.

Captain Sturt's favourable description of the country between Lake Victoria and the ranges of St. Vincent's Gulf induced the Governor of New South Wales to send Captain Barker to report on the suitableness of that region for a settlement. Captain Barker did not live to make his report,

---

[1] *The British Colonies.*

having been killed by natives; but his companion, Mr. Kent, brought back such a favourable description of the soil, pasturage, and fresh-water supplies, that a desire was immediately created in England to form a colony in South Australia. A committee was formed with a view to starting a colony on the "self-supporting system," of which Mr. Edward Gibbon Wakefield was the chief sponsor. Westgarth[1] thus describes this precious scheme: "He held that, by placing a high value on the unreclaimed lands of a new country, and forwarding a labouring population out of the sale of those lands, the emigrants would of necessity work at low wages, as the purchase of the dear lands would be above their means, thereby securing the capitalist investing in the land a large interest for his money, and forming at once a community of labourers and artisans who would minister to the benefits of the landholders. Besides these large landholders, a class of small farmers was to be induced to emigrate, by disposing of the land in small sections to be cleared and cultivated by their families."

This scheme was considered such an embodiment of wisdom that an association was eventually formed to carry it out. A charter was obtained, and a system of local government arranged, which was to come into operation as soon as the settlement numbered fifty thousand. A large sum of money was subscribed, and in 1836 a number of vessels set sail with officials and emigrants. The first arrivals landed on Kangaroo Island, but were afterwards

[1] *Australia*, p. 215.

conveyed to the Adelaide Plains, where the colony was formerly inaugurated, and Captain Hindmarsh proclaimed Governor, on the 28th of December.

The first months of the new settlement were marked by unseemly quarrels among the officials, which, in one instance, led to a free fight in the streets of Adelaide. These difficulties and disagreements, indeed, became so grave that, in 1838, Captain Hindmarsh, the Governor, was recalled, and Lieut.-Colonel Gawler appointed in his stead. He, however, proved so poor an administrator that he, too, ere long, had to be superseded. The failure of these gentlemen as Governors leads Martin very justly to animadvert on the folly of placing men in positions of trust for which they are totally unqualified, because, like Captain Hindmarsh, they may have distinguished themselves " at the battle of the Nile," or because, like Governor Gawler, they may have been " present at many of the great sieges and battles in the Peninsula." " It is quite true," he remarks, " that naval and military officers have occasionally (though seldom) made efficient Governors of colonies; but they are exceptions to a rule. Much of the long-protracted misrule of some of our colonies may be traced to the evil of appointing soldiers or sailors as civil Governors, irrespective of their aptitude or fitness for such important and difficult duties."

Notwithstanding the fact that Governor Gawler found the colony on the verge of bankruptcy, he immediately launched forth in redoubled expenditure on public works, although by so doing he raised the price of labour and kept men at work in town who should have been employed tilling the land; and in order to meet his payments he drew unauthorised bills on the Home Government. He was soon replaced by Captain (afterwards Sir George) Grey, who did his best to retrieve the disasters into which the colony had been precipitated. He was hampered, however, by the continued unwisdom of the projectors of the colony, and the Government had at length to step in and suspend the charter, making South Australia a Crown colony.

Although Captain Grey had a difficult task to perform, he did it with credit to himself and advantage to the colony. His first effort was to reduce expenses and to drive the settlers on to the land, and in both respects he was completely successful. In 1839 the population of the colony was 10,000; by 1840 it had risen to 14,610, and by 1845 to 22,390; while in the five years from 1840 to 1845 the amount of land under cultivation had increased from 2500 to upwards of 26,000 acres.

It remains to give some particulars of the pre-Victorian era in New Zealand, that New Britain of the Southern Ocean, with its three larger and many smaller islands, constituting an area of 106,240 square miles, or about one-eighth less than that of Great Britain and Ireland. With its temperate climate and fertile soil, it soon became a favourite resort for immigrants, who were not deterred by the danger they ran from the savage and warlike natives who peopled its slopes and vales. Braver and in every way superior to the degraded aborigines of Australia, the Maoris, with their painted skins, probably presented to the first white invaders of New Zealand a similar contrast to that afforded by the early Britons in their pigmental adornment to their Roman subjugators. Possibly they were a degree more degraded, in that, according to undoubted evidence, they were of cannibalistic tastes, which our Celtic forefathers were not. They were, indeed, one of the finest races with which the British in their world-wide colonisations have come in contact, and it is pleasing to know that so sturdy a race has not been completely wiped out of existence by our civilising methods.

From the time of Captain Cook's last visit until 1791, when Captain Vancouver touched at Dusky Bay during his voyage of exploration and annexation to the north-west coast of America, New Zealand appears to have been unvisited by Europeans. Two years later the *Dædalus*, under the command of Lieutenant Hanson, was sent thither by the Governor of New South Wales, and two natives were taken thence to Norfolk Island. The object of their deportation was to obtain from them the secret of the Maori method of dressing flax; but when asked, after their arrival at the little penal colony, to make known the process, they rather haughtily informed Governor King that flax-dressing was an affair of the women, of which they, being respectively a chief and a priest, knew nothing. After this ships frequently touched at New Zealand ports, particularly whalers and sealers, especially after the granting of a premium for the encouragement of whale-fishing in the South Seas.[1] In some cases the whalers established themselves on shore, and pursued their avocations from these stations with the friendly assistance of the natives. But in too many instances these early relations of Europeans with the Maoris led to wrong-doing and bloodshed. On one occasion an entire ship's company was sacrificed in consequence of the brutal conduct of the captain to a native, and out of this arose other murders and atrocities.

A better chapter for New Zealand opened when, in 1814, the first missionaries commenced their labours in the Bay of Islands. These were Messrs. Hall and Kendall, who were sent out by Mr. Samuel Marsden, colonial Chaplain of Paramatta, New South Wales, and one of the best friends the Maoris ever had. At the same time the Governor of that colony took the natives of New Zealand under his protection, and prohibited the removal of any of them without the express permission of their chiefs. Mr. Kendall was appointed, with the consent of the chiefs, Resident Magistrate of the Bay of Islands. This was the beginning of British authority in New Zealand. The mission established under the auspices of the Church Missionary Society did much to civilise the natives, and the more, doubtless, because the missionaries did not confine themselves to teaching the tenets of the Christian religion, but instructed their pupils in agriculture and other useful arts as well. Some years later the Wesleyans established a mission at Wangaroa, not far from the Bay of

[1] In the fifty-first year of George III.

Islands, and subsequently on the Hokianga River, thence extending their operations southwards as far as Port Nicholson on Cook's Strait.

The good effected by the missionaries, however, was too often undone, or, to a large extent, counteracted, by the evil examples set by the traders and others who settled along the coasts. These people not only sold the natives muskets and gunpowder, and gave them a taste for rum, but made them acquainted with other vices of civilisation that otherwise they would have known nothing of. Some notion of the state of affairs then existing may be gathered from a despatch addressed, in January, 1832, to the Governor of New South Wales by Viscount Gooderich, the Colonial Secretary. It was in answer to one in which Sir Richard Bourke deplored the condition of things in New Zealand, but confessed his powerlessness to set them right. " It is impossible," wrote the Secretary for the Colonies, " to read without shame and indignation the details which these documents disclose. The unfortunate natives of New Zealand, unless some decisive measures of prevention be adopted, will, I fear, be shortly added to the number of those barbarous tribes, who, in different parts of the globe, have fallen a sacrifice to their intercourse with civilised men who bear and disgrace the name of Christians. When, for mercenary purposes, the natives of Europe minister to the passions by which these savages are inflamed against each other, and introduce them to the knowledge of depraved acts and licentious gratifications of the most debased inhabitants of our great cities, the inevitable consequence is a rapid decline of population, preceded by every variety of suffering. Considering what is the character of a large part of the population of New South Wales and Van Dieman's Land, and what opportunities of settling themselves in New Zealand are afforded them by the extensive intercourse which has recently been established, adverting also to the conduct which has been pursued in these islands by the masters and crews of British vessels, I cannot contemplate the too probable results without the deepest anxiety."

These admitted evils, and a formal request made by a number of chiefs for British guardianship, led to the appointment, by the Colonial Office, of a Resident in the person of Mr. J. Busby. That gentleman's presence and influence, however, do not appear to have abated the evils complained of, although the fact that there was such a representative of British authority may have led many persons to establish themselves in the islands who would not otherwise have done so. It certainly had the effect of stimulating a movement for the acquisition of land that up to that time was almost unprecedented. Individuals and companies vied with each other in the most deplorable methods of securing large extents of territory. "The land fever," says Martin,[1] "in its different phases of 'sharking,' 'jobbing,' and *bona fide* speculation, literally raged in New Zealand. What gold was to the Spaniards in Mexico, land at this period be-

[1] *The British Colonies.*

came to the English in these islands, and as the warlike aborigines most coveted the acquisition of firearms, they divested themselves of their only possessions in order to obtain those deadly instruments which, together with ardent spirits, were the most potent means for the destruction of their race. Almost every captain of a ship on arriving at Sydney exhibited a piece of paper with a tattooed native head rudely drawn on it, which he described as the title-deed of an estate, bought for a few muskets, hatchets, or blankets, and as the Government had fixed a price of five shillings, and afterwards of twelve shillings, per acre on land in Australia, adventurers crowded to New Zealand, hoping there . . . to pursue their schemes with impunity. The extent to which the land mania prevailed may be best understood by the fact that, when to the claims of various associations and private individuals came to be added the enormous one of the New Zealand Company, the total area of the islands, including rocks, mountains, and swamps, would have been quite insufficient to satisfy them."

Jameson, in his *Travels in New Zealand*, says that one company, consisting of four individuals, claimed the whole of the Middle Island in consideration of a few hundred pounds in money and merchandise, and a life annuity of one hundred pounds; while another person, representing a Sydney firm laid claim to several hundred thousand acres, including the township of Auckland, purchased at the price of a keg of gunpowder. Even the Resident and the missionaries, with the notable exception of the

Wesleyans, were seized with the land-sharking mania.

The New Zealand Company, above referred to, was almost the biggest shark of the lot, having, for about £1500 worth of muskets, gunpowder, tomahawks, pocket-handkerchiefs, tobacco, Jew's harps, and other articles,[1] purchased a territory as large as Ireland. The guiding spirit of this enterprise was the same Mr. Wakefield who was chiefly responsible for the South Australia fiasco. It began as a New Zealand Association, whose purpose was to buy up large tracts of land from the natives, and resell it at a profit to whomsoever might be induced to seek his fortune in the new land which, it was supposed, must soon come under British domination. The charter it sought, however, was refused, whereupon the association was transmogrified into a company; and as the scheme had many supporters, the son of the projector went out with a party of pioneers, in 1839, and " purchased " millions of acres at the rate of about sixpence per thousand. As, however, the chieftains with whom Colonel Wakefield dealt had no right to sell, it may be imagined in what perplexities emigrants who dealt with the Company for allotments found themselves involved when they landed in Cook's Strait, and proceeded to take up their holdings.

It was clearly time for the Government to do something, especially as the number of British residents in the islands was increasing year by year. Including missionaries and their families, there was,

[1] Bourne.

in the early part of 1839, a European population of no fewer than two thousand persons. The most considerable settlement was at Kororareka, in the Bay of Islands, where, in the previous year, the inhabitants, following the inevitable Anglo-Saxon instinct, had established a form of government, and framed a code of laws, one of which was to the effect that every able-bodied person should provide himself as soon as possible " with a good musket and bayonet, a brace of pistols, a cutlass, and at least thirty rounds of ball-cartridge."

These doings, together with the less justifiable acts of the New Zealand Company, led to the taking of a decisive step by Lord Normanby, the Colonial Secretary, in June, 1839, when he instructed the Governor of New South Wales to regard all the settlers in New Zealand as under his jurisdiction, " and, both on their behalf and in the interests of the natives, to treat with the latter for the purchase of land."[1] It was explicitly set forth in these instructions that the natives " must not be permitted to enter into any contracts in which they might be ignorant and unintentional authors of injuries to themselves," and, further, that " one of the first duties of their official protector " would be to see that such was not done.

The despatch of the Colonial Secretary disclaims, on behalf of the Queen and her subjects, " every pretension to seize on the islands of New Zealand, or to govern them as a part of the dominion of Great Britain, unless the free and intelligent con-

[1] Fox Bourne.

sent of the natives, expressed according to their established usages, shall be first obtained." Careful directions were given for securing this end, and in accordance therewith Captain Hobson, R.N., who had been sent out for the purpose, sailed from Sydney with a commission as Lieutenant-Governor " in and over any territory which is or may be acquired in sovereignty of her Majesty" in New

AUCKLAND, THE FIRST CAPITAL OF NEW ZEALAND.

Zealand. Arriving in the Bay of Islands on the 29th of January, 1840, Captain Hobson forthwith established British law in place of the local authority with its " thirty rounds of ball-cartridge," and then proceeded to carry out the instructions of Lord Normanby. So well did he succeed in his mission that, with the consent of the chiefs, British sovereignty was within a few months established in New Zealand, and in the month of November following the colony of New Zealand established by charter. Captain Hobson was, of course, appointed the first Governor, with a legislative and an executive Council to aid him in the work of government. Auckland, situated on the neck of land between the Manukau Harbour and the Kauraki Gulf, was chosen as the Capital.

CHAPTER V.

A PEACEFUL REVOLUTION.

WHILE these developments were taking place in the south-eastern corner of the Empire a new era was being inaugurated in the old haunt at home. After a tense and protracted struggle the discredited landlord rookery at Westminster had been got rid of, its selfish and corrupt blood ejected, the place cleansed, and a new flock collected and installed—with momentous results, as we shall see. For generations the reins of power had been held by a debased and debasing oligarchy, which had on more than one occasion brought the Empire to the verge of ruin by pursuing a policy of intermeddling in the affairs of foreign states that was at once expensive and hurtful to the national welfare. On these external matters the attention of statesmen was so much absorbed that they had no time to devote to internal affairs, even if they had been so inclined. Domestic abuses that constituted their strength and profit were consequently allowed to accumulate, or if disturbed, it was only for party purposes, and when these were met, they were again left to increase and multiply. While rulers were possessed of intellectual powers of a high order, Government was entirely conscienceless. Men of nobler aims and aspirations might raise their voices, and point out broader and juster ends of government, but they raised them in vain.

It was a humiliating spectacle. Here were men of great gifts, educated, refined, holding that Providence had called them specially to govern a great Empire, and they ruled it almost solely with a view to their own profit and emolument. Nor was this the worst feature of the scandal. They abused their trust, and though found out and exposed, they were not ashamed. It had been proved to demonstration that this two-sided oligarchy had utterly failed in its legitimate purposes, that its rule was carried out more for the benefit of the administrators than the community, that the public money was squandered in the maintenance of useless sinecures and undeserved pensions, and that peers and commoners, their relatives, their dependents and connections, alike abetted, as they participated in, the general corruption. Official patronage was abused, and Cabinet Ministers were not above creating offices for their sons, and then abolishing them and retaining the compensation pensions. Nor did the evil attach only to the department of the public service; the gangrene was everywhere. Inequalities and abuses were not more rife in public offices than in the Church, in the courts of law, and in the great corporations of the kingdom. The entire system, the whole of the body politic, had become so corrupt and diseased that there was no possibility of restoration to health without a thorough renewal of the parts, almost from the foundation upwards.

Nothing was clearer than all this to men of sense and just and humane views. Fifty years previously the *quod erat demonstrandum* had been so thoroughly recognised that reform was on the point of being achieved by a national movement, when it was suddenly arrested by the "No Popery" riots of Lord George Gordon. On the top of that upheaval came the cataclysm of the French Revolution to further check and postpone the renovating process. But though for a time overwhelmed by reactionary forces, the regenerating leaven was still there, working silently for the most part, albeit sometimes giving forth a sound or a movement indicative of the living energumen within—innocent and harmless eruptions in the main, though too often envenomed by the touch of Government spies to suit the despotic purposes of their employers. But even these things in the end—indicating as they did the substitution of blind fury for wise guidance and government, as in the case of the Manchester massacre—told in favour of the health-promoting process. For long years it had seemed as though struggle and aspiration were vain, and that as things were so must they continue to be. But where there is growth there is still hope; and there was nothing to show that the people of these isles had lost the principle of growth and development. The signs were indeed all in the opposite direction.

Everything indicated expansion, moral as well as physical.

There had never been a time of greater intellectual and moral activity than that following the Revolution of 1789, and from then on to 1832. It is a period that, for brilliance of poetic achievement, equals the Augustan age of Elizabeth; while, taking the whole realm of intellectual conquest, it would be hard to find its parallel in any age or country. The general stir and awakening of mind affected the whole people. Movements in favour of national education, which had had their rise towards the end of the century, were now taken hold of and utilised with increasing vigour. Dr. Bell and Joseph Lancaster found a receptive public for their ideas on primary instruction. Eager for education, the people readily seized upon their simple methods of teaching, and gave them every advancement in their power by subscribing for the erection of schools, and for raising the necessary funds in lieu of endowment. From Dr. Bell the National School Society had its origin; from Lancaster, the British and Foreign School Society—both of which told immensely in the direction of a cheap, expeditious, and national system of education.

Not less important as regards the general movement was the institution of infant schools. The idea of these appears to have first originated in the fertile brain of Robert Owen of New Lanark, where he founded an asylum for the children of the adult population of that industrial centre. The example thus set soon had its imitators in all directions. In

1818, an infant school was established in the metropolis under the auspices of Lord Landsdowne, along with Macaulay, Mill, and Brougham.

LORD BROUGHAM.

The last-named was one of the most indefatigable men of his time in the cause of education. As chairman of a Parliamentary committee appointed to " inquire into the education of the lower orders," he collected a mass of useful information, showing, first, the large portion of the population that was without the means of education, and, secondly, the vast funds existing in the kingdom, piously bequeathed for the purpose, but which had been misapplied by the fraud and negligence of trustees. The result of his powerful exertions was the appointment of a commission to inquire into the abuses of public charities. Subsequently (June 28, 1820), in an able speech, he brought the subject of popular education under the notice of Parliament, and drafted a scheme of national education which, but for one inherent defect, would have been a forecast of the comprehensive system that was to take effect fifty years later. The main feature of this project was to render education subordinate to the established clergy. But these, though it was proposed to give so much into their hands, were not satisfied because they could not have dissenters excluded from its benefits; the dissenters, on their part, were, naturally enough, jealous of so much influence being placed in the hands of a hostile sect; and so the scheme came to grief.

But though the Government failed to do anything in the direction of popular instruction, much in this regard was effected by the people themselves. In the great work of teaching the poor all parties and persuasions united with the most laudable zeal. The belief that universal education could have any injurious effect upon the character of the community was very generally exploded; and the results of inquiries set on foot by Brougham in 1828 showed that immense progress had been made since the year 1818, when he instituted his first inquisition into the subject. The information obtained was far from complete; but, so far as it went, it showed that the number of children who attended unendowed day-schools had grown from 50,034 in 1818 to 105,571 in 1828.

Thus, in spite of Government interference, education continued to make headway. Nor was this effected in schools alone. There was an intellectual ferment in the air. In spite of prohibitions, meetings were held and ideas disseminated; the right of publishing Parliamentary debates had been already won, the newspaper press was growing in strength and importance; and though the output of cheap publications for spreading useful knowledge was small compared with that of our own day, it was for the time enormous. This literature arose in response to the general desire for information—a desire not limited to any particular section of society, but extending to all classes. The more opulent formed themselves into literary and philosophical societies; while the working people established mechanics', apprentices', and other institutions for mutual benefit and instruction. A new university was projected in the metropolis for the accommodation of the middle ranks of society. Science in all its more gainful aspects was pursued with avidity and success. The great names of the preceding generation—the Priestleys, the Bradleys, the Arkwrights, Smeatons, Brindleys, Dollands, Rumfords, Watts, Cavendishes, and Maskelynes—had their worthy successors in such men as Davy, Wollaston, Dalton, Ivory, Babbage, Faraday, South, Young, Arnott, Brewster, Herschell, Buckland, Talford, McAdam, Rennie, and a host of others. The advances made in chemistry, and in its application to agriculture, in geology, mineralogy, civil engineering, mechanics, and anatomy, and the geographical researches in Africa and the Arctic regions, constituted a justifiable boast of the period. Davy's safety-lamp well characterises the ameliorative science of the age. But the wonder of the time was the further application of the powers of the steam-engine—that as then unrivalled invention which had supported the war, and laid the foundation of commercial, manufacturing, and agricultural prosperity. Hitherto this marvellous agent had been chiefly applied to the manufacturing arts; but in its new developments it was extended to agriculture, to road travelling, to river and ocean navigation. It is significant of the new era to read that, in May, 1822, an iron steamboat, propelled by a thirty-horse engine, was exhibited on the Thames. This vessel was designed to open steam navigation between London and Paris. Four years later, Captain Johnson, in the *Enterprise*, won a prize of ten thousand pounds, subscribed in Calcutta as a reward to the first person who should make a steam voyage from England to India. The *Enterprise* left Falmouth in August, and reached the Hugli in December, after a voyage of sixteen weeks and three days—a poor record, but significant of the coming revolution.

The period was, in short, one of growing utility. Not only was science pursued in reference to its application to industry and the arts, but a fresh impulse was given to the study of chemistry, history, and natural and experimental philosophy as a means to the amelioration of the conditions of human life. Thus the age became more and more one of progress and humanity. Even in Parliament the intrigues of factions and their interminable conflicts fell into disrepute. Questions bearing more directly upon the common weal—the freedom and advancement of commerce, fiscal and judicial reforms, the mitigation of criminal law, the growth of indigence and population, and the improvement of police—all these received an increasing share of attention.

Concurrently, too, the period is remarkable as the beginning of a new era in commercial legislation; and those principles of unrestricted intercourse among nations which Sir James D. Stewart and Adam Smith showed to be most conducive to their mutual benefit, at length found their way into the Imperial Parliament. Lord Lansdowne in the Upper House, and Messrs. Huskisson, Robinson, and Poulett Thomson in the Lower, were the most indefatigable exponents of the new policy. Men, too, in the business walks of life began to occupy themselves with the same ideas, and petitions in favour of free trade were sent up by the leading merchants of London, Glasgow, and Bristol. Thus the repugnance of the Government to innovations was gradually overcome, and important changes in mercantile law were made during the administration of Lord Liverpool. Some hundreds of statutes relating to commerce, aliens, and denizens, were wholly repealed; the navigation laws, which required that the transit of goods should be in British ships, navigated by British seamen, was rendered less strict; bounties and other expedients for the encouragement of the fisheries of Britain, and the linen manufacture of Ireland, were done away with; wool was allowed to be exported, and manufactured silks and other products imported; and, lastly, colonial trade was partially opened to foreign nations.

The old mercantile idea respecting colonies had been that they were planted and protected entirely for the benefit of the mother-country. Hence it was held that the colonists had no right, as the Earl of Chatham once said, to make " a nail for a horseshoe for themselves," but that all they produced should be brought to Britain to sell, and all they consumed purchased exclusively in the same market. In short, according to the then prevalent notion, the whole Empire must be regarded as a big family circle, in which everybody not related ought to be treated as an interloper. It was a narrow and deadening system, and all parties to the bargain were reciprocally injured.

The healthy beginning in the direction of better things made during the reign of George IV. was not vigorously and uniformly continued in that of his successor, owing partly to the long-cherished prejudices, old monopolies, and often apparently conflicting interests against which it was necessary to contend, but more perhaps to the fact that the current of reform had taken another, and, for the time being, all-absorbing direction, leading in the end to that grand achievement of constitutional revolution, the Reform Act of 1832.

It is needless to go over the famous and well-remembered story, more momentous to the destinies of the people of these islands and their kith beyond the seas than the charter wrung from King John, or the Bill of Rights acknowledged and signed by William of Orange. It was a new Conquest, ushered in and sped upon its course by that magnificent act of resumption, effected by our friends across the water-way when the still unteachable Bourbon made his murderous fling at their liberties and their lives. The acclaim of that splendid victory rang throughout Europe, and gave renewed heart and zeal to the friends of progress here, who, though foiled for a time, eventually won their charter of popular rights —happily, too, without the destruction and bloodshed to which the French, in their self-defence, were compelled to resort. It was, however, by the narrowest verge that such result was escaped. The whole country was thrown into so intense a ferment and agitation that had the lords stood in the way much longer than they did there is no telling what might have happened.

The effect of the reform upon the country was immediate and profound. It was like the letting loose of waters upon a land that had long been parched for want of their fertilising streams. Fresh life was given to the community, and renewed energies to the people. There was hardly a single department of human activity that did not feel the change and respond with twofold vigour. These matters, however, relate to the general history of the country, rather than to the specific subject here to be treated. One or two legislative Acts, however, having reference to the extra-Britain of the colonies and dependencies, it is necessary briefly to record. The first of these was the abolition of colonial slavery, which has been justly designated as one of the most generous acts of legislation ever recorded of any Assembly. It was a fitting sequel to the abolition of the African slave-trade in 1807, and the price paid—twenty millions sterling—was not too great for the removal of the stain upon England's honour, she having taken so large a share in establishing the iniquitous system. The Act was a noble one, and altogether worthy of the first session of the Reformed Parliament.

Another measure passed during the same session was perhaps still more important in its general effects than the foregoing. By it the Government of Hindustan was entirely changed. Ever since the Act of 1813, which made the first great inroad upon the Company's exclusive privileges, there had been a growing agitation in favour of further concessions to the principle of free trade. A number of enactments and regulations had been obtained, all more or less subversive of the old monopoly. In 1820 Parliamentary committees were appointed to consider the foreign trade of the country, and to report upon the best means of extending it. India and

EARL GREY, "REFORM PREMIER."

China came in for a large share of attention, and it was felt both by Parliament and the trading community at large that the East India Company's monopoly of the Chinese trade should be abolished in the interest of commerce in general. However, with some slight modifications in favour of freer traffic, the matter was again shelved until 1830, when select committees of both Houses were appointed to consider the affairs of the Company, and the trade between Great Britain, the East Indies, and China. The reports of both committees were unfavourable to the Company; but again action had to be postponed in consequence of the reform agitation. That question settled, however, one of the first acts of the new Parliament was to place the Company on an altogether different footing. In short, it was decided that it should cease its connection with commerce, and devote its undivided attention, in conjunction with the Board of Control, to the duties of governing the vast empire of India. Thus the Chinese trade was thrown open, and the great John Company, from a trading concern, was transformed into a solely governing body, the Crown taking over all its effects and claims, along with its obligations, and paying to it a certain sum annually from the India revenue. On these terms the Company's charter was renewed for twenty years, dating from April 30, 1834. This wise enactment was coupled with others for the better government of the dependency, including provisions for the mitigation and gradual abolition of slavery in the East, and for the appointment of a law commission to inquire into and improve the existing laws, police, and courts of justice in India.

Thus quickly did the broadened constitution begin to have its effect upon the different parts of the Empire. It has been alleged that the abolition of slavery told upon the islands of the West Indies in the form of ruin. If lessening the speed at which fortunes are made be ruin, then it must be granted that the result was very ruinous to some of those colonies. But the entire system of wealth-getting there pursued was one utterly abhorrent to all right-thinking men; it degraded alike the white and the black; nothing could justify its continuance; and it would have been better for the whole superstructure of the Empire to go to pieces, like the inhuman monarchies of old, than that its wealth should be accumulated and its power built up on such a system of tyranny and cruelty as there prevailed. There are still people whom one hears deploring the slave days, when the negro could be forced to work by the terror of the lash; whereas now, free to do as he pleases, he cannot be induced by any bribe to labour as he formerly did, but prefers to toil on his little farm, and enjoy all the profit to himself. One cannot wonder that it is so. Generations must pass before the memory of those days of cruelty and wrong can be obliterated, even if they ever are effaced. Meanwhile, if the black chooses to live in simplicity and ease, unallured by the white man's fevered dreams of avarice, no one has a right to say that he shall not do so. And if the white inhabitant does not make as much money as formerly, he cannot create as much wrong, and so the world is happier. Certainly the time has gone by, or is rapidly going, when men can look upon and use their fellows as the mere instruments of their greed.

Looked at in this light, the West Indian colonies are not worse off, but immeasurably better, for the abolition of slavery. Naturally those islands are like veritable Gardens of Eden; everyone who has visited them speaks in terms of rapture of their beauty and fertility. Ceylon and Java alone, among the islands of the world, says Fox Bourne, can rival in external attractions " the Queen of the Antilles," with " its splendid harbours, its beautiful mountains, its luxuriant valleys, its fertilising streams." [1] Yet slavery made of Jamaica in particular a veritable hell, wherein the white man, degraded by the system on which he increased in wealth, easily outdid the black in savagery and loathsome cruelty. The story of its insurrections, the barbarity with which they were suppressed and the subjugated slaves afterwards tortured and slain, is one that can hardly be read to-day without feelings of shame and detestation. The insurrection of 1832 and the ghastly tale of its suppression had much to do with the abolition of slavery. The thrill of horror that passed through England when the records came to hand of the way in which the revolt was put down converted at once to the anti-slavery cause all who were not blinded by their selfish interests. " After the slaves had returned to their estates under a promise of pardon, they found that they had come back to be slaughtered. Martial law being proclaimed, they were shot and hung indiscriminately. At Montego Bay

[1] *The Story of our Colonies.*

negroes were often tried, sentenced, and hung, all within the space of an hour and a half, the corpses being cut down in order that fresh use might be made of the gibbets. . . . About a dozen white men had been murdered. For this more than fifteen hundred negroes were executed, and many others died under the lash of their enraged masters. The persecution lasted long, and fell especially upon those slaves who had dared to listen to the teaching of the Baptist missionaries, although those missionaries appear to have in no way instigated the turmoil."[1]

To change a condition of society in which such things could take place—to make it possible to live as Christian, or at least as civilised, men—was worth all the false and pernicious prosperity that grew out of slave labour. With such a change only could arise that true prosperity of which the other was but an unreal and degrading semblance.

If Jamaica and others of the West India Islands are not making money as fast as they formerly did, it is because they commenced wrong; and it is never an easy matter to make a new start, especially by those who were bred and born in the bad system, or have inherited its vicious taint. It may be that before the old prosperity of the islands can return a renewal of the race may be necessary by the introduction of fresh British blood. There is room enough for a large immigration; and a population with the healthy working instincts of the race, in place of one brought up in the tradition of a helot

[1] *The Story of our Colonies.*

class to do everything for them, would soon restore to those colonies some of the life and prosperity that abound so vigorously in the younger dependencies.

In India a similar, though a far more gigantic, task is laid upon the dominant race—one requiring the utmost tact, wisdom, and unselfishness. Year by year, as the generations have gone by, the British have shewn themselves more and more determined to do their duty to the people over whom their destiny has called them to rule. They make mistakes at times, and not in every instance, perhaps, is their rule just and beneficent; but when it is not so, the failure arises from temporary blindness, not from a wilful desire to play the tyrant merely. This is probably the reason why there are so few attempts to throw off the British yoke. The yoke is light, begotten of the instinctive genius the Briton possesses for governing the races subject to him. He may not be loved; it would be rather wonderful if he were, seeing that he is obliged to govern as a caste apart. But as compared with the rule of the Spaniard, the Portuguese, and the Dutch, that of the British is always endurable; and in very many instances the subject peoples supply most of the material for the army, which, while it keeps out the foreign invader, also holds them subject to their conquerors. No sooner has a stubborn race been subjugated than its warriors are formed into British regiments, soon to become as loyal and as proud of the service as any. Such was the case with the Gurkhas, such, later, the case with the Sikhs.

Under the Marquis of Hastings a new province,

the nucleus of what are now the Central Provinces, was formed out of the territory recovered from the Pindárés. During the administration of Lord Amherst, who succeeded the Marquis of Hastings as Governor-General in 1823, the first Burmese war arose, and was brought to a close in 1826 by the cession to the British of the provinces of Arakan and Tenasserim. Under the rule of Lord William Bentinck, whose praises are so enthusiastically sung by Macaulay, administrative reform and the moral elevation of the peoples of Hindustan were the chief subjects of consideration. According to the inscription upon his statue at Calcutta, penned by the historian, Bentinck abolished cruel rites, effaced humiliating distinctions, gave liberty to the expression of public opinion, and made it his constant study to elevate the intellectual and moral character of the nations committed to his charge. The two most memorable acts of his administration were the abolition of suttee and the suppression of the Thugs, a race of fanatics who regarded murder as a religious duty. It was during the governorship of Lord Bentinck that the Company's connection with trade ceased, and what we may call the new spirit towards the natives was inaugurated. His beneficent sway, however, had anything but a wise upholder in Lord Auckland, who took over the administration of affairs in 1836, and ere he had been long at the helm brought on the first Afghan war, which resulted in the annihilation of a British force in the defiles of Khurd, Cabul, and Jagdalak, Dr. Brydon being the sole survivor to reach Jellalabad. The disgraceful defeat was avenged the same year by General Pollock.

After the West Indies and Hindustan, Canada may be said to have been the first of the British dependencies to benefit by the new charter. For some time past affairs in that colony had been going from bad to worse. By the Quebec Act of 1774 the Canadians were granted the free exercise of their religion, and secured in their civil rights, laws, and customs. They were then chiefly French; but on the recognition of the independence of the United States, thousands of American loyalists sought new homes in Canada, and were rewarded with grants of land and presents of agricultural implements. A large number settled on the St. John's River, and had that district erected into the separate province of New Brunswick, while upwards of ten thousand settled in Ontario. In 1791 the colony was divided into two provinces—Upper Canada, or Ontario, and Lower Canada, or Quebec—in both of which representative institutions, although not responsible government, were established. The arrangement, however, did not prove satisfactory to either province, leading to conflicts between the popular and elected Assemblies and the nominated or official Council, and in the end to the brief rebellions of 1837 and 1838.

In consequence of the threatening state of affairs, the Earl of Durham, one of the framers of the Reform Bill, and a statesman of ripe wisdom and exceptional ability, was in 1838 sent out as Governor-General to settle affairs on a just and liberal basis. He made a thorough investigation into the grievances

and needs of the colony, visiting all parts of it, and
making personal inquiry in every quarter. The
report which he drew up as the result of his inquisi-

LORD DURHAM.

tion is one of the most important historical documents connected with the country. In it he recommended that the two provinces should be reunited,

with one legislative and administrative system. He also suggested such a confederation of all the British North American colonies as was destined years afterwards to be realised. How large-minded he was, and what a different conception he had of the duties of governments to that entertained by previous statesmen, may be gathered from one sentence of his report. "Our first duty," he wrote, "is to secure the well-being of our colonial countrymen; and if, in the hidden decrees of that wisdom by which the world is ruled, it is written that these countries are not for ever to remain portions of the Empire, we owe it to our honour to take good care that, when they separate from us, they should not be the only countries on the American continent in which the Anglo-Saxon race shall be found unfit to govern itself."

In accordance with Lord Durham's recommendation, the two provinces were, in 1840, reunited as one province, with equal representation in the common legislature, and the practical concession by the mother-country of responsible government. Thus Canada became the first of those nations, offshoots of the old home, that, without severing their connection with the Crown, practically took their destinies into their own hands, and, with the willing consent and heartiest good wishes of the parent Government, set up for themselves. When the colony thus made its fresh start its population numbered—in Upper Canada 450,000, in Lower Canada 650,000.

CHAPTER VI.

MOTHER OF NATIONS.

WHEN, on the death of William IV., in June, 1837, Queen Victoria, at the age of eighteen, was called to the throne, the dominions that owned her sway were probably in a happier position than had been enjoyed by them at any previous period of their history. It cannot be said that they were entirely at peace, although no considerable war was going on at the time. As we have seen, Canada was disturbed, and there was trouble brewing in Afghanistan, chiefly, it must be acknowledged, through the unwisdom of the Governor-General. Mere lust of conquest has probably very rarely, if ever, been the cause of the extension of British dominion in India. With perhaps the exception of the first Afghan war, almost every departure from a pacific and defensive policy has arisen from the ignorant ambition or the flagrant perfidy of the native powers. There was also in progress one of those small Kaffir wars which the generality of British proconsuls were so powerless to prevent and so indifferent about entering upon. But in so extensive and so detached an Empire it would be a marvel if at any one time profound peace reigned throughout.

Probably never before—certainly not in modern times—had a young woman been called upon to reign over dominions so extensive as those which, in 1837, acknowledged the sway of Great Britain. Nor had any previous British sovereign been acclaimed to so extensive an heritage. As we have seen, within a few years vast additions had been made to the possessions under the rule of the East India Company, and these were further augmented by the successful issue of the Sind war, which was a sequel to that against Afghanistan.

Several of the Australian colonies had been founded during the reign of William IV., notably that of Port Phillip, or Victoria, as it was afterwards called, in honour of the Queen, and South Australia; while a sporadic beginning of colonisation had been effected in New Zealand. During the same period, also, the British dominions in Africa had been considerably extended by the establishment of the colony of Natal. An attempt at colonising that district had been made in 1824, when Lieutenant Farewell, R. N., who, having put into Natal Harbour for provisions the previous year, and formed a most favourable opinion of its capabilities, returned thither with a few Europeans and some Hottentots, with the object of opening up trade and establishing a colony. He was given a considerable tract of land by Tchaka, the founder of the Zulu power. The settlement commenced well, but was not allowed to go on long in peace. In 1828, Tchaka was assassinated by his brother, who soon began to show his hostility to the little colony, and, in the end, after the murder of Farewell and some others, the settlement was well-nigh put an end to.

A small number of Englishmen, however, with some Cape Hottentots, continued on the shores of the bay, carrying on a trade with the natives, and appear to have been unmolested. In 1836 they were joined by a large body of Dutch farmers, who had quitted Cape Colony in consequence of their dissatisfaction with British rule. It must be acknowledged that there was great cause for their discontent. The English took so little pains to study their interests that the Boers came to scout the idea that they wished to see justice done as between man and man.[1] The first act of the Dutch was to obtain a grant of land from Dingan, the Zulu chieftain, but that sanguinary tyrant, while agreeing to their wish, treacherously slew a number of the Boers, including Retief, their leader, whilst in his kraal, and then fell upon their camp and massacred nearly every man, woman, and child in it. The rest of the Dutch, with the Englishmen and their Hottentots, now attacked Dingan, but were defeated. The Zulus, in return, were routed when they threw themselves upon the Boers in their laagers. In the end Dingan was deserted by a number of his own people, and, with their aid, the Dutch, in 1840, inflicted a severe defeat upon him, and he was shortly afterwards slain.

[1] Theal, *South Africa* (Story of the Nations Series).

The Englishmen settled in the bay had in vain petitioned the Imperial Government to declare Natal a British possession. The Dutch farmers, therefore, with Pretorius at their head, having settled matters with the Zulus, proclaimed the settlement a free republic, and proceeded to build the town of Pietermaritzburg. Umpada, the brother of the late chief, was proclaimed chief of the Zulus, but was compelled, as a condition of his elevation, to cede to the conquerors all the country from St. Lucia Bay to the St. John's River.

When the news of these proceedings reached Cape Town, steps were at once taken to bring the rebellious Boers to terms, although that was not effected without the aid of a military force. In consequence of this attempt the settlement was incorporated with Cape Colony in 1844. Some of the Dutch farmers decided to remain under the British flag; but the majority, with Pretorius at their head, again "trekked," and crossed the Drakensberg Mountains into the interior. In 1845 Natal was given a Lieutenant-Governor and an Executive Council.

In the meantime Cape Colony had been making immense strides, notwithstanding the unfortunate quarrels and devastating wars that were constantly recurring with the natives. In many cases there was small excuse for these "little wars"—little, truly, in that they related to the interests of a few thousand half-savage people, but too often big as regards the violations of right they perpetrated.

It would seem useless to hark back upon the struggles of sixty years ago were it not that we have just witnessed a repetition of the same evils, albeit on a larger scale, showing that there are still amongst us men who, though they bear the British name, appear to be devoid of the most elementary sense of that fair play which is held to be the distinctive British virtue.

We seem to be listening to the record of the late Matabele war instead of to a Kaffir affair of 1834 and 1835 as we read: " Their loss during our operations against them has amounted to four thousand of their warriors, and, among them, many captains. Ours, fortunately, has not in the whole amounted to a hundred, and of them only two officers. There have been taken from them also, besides the conquest and alienation of their country, about sixty thousand head of cattle, almost all their goats; their habitations everywhere destroyed, and their gardens and cornfields laid waste. They have been, therefore, chastised, not extremely, but perhaps sufficiently."[1] It is the Governor, Sir Benjamin D'Urban, who thus writes, in his report to the Colonial Secretary, Lord Glenelg.

Colonel Smith, who was one of the perpetrators of this " not extreme " chastisement, reports that, although the traces of the enemy were numerous, they " fled so rapidly that few were killed, and only three shots fired at the troops. The whole of the country has been most thoroughly traversed. Upwards of twelve hundred huts, new and old, have been burnt; immense stores of corn, in every direction, destroyed. Cattle of all sorts, horses and

[1] *Parliamentary Papers*, May, 1836.

goats, have fallen into our hands. It is most gratifying to know that the savages, being the unprovoked aggressors, have brought down all the misery with which they are now visited upon the heads of themselves and their families, and that the great day of retribution, and the punishment of the unprovoked atrocities committed by their murderous savages on our colonists, have arrived." [1]

It is such men as these that have been the bane and despair of British dominion the world over, and Lord Glenelg's condemnation of the acts of which Smith boasts is at once honourable to the head of the colonial department and well merited as a rebuke to the insensible Colonel. "I am affected by these statements," he said, "in a manner the most remote from that which the writer contemplated. In the civilised warfare of Europe this desolation of an enemy's country, not in aid of any military operation, nor for the security of the invading force, but simply and confessedly as an act of vengeance, has rarely occurred, and the occurrence of it has been invariably followed by universal reprobation. I doubt, indeed, whether the history of modern Europe affords an example even of a single case in which, without some better pretext than that of mere retribution, any invaded people were ever subjected to the calamities which Colonel Smith here describes—the loss of their food, the spoiling of their cattle, the burning of their dwellings, the expulsion of their wives and families from their homes, the confiscation of their property, and the forfeiture

[1] *Parliamentary Papers*, May, 1836.

of their native country. . . . The great principles of morality are of immutable and universal obligation, and from them are deduced the laws of war. Of these the first and cardinal is that the belligerent must inflict no injury on his enemy which is not indispensably requisite to ensure the rights of him by whom it is inflicted, or to promote the attainment of the legitimate ends of the warfare. . . . I must confess my inability to discover what danger could be averted, or what useful object could be attained, by the desolation of the Kaffir country."[1]

It is pleasing to be able to record that, in accordance with the principles of morality here laid down, Lord Glenelg caused the land and the property taken from the Kaffirs to be restored to them. He also inaugurated a new system of dealing with the natives, which, if it had been persistently carried out, would have caused the progress of the colony to be much more rapid than it was. "Treaties," says Mr. Fox Bourne, in his admirable *Story of our Colonies*, " were entered into with most of their chiefs, by which trade was encouraged, and their territories were reserved to them without interference, on condition of their respecting the rights which the Europeans had hitherto acquired by conquest."

For ten years peace was kept, and great improvements were made in the colony. The population nearly doubled in the time. In 1807—the year following the British annexation—the white, black, and coloured inhabitants of the colony amounted to 56,000. By 1836 they had reached 150,110, and in

[1] *Parliamentary Papers*, May, 1836.

1846 to 285,279. But in the latter year another war broke out with the Kaffirs, who resented the arbitrary proceedings of Sir Peregrine Maitland, a new Governor appointed in 1844. Treaties that had been made with them were broken, and the good feeling of years destroyed. The Kaffirs were, no doubt, in fault; but the burden of wrong lay on the superior race, with its tradition of doing as it would be done by. It is a dismal record, and need not be recapitulated.

There has, however, unfortunately, been a great deal of this forgetfulness, or wilful negligence, in the past; and, as was inevitable, it led to all sorts of trouble, not only with the natives, but, as we have seen, with the Dutch also. Though the area of the colony was increased, old sores, instead of being healed, were allowed to increase and to fester. The Dutch settlers, a brave and sturdy race, nearly akin to the English and the Scotch, were for their hardihood, if for nothing else, eminently worth conciliating. But instead of that they were made in every possible way to feel that they were under the domination of an alien race, until, exasperated beyond control, they were ready to dare the wilderness, with its wild beasts and wilder men, rather than be under British rule. Reference has been made to the " trek " of 1835–36, when between five and ten thousand descendants of the old Dutch settlers sold their property, and, passing to the north of the Orange River, settled down in the territories which now form the Orange Free State and the South African Republic.

The first legislative Council, consisting of official and non-official members appointed by the Crown, was formed about the same time. Under this semi-military rule the colony continued until 1853, when, with a civil Governor, aided by a legislative Council and a House of Assembly, comprising representatives elected by the town and country districts, it took its first step towards free and responsible government.

A few years before the colony had gone through a severe crisis over an attempt on the part of the Imperial Government to convert the Cape into a penal station. A number of convicts were ordered thither from Bermuda, but the colony would have none of them. The *Neptune*, with the moral refuse on board, actually arrived in Simon's Bay, whereupon " petitions to the Queen, to the two Houses of Parliament, and to the people of England were adopted; and the community entered into a solemn league to suspend all business transactions with the Government, in any shape or on any terms, until the order making the Cape a penal settlement was reversed, and the convict ship was sent away."[1] The contest was a sharp one, and lasted some months, but in the end the colonists won, the *Neptune* being finally ordered to convey its human cargo elsewhither. One cannot but admire the moral fibre and sturdy independence of the colonists in thus refusing to have their country contaminated by the failures of a civilisation that, by its inequalities, makes an inevitable declivity towards crime.

At this very time New South Wales was in a state

[1] Noble, *Handbook of Cape Colony*.

of commotion, occasioned by the attempt to revive transportation, which had been put an end to in 1840. The *Hashemy* arrived at Sydney with a cargo of convicts amid a storm of indignation. The difficulty was overcome by handing over the undesired immigrants to the squatters of the Darling Downs, who were only too ready to receive them. Two years later the colony was endowed with a legislative Council of thirty-six members—to be increased to fifty-four when Port Phillip was admitted a share in the new constitution—of whom one-third was nominated by the Crown, and two-thirds elected by the colonists. The new *régime* took effect during the governorship of Sir George Gipps, whose rule was not in all respects as wise and beneficent as it might have been. For a few years subsequent to the change the colony was far from prosperous, although it was increasing in population and importance. In 1846 the number of inhabitants had increased to 189,609, being considerably more than double what it was ten years before. Of this number nearly 33,000 belonged to the thriving district of Port Phillip.

With such energy as the colony possessed, however, and such vast resources, it was impossible for it long to remain under a cloud, and before many years had elapsed its sheep-farming and wool-growing had more than restored the prosperity which it had formerly enjoyed. Some idea may be gained of the growth of this industry from the fact that by 1851 something like ten millions of sheep were grazing on the different squatters' stations, and the wool yielded by them and exported to Europe was worth about a million and a half sterling. The prospects it afforded of speedy emolument were such as to attract to the colony a very different class of persons to the ordinary emigrant. " Young men of good family and connection in England, retired officers of the Army and Navy, graduates of Oxford and Cambridge, are all amongst them," writes one who was long in the colony.[1] " To these must be added most of the settlers, a class of persons who have large tracks of land in their own right, obtained by purchase or free grant from the Crown, but which, by reason of the land soon becoming insufficient for the support of their rapidly increasing herds and flocks, oblige them to take up stations, as it is termed, in unoccupied parts of the country; so that the principal settlers are also the principal squatters —settlers as to their own lands, squatters as to the Crown lands they occupy."

During the first decade of the Queen's reign similar progress took place in New Zealand, that " Britain of the South," as it has been well called. In the four years from 1839 to 1843 the New Zealand Company alone sent out nearly nine thousand emigrants. Within that period a number of little centres of colonisation were established, and all, after some initial difficulties, throve. Auckland, the most northerly of them, and for a time the most prosperous, has been already mentioned. At the southern extremity of North Island the settlement of Wellington, on Port Nicholson, in Cook Strait,

[1] Therry.

was established by Colonel Wakefield, under the auspices of the New Zealand Company, in 1840. In the following year the settlement of Taranaki was founded on the western side of the island by the New Plymouth Company, who had purchased fifty thousand acres of land from the New Zealand Company. On the opposite coast, Napier, established soon after, subsequently became the capital of the province of Hawke's Bay, stretching up from Wellington to Auckland.

Nelson, occupying the northern portion of Middle Island, and separated from Wellington by Cook Strait, was planted by the New Zealand Company in 1841. Its eastern half was afterwards converted into the province of Marlborough, with Picton (formerly Waitohi) as its chief town. The next settlement in point of date was that of Port Chalmers, in the southern part of the island, with Dunedin as its centre, sent out by the Otago Association in 1848. This was an attempt to establish a model religious settlement, consisting principally of members of the Free Church of Scotland. As far as its sectarian character was concerned, it was a failure, as was also a similar Episcopalian scheme, made a year or two later near Port Lyttleton, in the province of Canterbury, occupying the middle portion of the island. During the decade ending in 1849 the European population of New Zealand, with a total area of about 104,471 square miles, had increased from about 2000 to upwards of 20,000.

All this had not been done without difficulties and conflicts with the Maoris. The successive Governors and the Home Government did their best to prevent all such troubles; but the greed and unwisdom of some of the colonists were often too much for them. The agents of the New Zealand Company, which had obtained a charter in 1841, and thus constituted a dual authority, were especially difficult to control. Here is an instance in point. In 1843 Colonel Wakefield, the Company's agent at Nelson, insisted on surveying some land which he professed to have bought from the natives on the banks of the river Wairau. Two chiefs asserted that the land in question had not and could not be sold by the Maoris, and, by way of protest against the survey, burnt down a surveyor's hut.

"The police-magistrate at Nelson issued a warrant for the apprehension of the chiefs, and himself proceeded with Colonel Wakefield and a body of forty settlers (most of them armed) to execute it. The chiefs were soon discovered, but they declined to surrender. While the parley was proceeding, a shot, fired by one of the English party, struck a Maori woman. . . . The Maoris then poured a volley into the arresting party. Nineteen white men, including Colonel Wakefield, were killed; the Maoris only lost four of their number."[1] "So manifestly illegal, unjust, and unwise were the martial array and the command to advance," said Lord Stanley (afterwards Earl of Derby), who was at the time Colonial Secretary, "that the authors of that order must be held responsible for all that followed in natural and immediate sequence upon it. The

[1] Jenks, *A History of the Australasian Colonies.*

natives only exercised the rights of self-defence and of mutual protection against an imminent, overwhelming, and deadly danger. Revolting to our feelings as Christians, and to our opinions as members of a civilised State, as was the ultimate massacre, it is impossible to deny to our savage antagonists the benefits of the apology which is to be urged in their behalf. They who provoke an indefensible warfare with barbarous tribes are hardly entitled to complain of the barbarities inseparable from such contests."

As was to be expected, the effect of this unjustifiable act was to arouse passions that were not allayed for years. Nor were the resulting hostilities confined to Middle Island. In 1845 the settlement of Kororareka—now Russell—in the Bay of Islands, was destroyed, with the exception of the missionaries' quarters. Fortunately the Maoris almost invariably recognised the friendly character of the missionaries, and so were often induced to show moderation, if not to keep the peace, when excited to acts of violence. As in South Africa, so in New Zealand, the missionaries effected much good, partly because they did not confine their teachings to doctrinal matters, but laboured diligently to give the Maoris a taste for agriculture and other civilised arts, and to check as far as possible the evils of gunpowder and rum.

Captain Fitzroy, who succeeded Governor Hobson in 1842, and Sir George Grey, who ruled from 1845 to 1853, did much by their wisdom and moderation to pacify the natives, although quiet was not thoroughly established until 1848. Sir George Grey's rule was especially wise and beneficent. Not merely did he find the colony " in a position of imminent peril " from the war that was being waged against the natives, but in a condition of actual bankruptcy. He succeeded in restoring it to peace and putting it on the highway to prosperity.

It was during his administration that an Act granting representative institutions to the colony was passed by the Imperial Parliament. By it the constitution of a General Assembly was provided for, to consist of a legislative Council, the members of which were to be nominated by the Governor, and of an elective House of Representatives. The first session of the Assembly was opened in May, 1854; but the members of the executive were not responsible to Parliament. The first ministers under a system of responsible government were appointed in 1856. The franchise amounted practically to household suffrages.

Thus was the work of nation-making in the southern hemisphere carried on during the earlier years of the Queen's reign—on the whole, probably, as regards the Australasian colonies, with less injustice to the native races than in any other part of the world. It was, perhaps, unavoidable that wrongs should be inflicted upon the more unsophisticated race when brought in contact with a more energetic people, possessed of superior culture, and endowed with an earth-hunger that a large share of four continents has not been able to satisfy.

There were many causes at work to stimulate the enormous outflow of emigration from 1820 onwards, the difficulty of procuring land and of making a living upon it at home being undoubtedly one. Probably the general dissemination of knowledge and the breaking up of old notions and associations was another. Railways, too, which were now becoming common all over the country, were familiarising the people with the idea of cheap and rapid transit from place to place. Steam navigation likewise had its influence, although, of course, there were as yet no steamships making such distant voyages as Australia.

But even so early as 1838 repeated voyages were made between Bristol and New York with steam as the only motive-force, the three thousand miles of ocean being traversed in fourteen or fifteen days. Such a rate of travel seems sluggish to us at the latter end of the nineteenth century; but the feat was a real marvel then. Similar services were soon started from Liverpool and London. The same mighty agent was put under requisition to facilitate communication with India. In the early part of 1837 an arrangement was concluded between the Government and the directors of the East India Company for the establishment of a regular monthly steam service between this country and Bombay, by way of the Mediterranean, Suez, and the Red Sea. This route, in lieu of that by the Cape of Good Hope, reduced the distance nearly one-half, so that by this means letters could be transmitted from London to Bombay in from forty-five to sixty days. A further saving of from four to six days was effected by sending the mails overland to Marseilles, to be conveyed thence to Alexandria by the French mail-packets.

Some idea of the rapidity with which steam navigation progressed when once fairly started may be gathered from the fact that, while in 1814 there was in the United Kingdom but one steam-vessel plying under the British flag, in 1837 there were 632. In the same period the steam tonnage increased from 69 to 71,031. These figures are exclusive of steamers employed in river traffic. Thus, with the need, arose the power of accelerated communication between the different parts of the Empire.

Nor is it without significance that the commencement of the new era which was ushered in by her Majesty's accession was marked by the suggestion of the penny postage and the first experiment with the electric telegraph—both of which, as links to bind persons and places closer together, were destined to have so enormous an influence ere many years had passed. Equally significant in its way was the great stride forward which the newspaper press made between September, 1836, when the reduction of the stamp duty came into operation, and the corresponding period of 1837. At the former period there were 397 newspapers in existence, with a united circulation of 35,576,056. Within the year following the number of journals had increased to 458, and their combined circulation to 53,496,207.

CHAPTER VII.

THE DISCOVERY OF GOLD.

The year 1851 was marked by an event of the first importance in the history of Australia, and, indeed, of the whole British Empire. That was the discovery of gold in New South Wales and Port Phillip, or Victoria, as it is now called, having been separated from the mother-colony, and started on its course as an independent colony the same year.

It had long been suspected that the soil of Australia was in parts auriferous. Samples of the precious metal had been picked up here and there from time to time, although the story of their finding was at first received with incredulity. A convict is said to have been given a hundred and fifty lashes for shewing a lump of gold which he affirmed he had found in the interior, the supposition being, of course, that he had stolen a watch and melted it to prevent detection. This was in 1836. But as early as 1823 James McBrian, the assistant-surveyor of the colony, had noted in his field-book the fact of having discovered particles of gold in the vicinity of Fish River, fifteen miles from Bathurst. In 1840

Count Strzelecki, while exploring the southern part of the dividing range known as the Australian Alps, found traces of the precious metal, and inferred from his observations that it abounded in the district. The Count communicated his discovery to Governor Gipps, who requested him to keep the matter secret, lest a knowledge of the existence of gold should imperil the safety of the colony, seeing that there were forty-five thousand convicts in New South Wales, Tasmania, and Norfolk Island. In the following year gold was found in the Macquarie Valley and the Vale of Clwydd by the Rev. W. B. Clarke, although, for some unexplained reason, he did not make his discovery known at the time.

It is astonishing to think that, notwithstanding reports like these, and the stories of chance finds that were constantly cropping up, nothing should have been done to ascertain whether the precious metal existed in such quantities as to make it payable to work. However, in the early part of 1851, a Mr. E. H. Hargraves, an old New South Wales settler, who had recently returned from a visit to California, where gold had been discovered in 1848, was struck with the similarity between the geological formation of parts of New South Wales and the gold regions whence he had come, and began to make careful investigations. He was successful in his efforts, and in the month of May made known his discovery of alluvial gold in a stream known as Lewes Pond Creek, a tributary of Summerhill Creek, itself a tributary of the Macquarie River. The announcement had an electric effect, an immediate rush of diggers taking place to the district in question, about fifteen miles from Bathurst. The excitement that ensued was tremendous, and affected all classes. Trade was bad at the time; but not only those who were out of work, but men in the best positions, left their employment, obtained implements, and set out for the diggings. Nor could the news, of course, be confined to the colony; but before many months had elapsed the existence of gold in Australia was known all over the world, and a wave of emigration set in towards the southern hemisphere, which continued with unabated vigour for years.

As may be well imagined, in the newly separated district of Victoria the public mind was excited to the highest pitch by the discovery of one gold-field after another made in the neighbouring colony, and some burgesses of Melbourne subscribed a considerable sum to be offered as a reward to anyone who should discover a workable gold-field within two hundred miles of the capital. It had long been currently reported and believed that there was gold in the district. A watchmaker and jeweller of Melbourne was reported to have had native gold in his possession in 1849—"one lump," says Martin,[1] "of great purity, weighing twenty-two ounces," was "more than an inch in thickness." The same tradesman was said to have had a nugget weighing seventy-two ounces. A Mr. Campbell, while staying with a friend at Clunes, found gold in March, 1850, but kept the matter secret until July, 1851,

[1] *British Colonies.*

when gold was obtained in the Yarra hills and in the quartz rock of the Australian Pyrenees. In September the famous Ballarat mines were discovered; immediately afterwards came the news of the rich finds at Mount Alexander, followed by the disclosure of the still greater wealth of those at Bendigo. As one after another of these gold-fields became known, the crowds that packed up and set out for the diggings became daily larger and larger.

Westgarth, in his work on Victoria, says, " Ere the first month expired, nearly 10,000 diggers, of all classes of society, who had rushed promiscuously to the attractive scene, were up and around the famous Golden Point, the original nucleus of Ballarat mining. But hardly was this miscellaneous crowd settled at work ere it commenced shelving off to Mount Alexander, which rumour proclaimed to be a still richer gold-field. In October and November Mount Alexander lived in a blaze of predominant fame; but it was in turn dimmed by the superior lustre of Bendigo, which made good its pre-eminence during several subsequent years. Bendigo was, indeed, a wonder of its day, and the extent and activity of the industrial field it presented at this early time have hardly since been exceeded in any colony. In the middle of 1852, the winter of the antipodes, there were reported, no doubt with some exaggeration, to be 50,000 diggers along the Bendigo Creek. Two thousand carts and drags and other vehicles were said to be simultaneously toiling along the roads to the different gold-fields. Bendigo was a hundred miles distant from Melbourne, and a pound per ton per mile and upwards were the rates of carriage of the day. A ton of flour, which cost £25 at Melbourne, had risen to £100 before it reached the hungry consumer at Bendigo."

In the autumn of 1852 it is said that fully 70,000 men were "grubbing for gold" in the Victorian fields. Two years previous the entire population of the colony did not much exceed that number. In 1855 it had leapt up to 364,000, in consequence of the rush to the gold-fields, and by 1861 it had risen to 540,322.

Fortune was fickle at the gold-diggings, as elsewhere; and while some grew rich, others remained poor, even if they did not return poorer than they went. The turmoil the colony went through for years was such that old settlers wished the glittering hoards had never been laid bare. The overpowering attraction drew to Melbourne men of all classes, from the highest to the lowest, not excluding escaped convicts and ticket-of-leave men. Many, of course, were characters of the worst description, and the riot and demoralisation they introduced into the province had the most deplorable effects. However, in the end, the underlying moral grit and stamina of the race proved its salvation here, as it had elsewhere under equally deleterious influences.

Multitudes who at first rushed to the diggings were soon making their way back to the quieter and more wholesome pursuits of trade and agriculture, and found in one or the other the competence, if not the fortune, denied them at the gold-fields. There was, indeed, such a demand for supplies of all sorts that every branch of business flourished. Melbourne leapt in the course of a few years from the status of a small, straggling village to a thriving city. "In 1845," says Therry,[1] " Bourke Street contained but a few scattered cottages, and sheep grazed on the thick grass then growing in the street. It was only known to be a street in that year by a sign indicating, ' This is Bourke Street.' In 1856 it was crowded with fine buildings, and as thronged and alive with the hurrying to and fro of busy people as Cheapside at the present day. In 1845, from my residence on the Eastern Hill, it was a pleasant walk through green paddocks to the Court House. Ten years afterwards the whole way from that house to the Court House was filled up with streets. Two branches of Sydney banks supplied the district in 1845 with banking accommodation that only occupied them with business a few hours each day. In 1856 eight

MELBOURNE IN THE FORTIES.

[1] *Reminiscences of Thirty Years' Residence in New South Wales and Victoria.*

banks could scarcely meet the pecuniary exigencies of the community. In the principal street —Collins Street—there was, in 1845, but one jeweller, who displayed a scanty supply of second-hand watches and pinchbeck brooches in a shop similar to those in which pawnbrokers display their articles of used-up jewellery in the by-streets off the Strand. In 1856 might be seen, in the same street, jewellers' shops as numerous and brilliant as those that glitter in Regent Street. The harbour of Hobson's Bay, on the morning on which I left it for Sydney, in 1846, contained two large ships, three brigs, and a few small colonial craft. In 1856 the same harbour was filled with about two hundred large London and Liverpool ships, and countless other vessels from America, New Zealand, and other parts." In short, to quote the same writer, Melbourne " presented such a transition from poverty to splendour as no city in the ancient and modern world had heretofore exhibited in a corresponding period."

Such was the magical effect of Victoria's golden harvest, which soon outdid the almost fabulous yield of the Californian gold-fields. The value of the precious metal obtained in Victoria in 1851 was £600,000. In the following year it rose to £10,900,000, and in 1853 to £12,600,000. Subsequently it decreased somewhat; but during the first eighteen years of the gold-mining industry the total produce of the colony amounted to something like £150,000,000.

New South Wales profited in like manner, though

not to the same extent as Victoria, from its goldmines. During the corresponding eighteen years, from 1851 to 1868, the entire yield of its mines amounted to only about one-fifth of those of Victoria. Even that was a generous rain, and the effect upon the colony was, as in the neighbouring province, to give an impetus to every branch of industry, but especially to that of sheep-farming, for the production of wool and of tallow; for not many years after the establishment of wool-growing as a profitable staple, a subsidiary source of wealth was discovered in the fat obtained by boiling down the carcases of sheep. The result of the general prosperity was that squatters went farther and farther afield, taking up little by little the unoccupied lands to the confines of Victoria and South Australia, and then spreading out northwards over the rich lands very soon to be separated from the mother-colony, to form the new settlement of Queensland.

In 1851 New South Wales counted a population of 189,951. By 1856 it had increased to 266,189. In 1861 it was 358,278, although a couple of years previously two-thirds of her territory had been taken from her to form the colony of Queensland, leaving her 323,437 square miles, as against the 678,600 with which her younger sister was endowed.

When the new colony started on its career it had a population of under 30,000, Brisbane, the capital, claiming 7000 of them. By 1861 the population had increased to about 35,000. At that time it had an export trade of £709,599, composed almost wholly of the wool, tallow, and skins yielded by its sheep and cattle. In two years from that time the population had gone up to nearly 62,000, while the numbers of its flocks and herds had increased one-half.

In 1858 gold was found in the colony, though at first it was obtained only in small quantities. Between 1863 and 1868, however, the yield of the metal rose in value from £144,802 to £593,516. Great impetus was given to trade and immigration by the finding of a nugget, weighing nearly a hundredweight, in 1867. In the following year there was a total yield of 166,000 ounces, worth £664,000—but a faint promise of the wealth that was to come later. A few years after the discovery of gold in Queensland, an important step was taken in the commencement of cotton-growing, to be followed ere long by the production of sugar.

The growth of the colonies in population and wealth necessitated the granting, in 1855, of a large measure of self-government to both Victoria and the neighbouring provinces. Victoria led the way in the demand for a thoroughly democratic system. The points of its charter were the abolition of all property qualifications, equal electoral districts, manhood suffrage, and vote by ballot. The contest was a warm and stubborn one, fought for as vehemently as the Victorians fought for their gold. They won, the Home Government deeming it wise to let these virile colonials have their own way, even though, as regards the extent of their self-government, they outstripped the old country—the poor old country that, like a worn-out old grandmother sitting by her chimney-corner, refuses to let her stay-at-home children go until they kick over the traces, or some latter-day Moses turns up and conjures.

The result in Victoria was a new constitution, by which the colonists obtained complete powers of self-government through the instrumentality of two legislative chambers, both of them elective, presided over by a Governor, who exercised little more than the functions of a chairman. The first Parliament under the new *régime* was opened in November, 1856.

In New South Wales the machinery of government, under the enlarged constitution, was much the same as in Victoria. Except that the Upper House, in place of being elected by the people, as in the neighbouring colony, continued to be composed of members nominated by the Crown, the Government was almost as democratic as that of Victoria. The seventy-two members of the popular House were elected by universal suffrage under the security of the ballot.

Tasmania, in due course, followed the lead of New South Wales as regards transportation, and after 1853 received no more victims of old-world civilisation; at least, not in the form of criminals from British gaols, although for long years the blight of the abolished system remained upon the colony. There, too, the extended liberties of 1855 were enjoyed, though in a narrower measure than in the other and more vigorous colonies. The first representative Parliament was opened in December, 1856. Tasmania was for a time the least enterprising of the

Australasian countries. The circumstance is attributed by Sir Charles Dilke in part to its " cool, but winterless, climate," which disposed the people " to dream away their lives in drowsiness." If the reproach was at any time deserved, it does not appear to be so now; but whether the change be attributable to the fresh blood and new spirit infused into the people by the gold-fever, consequent on the finding of the metal, or the gradual elimination of the convict stain, is not quite clear.

South Australia yields but little of the precious metal, although she makes up for the lack by her wealth of copper, together with the unbounded facilities she affords for the production of wheat, wool, and wine. For a time the colony suffered from the rush of its miners and others to the goldfields of Victoria; but they soon began to return again, and, instead of digging for the metal, the South Australians attracted it to their shores by offering to barter their produce for uncoined ingots of slightly higher intrinsic value than the coins they were supposed to represent. This system continued until the establishment of colonial mints in 1853. The trade thus opened up was carried on by means of both land and river traffic routes, the steam navigation of the Murray being especially profitable.

Thus began an era of renewed prosperity and development. The colony was blessed with a series of able Governors, the most notable of whom was, perhaps, after Captain (subsequently Sir George) Grey, Sir Richard M'Donald, whose rule extended from 1853 to 1862. " During his term of office," says the author of *South Australia: Its Progress and Prosperity*, "responsible government was inaugurated, and the political changes were introduced which materially altered the position of her Majesty's representative. Sir Richard readily adapted himself to the new state of affairs, and settled down as a constitutional Governor, directed by the wishes of his ministerial advisers." The Act granting responsible government was proclaimed in October, 1856, and the first Parliament was opened in the month of April following.

Queensland, the youngest of the seven Austral lands, did not get her charter until three years later, the constitution being proclaimed in 1859, and the first representative Parliament opening in May, 1860. The colony began with a constitution similar in most respects to that of New South Wales, having a nominee council. "It is remarkable," says Mr. E. Jenks,[1] "as being the only Australian community which at once entered upon both separate existence and political self-government."

New Zealand did not unearth her initial hoard of gold until 1858, and for several years the yield was not very great. The first two years it hardly reached £90,000 in value. In 1861, however, it rose to £752,657, after which an average of nearly £2,500,000 a year was maintained, thus placing the colony next to Victoria in respect of its wealth of the precious metal. As in the case of the other colonies, the energies of New Zealand were vastly stimulated by the discovery of gold. Until that

---

[1] *History of the Australasian Colonies.*

time trade and enterprise had been sluggish; but with the influx of new blood, consequent upon the fame of its gold-fields, the aspect of things totally changed. In 1852 the imports were valued at only £359,444, the exports at £145,972. By 1863 they had gone up to £7,024,674 and £3,485,405 respectively. Gold and wool were the chief staples.

This account of the discovery of gold in the British colonies, and the revolution brought about thereby, would be imperfect without a brief retrospect of the influence of the precious metals upon the destinies of the British possessions in other parts of the world. Curious to relate, the same decade in which occurred the discovery and development of the gold-mines of the Australasian colonies witnessed also a rush of gold-seekers to British Columbia and Vancouver Island. Although, as we have seen, both Drake and Cook had touched upon the north-western coast of America in the course of their famous voyages, and Vancouver had thoroughly explored, and in 1791 taken over the country from the Spaniards, who had laid claim to it, little or nothing was done in the way of colonisation until, in 1804, the Hudson's Bay Company erected a factory on Fraser River, New Caledonia. Subsequently other forts were established, and finally, in 1843, a trading station was started on Vancouver Island, not far from the spot on which the town of Victoria was afterwards founded. The new factory proved so successful, and the district seemed to promise so well for general colonisation, that the Company obtained a grant of the island for ten years. The proximity of the new settlement to the Californian gold-fields proved highly advantageous, not only affording a market for much of its produce, but bringing thither many settlers, who, wearying of the turmoil of the diggings, settled down to the tranquillity of agricultural life under the old flag.

The colonisation of Vancouver Island and British Columbia, thus begun, soon benefited by a similar stimulus to that which proved so effective in the case of Australia and New Zealand. Gold was found in British Columbia in small quantities as early as 1850. During the next few years richer deposits were disclosed, and a steady influx of immigrants began about 1857. The movement was greatly accelerated by the discovery of the Big Bend gold-field in the year 1865. The previous year had witnessed the opening of rich mines of the precious metal within a short distance of Victoria, which, from a quiet seaside village, was thus suddenly converted into a busy port, with thousands of gold-seekers and settlers passing through it every month.

In the course of a few years the increase of population was so great that it was deemed advisable to relieve the Hudson's Bay Company of all control over British Columbia and Vancouver Island, and to form them into regular colonies.

This step was but the first of a series of important changes affecting the dominions under the British Crown in which the Hudson's Bay Company was involved. In 1868 the Company's charter was taken away, and thus the oldest trading corporation at that time in existence came to an end, its territories for a money consideration being transferred to the Dominion of Canada. The Act constituting the Dominion was passed by the Imperial Parliament in the year 1867, and under its provisions the provinces of Upper and Lower Canada, Nova Scotia, and New Brunswick were united in a confederation for general governmental purposes. The Federative Act provides that the Constitution of the Dominion shall be " similar in principle to that of the United Kingdom, and that the government shall be carried on in the name of the sovereign by a Governor-General and Privy Council, and that the legislative power shall be carried on by two Houses of Parliament, called the Senate and the House of Commons."

Provision was made in the Act for the admission of British Columbia, Prince Edward Island, the North-West Provinces, and Newfoundland. The first addition made to the Dominion as originally constituted was that of the Hudson's Bay Company's domain known as the North-West Territory. A portion of it, however, was converted into the province of Manitoba, which was admitted into the Confederation in 1870. In the following year the province of British Columbia, with which was incorporated Vancouver Island, and in 1873 the province of Prince Edward Island, respectively, joined the Confederation. Newfoundland alone of the British possessions in North America has not availed herself of the permission to become part of the Dominion.

The history of colonial confederation is a singular

one. In drawing up his report on Canada Lord Durham had thrown out the idea as one for consideration in regard to the future of British North America; at that time, however, the materials did not exist for such a union. But twenty years later the conditions for an experiment of the kind existed to perfection in South Africa. It was the needed solution for a great difficulty; it was asked for, and the man was there to carry it out. Only one thing was wanting, but it was a great want—the wisdom in the rulers at home to see the need and the opportunity, and to say "Go ahead." They said the very opposite, and recalled the great proconsul who dared to think differently from themselves.

The folly of that act of the Government of 1858 is to-day still working its mischief along the banks of the Orange River, the Vaal, and the Limpopo, and probably will for many a year to come. We have seen how the Boers were driven by harsh and unsympathetic treatment to seek homes and a country for themselves beyond the confines of Cape Colony. No one can for a moment doubt that they were a difficult class to deal with; but they were in a hard position, and one which the English, of all people, ought to have been able to sympathise with. A proud, unconquerable race, they were made by numberless acts to feel that they were under the rule of an alien people; whereas, by a little consideration given and a little trouble taken, they might, in course of time, have been brought to acknowledge a common bond and cherish a common national sentiment. It was only a matter of

ordinary justice, with a little increase of ordinary
forbearance, which was the more incumbent upon
the English, because upon them fell the government, and true government means forbearance.

However, these qualities were not exercised as
they should have been, and the Boers went out, and
formed their free states. But at length a real man
was made Governor—one with all the best qualities
and the best training for such a position—just,
unselfish, painstaking, sympathetic, loyal to the
noblest English traditions and to a great ideal.
Such was Sir George Grey, whose memory is revered
in South Africa by the truest friends of that country
and of humanity. But he had the misfortune to
differ from the administration in power at home, as
he had differed from its predecessor, touching colonial questions. The country had just come through
such a trying time in consequence of the Crimean,
Indian, and Chinese wars, that a policy of scuttle
seemed to be the leading card at Downing Street.
At any rate, there was a disposition to regard South
Africa as a useless incumbrance, and to get rid of as
much of it as possible. It was worthless as an outer-England for British expansion, it was vexed with
disaffected people, and made uninhabitable by
hoards of unteachable savages. Such appeared to
be the Colonial Office view; and Sir George Grey
was expected to support the red-tape official. However, he did no such thing, but, on the contrary,
placed the true facts of the country and the colony
before the Ministry. "The countries which lie beyond the Orange River," he wrote, "are very fertile

SIR GEORGE GREY.

and productive. Some of them are so to the highest degree. Their extent may be said to be boundless, and in many portions they are capable of carrying a very dense population."

Taking a broad and enlightened view of the situation, he suggested a policy of federating the European peoples and civilising the blacks : and, in making his proposition, he knew what he was about —knew, in short, that the thing was feasible. A few months after his despatch had been written, the Volksraad of the Orange Free State passed a resolution in favour of union or alliance with Cape Colony. When the Cape Parliament met in 1857 Sir George Grey laid the matter before it, and suggested the consideration of a scheme of a federation for the whole of the South African States, as the most hopeful means of providing for the future prosperity of the country. For this action the Governor was censured, and, upon his defending it, was recalled. He was almost immediately reinstated by Lord Palmerston, who now took the helm of State; but that "noble lord" was as incapable of taking a large idea as his predecessor, and so the opportune moment for friendly union and conciliation was allowed to pass—years afterwards to be sighed for and sought after in vain.

It is curious to note that at the very time Sir George Grey was penning his famous despatch to the Colonial Secretary on the value of South Africa as a field for British enterprise, gold was discovered in the colony, to be followed soon after by the finding of diamonds; so true is it that on whatever soil a Briton sets his foot, there surely he will presently find gold. The story of African gold, however, need not be related here. Its later history is in everybody's memory, and a discreditable history in many respects it is. Suffice it to note that the first outturn of the precious metal was in the golden decade of the fifties—a decade which saw golden deeds more precious for the permanence of the Empire than all the wealth that was being grubbed up by British picks and spades between the northern and the southern poles. The Crimea had seen treasures of British blood spilt and valour wasted for the continuance of an utterly detestable power in Europe which, if the Christian Powers had been one-quarter as Christian as they pretended to be, would have been bundled beyond the Hellespont centuries ago. Barely was that fatuous enterprise at an end ere the British were fighting for very life in India.

Since the Afghan and Sind wars that theatre of British influence had witnessed the final struggle with the Mahratta power, which ended with the capture of Gwalior, followed, in 1845, by the first Sikh war, and the second in 1848. These two wars were famous for the great battles of Moodkee, Sobraon, Chillianwallah, and Goojerat, and it was from the spoils of the Rajah of Lahore that the Queen obtained, as a gift from the directors of the East India Company, the world-renowned Koh-i-noor diamond. The Punjab was thus annexed to the British dominions, and the Sikhs, who had shown themselves among the most formidable of our foes in India, thenceforth proved the most devoted in their loyalty to the Queen, and, as soldiers under the British flag, as brave as they were loyal. In 1852 occurred the second Burmese war, ending in the taking over of Lower Burmah, and, during the governor-generalship of Lord Dalhousie, there were the doubtful annexations of the great states of Oudh and Nagpur.

Then came the terrible episode of the Indian Mutiny, which made for ever memorable the years 1857 and 1858. Of the errors by which it was brought about nothing need be said here, further than to note that at the bottom there was an overweening confidence in the power of the sword and too little care that justice should be done—that justice which is due even to a poor little dark-skinned Bengalee fakir, and that an Englishman ought to be too proud to withhold. The revolt, however, brought out some of the best qualities of the British, as well as of many of the varied races of the dependency, including the Sikhs, so recently reduced to submission. The outbreak found the Company almost wholly unprepared, with but forty thousand white soldiers in all India as against two hundred and fifty thousand Sepoys. Fortunately, not all these native troops were affected, or it might have gone hard with Uncle John in Hindustan; even as it was, with Bengal, Oudh, and the northern provinces wholly in the hands of the rebels, it was a Herculean task, and but for the heroism which in that supreme hour rose to the height of the need, the British might have been driven into the sea. Their fiery courage, however, was kindled to its fiercest by the infamous massacres at Cawnpore and other places; and neither English, Irish, nor Scotch, in all their miscellaneous fighting, ever shewed to better advantage than in the heroic defence of the Residency at Lucknow under Sir Henry Lawrence, in the brilliant march of General Havelock from Allahabad, in the siege and capture of Delhi, and in the second relief of Lucknow by the veteran Sir Colin Campbell. Taking it all in all, it is a marvellous episode, and, in a more romantic age, would have been enshrined in an epic.

The Mutiny was not without its effect for good. It shewed the rulers of the nation that if India was to be retained for the country's benefit and ours, the bonds of unity must be drawn closer. Hence, on the final suppression of the outbreak, the East India Company was abolished, and India passed under the control of the Crown. Since then the policy of the Viceroys and the Councils of India has been to observe a strict neutrality between the rival religions of the country, to interfere as little as possible with the customs and religious observances of the people, and to convince them more and more of the absolute justice of British rule. That policy has been, on the whole, successful, although, it need hardly be said, there is still room for improvement. Enormous sums have been spent in developing the railways of India, in irrigating the country districts, as well as in promoting the physical and moral welfare of the people in many other ways.

CHAPTER VIII.

THE CHARTERED COMPANIES.

THE story of the making of the Empire would be incomplete without a brief account of the chartered companies that are playing such important parts in their several spheres in the name and under the auspices of Great Britain. It was generally thought that, with the abolition of the East India and Hudson's Bay Companies, we had seen the last of colonial development and governance by means of chartered companies. The system, however, appears to offer advantages that cannot altogether be dispensed with, and so within the past seventeen years we have seen the old method revived, and four chartered companies set on foot, and given almost a free hand over enormous territories.

The first of these in point of date was the British North Borneo Company, which came into existence in 1881. Various attempts had already from time to time been made to form English settlements in Borneo, after Australia and New Guinea the largest island in the world; but none of them were successful until the establishment by James Brooke, in 1841, of the independent state of Sarawak. Brooke was a fine type of the Englishman, possessed at once of the spirit of adventure and of the genius for rule, a combination by no means rare among educated Britons. Quitting the service of the East India Company in 1830, he conceived the idea of putting down piracy in the Eastern Archipelago, and of carrying civilisation to the inhabitants of those islands; and being opportunely left with a considerable fortune by the death of his father in 1835, he set about the execution of his purpose. Purchasing a schooner-yacht, he sailed for Sarawak, where he arrived in 1839. On his arrival he found that the uncle of the Sultan of Borneo was engaged in a war with some rebellious chiefs. At Muda Hassim's request, he lent his assistance to put down the revolt, and in return for his services was given the greater part of the territory which now forms the state of Sarawak, with the title of Rajah. Brooke immediately set about reforming the government of the province, framing a new code of laws, and—taking a lesson from the achievement of Richard Cobden and Sir Robert Peel—introducing free trade. A vast improvement soon became apparent, both as regards the orderliness of the country and the increase of trade; but it took years to put down head-hunting and piracy, practices to which the natives were greatly addicted.

In 1846 the Sultan of Brunei ceded the Island of Labuan to Great Britain, in order to secure British aid in the suppression of piracy. The island contains only about thirty square miles; but as it possesses valuable coal-mines, it is of great importance to English trade in the East. Sir James Brooke (as he now was) on its cession was appointed Governor, as well as British Commissioner and Consul-General in Borneo, which position he continued to hold until his death in 1868, when he was succeeded by his nephew, Sir Charles Brooke.

Sir James Brooke had the satisfaction of seeing the independence of Sarawak recognised by the English Government, and the country greatly prosper under his rule. He found Kuching, the chief town, a place of some thousand inhabitants; he left it with twenty-five thousand; while the exports to Singapore, which in 1840 amounted to £25,000, were in 1858 £300,000.

This success, and the adventures generally of the English Rajah, which read more like a bit of romance from the days of Queen Elizabeth than doings of the prosaic nineteenth century, had the effect of calling attention to Borneo, and in 1881, as the result of concessions made to private individuals by the Sultans of Brunei and Sooloo, the British North Borneo Company was launched, with a view to acquiring the rights of the concessionaires, and developing the resources of the country. The territory thus acquired includes the whole northern portion of Borneo, from the Sipitong Stream on the west to the Sibuku River on the East, and is conterminous with the northern boundary of the State of Brunei on the west coast, and approaches that of the Netherlands on the east. It has a coast-line of upwards of 900 miles, and an area of a little over

31,000 square miles. The population is estimated at 175,000, and is composed of Malays, Sooloos, Dyaks, and various other tribes.

RICHARD COBDEN.

The territory is administered by a Governor, who is assisted by a Council and by residents appointed to preside over provinces and districts, the machinery being similar to that in Crown colonies. Labuan has been subject to the Company since 1889; its Governor, whose appointment is subject to approval by the Crown, being also the Governor of North Borneo. In 1888, by an agreement between the Imperial Government and the Company, North Borneo was constituted an independent state under the protection of Great Britain. The internal government is thus left in the hands of the Governor and his Council, subject to the court of directors in London, whilst the relations with foreign states are conducted from the Foreign Office.

The country is as yet almost entirely undeveloped, but it appears to possess practically unlimited possibilities of wealth. It exports gutta-percha, india-rubber, edible birds'-nests, timber, sago, and tobacco; and pearls, tortoise shell, and *bêche-de-mer* are found in the neighbouring seas. Gold, diamonds, iron, coal, and mineral oils are among its mineral resources, although as yet little has been done beyond some prospecting and exploration.

Between North Borneo and Sarawak lies the State of Brunei, which, ruled by its Sultan as regards internal affairs, has, since 1888, been virtually under the protection of Great Britain. Thus the whole of the northern part of the Island of Borneo is under British protection.

The direct trade of both Sarawak and North Borneo is chiefly through Singapore, which is 1000 miles distant, but they have also commercial relations with the Australian colonies and Hong Kong.

SIR ROBERT PEEL.

The nearest Australian port is Port Darwin, which is 1500 miles distant, while Hong Kong is 1200 miles distant. Some idea of the importance of North Borneo may be gathered from its central position in regard to these places.

The Island of Hong Kong was occupied by the British during what is known as the "Opium War" in 1841, and was formally ceded to Great Britain in the following year by the treaty of Nanking. It lies at the mouth of the Canton River, and is distant about ninety miles from the city of Canton. The colony includes a number of small islands, besides an area of two and three-quarter square miles on the mainland opposite to Hong Kong, which bears the name of British Kowlong. Hong Kong itself has an area of twenty-nine square miles.

When first occupied it was a bare island, a few fisherman being the sole inhabitants. Within three months of its occupation sixteen thousand Chinese had already taken up their abode in the colony. It soon became an *entrepôt* for the foreign commerce of China, and being a free port without customs' dues, speedily developed an enormous trade. The compilers of the Colonial Office List estimates the annual imports at twenty millions, and the exports at twenty-five millions sterling. The foreign commerce is mainly carried on with Great Britain, India, and the Straits Settlements. The chief town, Victoria, is situated on a splendid harbour on the north side of the island. It is well laid out with broad and airy streets, possesses some fine public edifices, while handsome houses of the merchant class are scattered about the town and its suburbs. The population of the colony in 1891 was 221,441, of whom more than nine-tenths were Chinese.

In its early days Hong Kong was decribed as the " most filthy and disgusting colony of the British Empire," and Mr. Montgomery Martin, who was Treasurer to the Government there, referring to 1855, said the European inhabitants were generally obliged " to sleep with loaded pistols under their pillows, and not unfrequently had to turn out of their beds at midnight to protect their lives and property from gangs of armed robbers." However, that sort of thing is now at an end, and Hong Kong is as orderly as most British settlements in which there is so large a proportion of natives. Such is the influence of a few men with brains in the right place. The colony is governed, like most Crown colonies, by a Governor, with an executive and a legislative Council.

The three other companies which have received charters since the granting of that of the North Borneo Company all relate to districts in the continent of infinite possibilities, and of late years a bone of contention amongst the Powers of Europe.

The first of these was the Royal Niger Company, chartered in 1886, which has control over a territory covering a million and a half square miles, and containing a population variously estimated at from twenty to thirty-five millions of people. It takes its name, of course, from the Niger, a river the course and origin of which for years gave rise to almost as much speculation as the source of the Nile. It has its rise on the north side of the Kong Mountains, and after a devious course of 2600 miles, empties its waters into the Gulf of Guinea. It is known by various names in different parts of its course, as the Joliba, the Mayo, etc. After joining the Benué it becomes the Quorra. At Aboh about a hundred miles from the sea, the great delta of the Niger begins. This delta extends along the coast for about one hundred and fifty miles, and is intersected by a network of channels and islands, the chief navigable streams being the Nun, the Mari, and the Bonny.

On the Gulf of Guinea the Niger Company has a coast-line of one hundred and twenty miles extending from the Forcados to the Brass River. The eastern frontier of the Company's territories runs from Old Calabar, or Cross River, in a north-easterly direction to some miles east of Yola on the river Benué, and thence to the south shore of Lake Tchad, thirty-five minutes east of Kuka, the capital of Bornu, the German sphere of operations in the Cameroons lying on the south-east. The northern frontier, marking the line of delimitation between the French and British possessions, extends from Barrawa, on Lake Tchad, westward to Say, on the Quorra, or middle Niger. The Company's territories, therefore, comprise the whole of the kingdom of Sokoto and the large western portion of the kingdom of Bornu, as well as over the kingdoms of Gando and Borgu.

The Fulah empire of Sokoto is the largest, the most populous, and extensive in the whole of the Sudan. The King of Gando, in the middle Niger valley, as well as all the other Fulah chiefs, recognises the suzerainty of the Emperor of Sokoto. Sokoto and Gando together cover an area of 219,500 square miles, with an estimated population of fifteen millions. The empire, which is conterminous with Bornu on the east, is bounded by Borgu and the Mossi country on the west. On the north it has the Sahara desert, while southward it stretches to the unexplored regions beyond Adamawa. The reigning sovereign of Sokoto has conferred on the Niger Company sovereign power over a large part of his dominions, and complete jurisdiction over all other than natives throughout the remainder.

The Fulahs, who are Mohammedans, and supposed originally to have been of East African origin, founded the Sokoto empire at the commencement of the century, and have maintained a paramount power in those vast districts ever since. Although divided into the two kingdoms of Wurno and Gando, the suzerainty of the former is fully recognised by the western state. Other states are independent, except that they pay an annual tribute.

Borgu, which is attached to the Niger Company by a treaty similar to that with Sokoto, occupies a considerable portion of the right bank of the Quorra, to the south of Gando and north of Illorin, another province of the Sokoto empire. Borgu extends westwards to the meridian of Greenwich, and forms the northern boundary of Dahomey. The people are pagan, and have successfully resisted the attempts of the Fulahs to bring them under subjection to Sokoto rule.

The Sokoto countries are for the most part extremely fertile, and are especially rich in agricultural resources, exporting considerable quantities of rice and other grains, besides onions of excellent flavour, the fruit of the butter tree, the parched seeds of the doria, dates, and honey. Cotton is largely grown, and manufactured into durable material coloured with indigo and other native dyes. Leather ware is also exported in exchange for salt from the Sahara and European goods.[1]

Reclus is of opinion that the easy access to these rich and populous provinces afforded by the Niger and the Benué will in the future constitute those rivers the most important of all commercial routes into the interior of the Black Continent. They afford uninterrupted navigation for steamboats for a distance of 1500 kilometres from the sea. By the memorable expedition of Baillie in 1854 the English became, says Reclus,[2] "les vrais suzerains des peoples de la Mesopatamie Nigritienne." He goes on to affirm that, though "England possesses only the moving and living part of Nigritia, formed by the fluviatile current, the rest appertains to her by a phenomenon of natural gravitation." He speaks in high terms of the wonderful fertility of many parts of the country, and of the enormous population it sustains. The cities, and there are many of them, are nests of industrial life, despite the wars that from time to time decimated whole districts, and the inhuman sacrifices that are constantly being

[1] Stateman's Year Book.
[2] *Nouvelle Geographie Universelle, L'Afrique Occidental.*

offered up in the pagan districts; for even where Islam is the dominant power, paganism still holds the greater part of the population.

The administrative centre of the Company's territories is at Asaba, about half-way between Lokoja, at the confluence of the Niger and Benué Rivers, and Akassa, on the Nun mouth of the Niger. The latter is the chief naval centre, while Lokoja is the headquarters of the trained native troops composed of Housas, officered by Europeans. Amongst the other chief towns are Wurno, the capital of Sokoto on the Gandi, Gando, the capital of the kingdom of Gando, Yola, the capital of Adamawa, Yakoba, Kuka, near Lake Tchad, etc. Some of these places have very large populations. Yakoba is said to have 50,000. Bida, the capital of Nupé, recently taken by the Company's troops, was credited in 1879 with a population of 100,000. Occupying a very favourable position near the Niger, and surrounded by fertile hills, it is a place of many industries. Stuffs are woven and dyed, iron is smelted and forged, leather is manufactured into various articles, and glass is made and applied to useful and ornamental purposes. The children are taught to read and write Arabic in the Mohammedan schools.

Rabba was formerly one of the largest cities in Africa. At the beginning of the century the slave-merchants made it their chief depot. It was ruined by the Fulahs. Richard Lander, who, along with Captain Clapperton, did so much to make known the Niger region, and settled the question of its outfall, visited the place in his second journey. Of

Illorin, Reclus says its streets are broad, with open places lined with booths, in which may be seen the merchandise of Europe and Africa, including stuffs from Egypt by way of Kuka and Kano. Illorin is a republican city, founded in 1790 by fugitives from all parts of Yoruba, and at the time of Lander's visit was divided into a dozen quarters, each belonging to a distinct tribe, and represented in the council by an elder. Fairs follow each other every five days.

Twenty steamers navigate the Niger and its tributaries, and afford a ready means for the security of peace and order. The importation of rifles and cartridges is forbidden, and the introduction and sale of spirits are under some restriction, although its civilising influence continues powerfully at work.

The countries under the Royal Niger Company form only a part of the sphere of the British influence in this part of Africa. A British protectorate was established in 1884 along the west coast from the boundaries of Lagos at the mouth of the Benin River to the mouth of the Rio del Rey, including the mouths of what are called "the Oil Rivers." Until 1873 it was called "the Oil Rivers Protectorate." Inland it includes the entire Benin region, the Niger delta, and the Old Calabar, or Cross River, from the rapids to the sea. It is bounded on the north-west by Lagos and Yoruba. The country, which gradually rises as it recedes from the coast, is well wooded and watered, and rich in vegetable productions. The territory is administered by an Imperial Commissioner, with a number of vice-consuls. The trade is carried on chiefly by the African Association, Limited, which has its headquarters at Liverpool.

RICHARD LANDER.

It would seem as though Great Britian had a great future before her in this vast region, the resources of which are almost inexhaustible. With peace to aid the natural fertility of the soil and the industry of the inhabitants, it may prove, as Reclus remarks, another India under the hands of the Niger Company. Within the last few months two campaigns have been conducted against native powers in the Hinterland of the Protectorate. One was necessitated by the massacre of a peaceful mission to the chief of Benin. He had consented to receive a deputation, which, in consequence, marched without arms, and was thus completely at the mercy of an ambuscade with which the savage potentate waylaid it. As a result of this piece of treachery a punitive expedition, composed of British marines and blue-jackets and a force of Housas, was at once prepared and despatched to take Benin, the capital, and annex the country of its chief to the Niger Protectorate; which was done.

The other campaign was conducted by Sir George T. Goldie, the Governor of the Royal Niger Company, against a body of Fulah usurpers from Nupé. The enemy was first cleared out of the country south of the Niger, after which the Company's forces directed their march upon Bida, the capital of Nupé. That, after a decisive victory, was occupied, and peace finally restored.

Shortly after the conclusion of the convention between Great Britain and Germany in 1886 regarding the Sultan of Zanzibar's territory in the mainland of East Africa, Sir William Mackinnon received from Sultan Burghash a concession of the strip of land ten miles in width along the coast. To work this concession a charter was obtained, and the Imperial East Africa Company incorporated. Under this charter, which was signed on the 3d September, 1888, the Company was given the " entire management of those parts of the islands and mainland of the Zanzibar dominions on the East Coast of Africa, appertaining to the territory lying between Wanga and Kipini, both inclusive . . . together with any further rights of a similar nature in East Africa." The Company's territories were subsequently greatly extended; but after it had been at work opening them up for several years, negotiations were entered into with the Imperial Government for the surrender of its property, and by arrangement with the Sultan of Zanzibar, the transfer was effected in 1895.

The territories thus taken over by the Government, which constitute British East Africa, extend into the interior from a coast line of about four hundred miles in length, running from the Umbe River in the south to the Juba in the north. The southern boundary runs from the mouth of the Umbe to the Victoria Nyanza at the point where it is intersected by the first parallel of south latitude, follows the northern shore of the lake, and continues in the same line westward until it meets the eastern boundary of the Congo Free State. On the north the boundary line begins at the mouth of the river Juba, and follows the course of that stream to its intersection with the sixth parallel of north latitude, whence it runs to the 35th meridian of east longitude, which it follows to the Blue Nile. The Congo Free State and the western watershed of the Upper Nile form the western limits of the territories thus under British influence. The total area is estimated at about a million square miles, and embraces a large part of Somaliland, the Equatorial Province,

Uganda, Usogo, Unyoro, etc. It also includes Witu on the coast, with the islands of Patta Manda, and the islands of Zanzibar and Pemba. These various territories are comprised under the three protectorates of British East Africa, including Witu, Uganda, and Zanzibar. Uganda is nominally under the rule of its king, as Witu and Zanzibar are under their respective sultans; but the administration is in the hands of British officials.

The chief ports are Mombasa, on the island of that name, Wanga, Malindi, Mambrui, Lamu, Kismayu. Mombasa, which is the capital of the coast protectorate, possesses the finest harbour on the eastern side of Africa. The railway which is being constructed to Uganda starts from this port. Its terminus will be on Lake Victoria Nyanza.

The principal products of the country are cloves, ivory, india-rubber, copra, hides, etc. The trade is mainly in the hands of Indian merchants. Pending the completion of the railways, the country is being peaceably opened up by exploring caravans carrying trade goods, and by missionaries, who have already done much good work for civilisation in these regions. The importation of arms and ammunition is prohibited, and every endeavour is made to check the consumption of spirits, as well as to put an end to the slave-trading.

The largest and most important of all the existing chartered companies is that which bears the name of the British South Africa Company, of which the world has heard so much of late, and is destined to hear so much more. Its charter, granted on the

29th of October, 1889, confers upon it large administrative powers in the region north of Cape Colony,

SKETCH MAP OF SOUTH AFRICA.

and authorises it to promote trade and commerce, and to work mineral and other concessions therein.

The boundaries of the Company's territory are, roughly speaking, Cape Colony and the Transvaal on the south, Portuguese East Africa and the British East Africa Protectorate on the east, the Congo Free State on the north, and German South-west Africa and Angola on the west. Thus the Bechuanaland Protectorate, Mashonaland, Matabeleland, and British Central Africa, all lie within the sphere of its operations, which extends from Mafeking to Lake Tanganyika, and comprises an area estimated at 750,000 square miles. The river Zambesi divides the territory into two parts, named respectively Northern and Southern Zambesia.

The country is said to be rich in minerals, including gold and silver, although up to the present it has not justified all the fine things said about it. But that may be the result of untoward events. The opening up of the country was commenced with great energy under the direction of Dr. Jameson. Salisbury, the capital of Mashonaland, was founded, and the Company's field of operations extended to the territory north of the Zambesi, excepting the British Central Africa Protectorate, which comprises the eastern portion of British Central Africa, lying to the west and south of Lake Nyassa. Other centres of activity soon sprang up at Buluwayo, Tuli, Charter, Umtali, etc. But some evil genius was at work marring progress. First came a fierce, and, as would seem, unjust, war with the Matabele; then followed the invasion of the Transvaal by Jameson and his unlucky force, set in motion, apparently, by the most evil of evil

DAVID LIVINGSTONE.

genii; to be succeeded like a thunderclap by another sanguinary conflict with the natives, which, like its predecessor, there is too much reason to believe was brought on by a lack of due consideration for the rights and feelings of the blacks.

A good deal has already been done in the way of railway building to open up the country. The line from Kimberley to Vryburg, opened in 1890, has now been extended beyond Mafeking. Another line, from Beira to Salisbury, through Portuguese territory, is in course of construction, and, it is hoped, will soon be completed. But the successful development of the territory depends on the appointment of wise and just administrators free from what a settler called " the Helldorado fever."

The Central Africa Protectorate is fortunately far removed from this turmoil and trouble, pursuing its own quiet way of progress, under the direction of its special Commissioner and Consul-General, and more in the spirit of the noble man who first explored that region, and discovered the lake which gives its name to a large section of the country. The Protectorate includes all British Nyassaland, as well as the Shiré Highlands and the greater part of the course of the Shiré River, which is a tributary of the Zambesi. It is divided into two provinces, the Shiré Province and the Lake Nyassa Province. Its chief towns are Blantyre, named after the birthplace of Dr. Livingstone, which was founded in 1876 as a mission by the Established Church of Scotland, and now the centre of settlement and trade; and Zomba, the headquarters of the administration. Several steamers ply to and fro on the lake, which is three hundred miles in length, and there is also communication between the junction of the Ruo and Shiré Rivers and Chinde, at the mouth of the Zambesi, by means of steamers. A railway is projected between Blantyre and Chiromo, at the junction of the above rivers.

The population of the Protectorate is estimated at 845,000, of whom under three hundred are Europeans. The principal exports are ivory and coffee. The plantations of the latter are becoming more successful every year. In 1894 the quantity of coffee exported amounted to 165,320 pounds; in 1895 the amount had doubled. Rice, tobacco, sugar, cotton, and tea are also grown. The expenses of the administration are met partly out of the revenue and partly by an annual grant from the Imperial Government. The Protectorate so far promises to be one of the fairest spheres for British enterprise and colonisation in Africa, although, unfortunately, it has of late been much disturbed by Arab slave-traders—a set of ruffians, who, if there is any vitality left in the noblest of English traditions, will soon be a phantom host flitting, ghost-like and disgraceful, through the pages of history. With France to aid on the west, the last of them should be well hung in ten years.

CHAPTER IX.

THE WORK STILL TO DO.

THUS has the colossus of Empire grown and expanded. It would seem at the first view as though the overburdened giant would sink beneath his load; and probably he would have done so ere this had it not been for the fact that, like the wise parent, the mother-country keeps her children in leading-strings no longer than necessary, but makes it her task to prepare them to take their own share of the load— to fit them for self-control and self-government—as soon as possible. In some cases the Australasian colonies were allowed to become practically independent ere they had in a sense reached their majority. Western Australia, it is true, was a backward child; but, finally, in 1870, that colony also was granted a legislative council. It consisted partly of elected and partly of nominee members, on the model of the constitutions of 1850. Five years previously the colony had seen the cessation of transportation. Twenty years more of steady progress brought it abreast of the sister-colonies; and in 1890 Western Australia was ready to receive a bicameral Parliament, with full powers of responsible government.

The policy of allowing such a free hand to dependencies, however, is a development of the present century, almost of the present reign. Formerly the method of the parent-land was not to make nations, but to keep its colonies in a state of semi-subjection. The ideal of rule was a bit in everybody's mouth, and a whip in the hand of the sovereign. Gradually all that has been changed; and now, instead of governing, the sovereign reigns only. The saying is probably truer of the Queen than of any previous occupant of the throne of these realms. But every personality has an influence, and that influence tells strictly in accordance with character and position. Hence it is not too much to say that, despite the fact that in theory her Majesty does not govern, there is not, and has not been during the past sixty years, a single individual, nor, indeed, any half-dozen individuals, who have exerted so great an influence upon the growth and destiny of the British Empire during the nineteenth century as the Queen has. One is led to infer that, as was the case with Queen Elizabeth, so her present Majesty takes delight in seeing her people put forth their strength and their prowess, and that, too, not so much on the field of battle as in every sphere of peaceful human endeavour. Moreover, the Queen has set her subjects an example of doing the best and the worthiest that it was in her power to do that will serve as a heritage for good for generations to come.

> "Had all of you done like her, there had been
> Small need for me to come as now I come."

If there had been a king instead of a queen upon the throne, it is possible that he might not have been so content simply to reign, but would have wished in some measure to rule also; and so the age would not have witnessed the unique spectacle of a people allowed to "go as they pleased," the only check being that they should go according to the rules of the game. It is true that the said rules have not always been so strictly observed as they might have been, and in one instance—that need not be named—there was a flagrant and disgraceful departure therefrom. But on the whole, subject to human imperfections, the enormous growth of the Empire during living memory has been one of manifest destiny—the result of inherent racial strength, rather than ambitious striving—more truly than at any previous period of the nation's history.

The sword has by no means been left to rust in the scabbard; but what it has won for the Empire during the present reign is insignificant in comparison with that which has been acquired, as one may say, by the pick and the ploughshare, and by sovereign inheritance, or what Reclus calls the "phenomenon of natural gravitation." Of the latter description were the rights acquired over the group of islands in the Pacific named collectively Fiji, which, in the year 1874, became vested in the British Crown by surrender of the native chiefs, and was incorporated as a colony—to which Rotumah, to the north, was added in 1881. The government is in the hands of a Governor and a legislative Council, of whom half are official and half non-official. This cession took place by virtue of the paramount influence which England has for a century exerted in the Pacific— the effect of the Englishman's long-acquired habit as a sea-rover, settling and pushing his fortune wherever he can get a foothold or a living is possible.

The incorporation of Fiji with the dominions of Great Britain had the effect of raising a host of questions relating to that quarter of the globe. The title of "High Commissioner for the Western Pacific," given to the Governor of Fiji, seemed to other nations an unwarrantable assumption of dominion on the part of England over all the seas and lands in that region. Jealousies, natural under the circumstances, were at once aroused, and the warships of the United States, as well as of European nations, began to "crowd round Samoa, and other tempting spots, like eagles round a dying traveller."[1]

Amongst other questions, it brought to the front that of New Guinea. On the organisation of Fiji, representations were made to the Imperial Government as to the desirability of taking a similar course with regard to that island, or to the eastern part of it, the western portion being already under the dominion of Holland. But the Secretary of State (Lord Carnarvon) refused to take the proposed step unless the Australian colonies were willing to share amongst them the expenses that would be incurred by the annexation. This the colonies did not appear inclined to do, and so the matter remained in

[1] *History of the Australasian Colonies.*

abeyance until 1877, when the reported discovery of gold in the island sent a crowd of adventurers thither.

Measures were taken by the Queensland Government and the Imperial authorities to secure order at Port Moresby (afterwards to become the capital), and in the islands of Torres Strait, where various industries, as pearl-fishing and trepang-curing, were springing up. The islands were subsequently brought within the Queensland boundary; but still the Home Government declined to move from the position they had taken with respect to New Guinea, even though in 1878 the High Commissioner for the Western Pacific, Sir Arthur Gordon, recommended its annexation.

In this condition matters remained until 1883, when the Queensland Government, through its Premier, Sir Thomas McIllwraith, made a formal offer to the Home Authorities to undertake the cost of administering New Guinea, if the Imperial Government would sanction the annexation. This was in February; and as the Colonial Office appeared to be in no hurry to come to a decision in the matter, while at the antipodes public opinion was becoming more and more urgent, Sir Thomas McIllwraith, in April, took formal possession of the island in the name of her Majesty.

This step was resorted to because of a report reaching Australia to the effect that a German association was in course of formation for the exploitation of the unowned portion of New Guinea. Nevertheless, Lord Derby repudiated the act of the Queensland Government. The question, however, was of such momentous importance to the eastern colonies of Australia that in the end the colonials had their way, although not to the extent that they at first wished. By an arrangement signed at Berlin in 1886, the eastern half of New Guinea was divided between Germany and Great Britain, the former taking the north-eastern portion, thence known as Kaiser Wilhelm's Land, and England the south-eastern portion. The latter, by an Act of Parliament passed in 1887, was, in the following year, formally created a possession of the British Crown. It embraces the group of islands lying within the 141st and 155th meridians of east longitude, and the 5th and 12th parallels of south latitude.

The government of the colony of British New Guinea is vested in an Administrator, aided by an executive and a legislative Council. For judicial purposes it forms part of Queensland, which is responsible for the expense of its administration to the extent of £15,000 a year, towards which New South Wales and Victoria contribute each £5000. The area of the colony is estimated at nearly 90,000 square miles, and the native population at 350,000. Very wisely, the sale of firearms, spirits, and opium to the natives is forbidden.

With perhaps the exception of several of the southern Solomon Islands, formally taken possession of a year or two later, New Guinea forms the last important accession to British territory, always barring, of course, the gradual and inevitable accretion in India. But even there little in the way of fresh conquest or annexation has taken place since the incorporation of Upper Burmah in 1886. The chief item has been the strengthening of the northern frontier by the occupation of Chitral, after a brilliant little campaign, in 1895.

The vast territory of India now enjoys, as it has for years enjoyed, the blessings of an Imperial British peace, under which the people have prospered as they could not have done under any native rule of which the world has the record. No one can doubt that the British have yet much to do in the dependency in the way of organisation and development. But how much has been done, and how much the country has thriven under English rule during the present reign is evidenced to some extent by the country's imports and exports. In 1837 they stood at thirty-seven millions sterling; they have now risen to one hundred and sixty millions. When it is realised that the total population of the dependency amounts to two hundred and eighty-seven millions, or fifteen per cent. of the estimated population of the globe, far and away in excess of the population of the remaining areas under British sway, some idea may be gathered of the gigantic work that is yet to be done in that most important of British dominions.

Few will question the capacity of Englishmen for the task. The only fear is lest the destinies of the nation should fall into the hands of men with more tongue than general brain-power, with a policy of show rather than of substance; or lest the people should be so corrupted by wealth as to lose all moral stamina. That there is some cause for fear no one can doubt who notes the fawning worship which wealth, and the paraphernalia of wealth, receives from a section, and an important section, of the public press, the visible sore that attests the widespread disease.

But this glamour will surely pass, and the day come when a real man will be ashamed to be lauded as a millionaire, nay, even to be such, not only because it is childish to grasp more than one can make good and noble use of, but for the still more cogent reason that the cases are, and must of necessity be, exceedingly rare in which a man has gained a million of money without trick or reproach.

But there has been of late years, and is still, so much idolatry of wealth, that it has occasioned, even in quarters where a higher spirit ought to have prevailed, such a frenzy for gold, that right and justice and fair dealing have been too often relegated to the lumber-room of forgotten ethics in the mad and disgraceful scramble for it. Amid the welter of South African politics for the past few years the slime of that serpent stain is everywhere visible. Into what a danger it has brought the Empire everyone who watches contemporary events must be aware. It will take England years to undo that mischief, and yet the great conscience of the country is entirely free from any part or wish in the wrong.

President Steyne, of the Orange Free State, told Mr. Poultney Bigelow that he was of opinion that when English legislation, in regard to South Africa, had been oppressive, it was because it had been done under misapprehension. That is doubtless true. Englishmen, as a rule, desire to be fair and to be just. But, unfortunately, the ordinary Briton is insular, and in consequence too apt to allow interested people, from whom he obtains his information, to prejudice him. There are Englishmen enough who travel about the world, and who are capable of seeing things with a clear eye, but they are for the most part men who have got their business to attend to, and who are so absorbed therein that they have little time to give to matters outside their little sphere.

This is the case with the ordinary Englishman; but there is another type of man who is often enough but half-British—one who has his axe to grind, and whose axe is best ground by misrepresentation. It is this man's business to misrepresent; it is his interest to make his voice heard, and he takes care to raise it till it sounds like a thousand. Hence this man and his colleagues, with their greed, their inveracity, and their strident jingoism, are too often accepted as the guides of truth, when, in reality, they are but the instigators of falsehood and deception, and the British public is misled.

Allied to these are the falsely patriotic—men and women who imagine that patriotism will cover any wrong. England has no worse enemy than these; and if the lordly Empire, over which reigns probably the best Queen that ever lived, should at any time come to grief and suffer dismemberment it will be the fault of those who, for their hoards of shining dust, degrade their manhood and soil the British name.

England has undoubtedly benefited from the finding of gold in her dominions; but her best wealth always has and ever will come from the deft alchemy that transmutes the common earth into gold, and her best and solidest interests are bound up with those—the common, everyday stuff of humanity—who pursue such steady and unpretending industry. The Empire owes much to that sterling commodity—the common man. His virtue may not be very shining, but it is real and substantial. There is nothing like it. With no great extremes, either of ambition or of greed, he is content to do the task that falls to his lot, and to earn enough to pay his way and to bring up his children in decency and "the fear of God." Year in and year out, from the cradle to the grave, he may be uniformly counted on. His labours are steady and constant, his work is well done, he builds to endure. The veritable salt of the earth, he gives it health, he gives it strength. He is the mainstay and backbone of the Empire. Stolid and silent for the most part, he is yet full of the religion and passion of his race, and will fight for an idea—die for it if need be. The classes have doubted him, and in times past have scanted his liberty—would do so still; but he has been more to the Empire than they, and will be yet. His loyalty is deeper; it is innate, seeking no pay. That of others often stands on favour; his is part of his being.

Since his enfranchisement the world has made a

surer, because a broader progress. His ideals are prevailing, and will prevail. They are the ideals of the common humanity. Fears were expressed at the time of the first Reform Bill that the broadened base of the nation's liberties would prove its ruin. So far from that having been the case, additional strength has come with every extension of constitutional rights. Moreover, the lesson of the colonies goes to prove how blind and stupid was all the rage of Governmental repression and rejection in the earlier decades of the century. The demand for triennial or quinquennial Parliaments, for manhood suffrages, for the ballot, for paid members, and a score other political novelties seemed to the rulers of our grandfathers' days the outcries of revolutionary miscreants, who were only aiming at the overthrow of the throne and the Constitution. In reality they were the voices of the saviours of society. All these ideas, and more, have been introduced into the political structure of the colonies, and have been found to fit beautifully into the constitutional scheme. "The effect of modern changes," says Jenks,[1] "has been practically to give the franchise for the popular House to almost all resident males of full age—a position taken up by South Australia from the beginning; while New Zealand[2] has even extended the suffrage to women. The introduction of the 'one man, one vote' principle has been effected in South Australia, New Zealand, and New South Wales. The ballot system of voting was

[1] *History of the Australasian Colonies.*
[2] And South Australia.

adopted very shortly after the introduction of responsible government, and is now in force throughout the Australasian colonies. In most cases the extreme limit for the duration of a Parliament has been reduced to three years; but Tasmania and Queensland retain the old term of five years, and the new Constitution of Western Australia has adopted the intermediate number of four. Payment of members is (it is believed) now universal in the case of the Lower Chambers of the Australasian colonies, with the exception of Western Australia; in the case of New Zealand, members of the Upper Chambers also receive remuneration."

Yet, notwithstanding this realisation of "Chartism," the predicted ruin has not only not come, but the Empire has gone on growing and expanding, and with every expansion prosperity has broadened and security deepened. Nor has the throne or religion suffered. As for the throne, loyalty is as deep and sincere in the most democratic of the colonies as it is between the four seas of the Home lands. All this is a good augury for the preservation and consolidation of the Empire.

There cannot, one would think, in the nature of things, be much more room for annexation or conquest. The task that remains, therefore, for Great Britain is one of development—the completion of the work. That is a sufficiently gigantic labour to occupy all the best energies of the race for generations, possibly for centuries. There have been conquering nations before—nations that have spread wide arms over subject races; but they have in every

instance failed in that which now devolves upon the
English to do—to apply the blessings of a higher
civilisation to the various nations under British rule,
and, in order to do that, to strive to attain fully that
higher civilisation herself. For in not a few depart-
ments of the national life there are still to be found
relics of low and barbarous ideals.

As regards government, the task becomes more
and more one of doing justice. It may be—indeed,
undoubtedly is—a leading trait of a great people to go
on conquering and adding possession to possession,
holding them against the world, if need be, and administering them wisely. But that has been done
before, albeit not perhaps so successfully.

There is, however, a step beyond that. To
achieve a still higher greatness is to do what was
never done before—so to treat the subject races that
they shall feel that their subjection is one of education merely—that they are being surely trained to
know and rightly enjoy freedom.

Such appears to be England's better destiny.

Her greatest task, however, will be to subdue herself. Her greatest enemies are those spirits at home
who, without justice or consciousness of others'
rights, are at all times willing to force the country
to any lengths for the sake of national aggrandisement or personal greed.

Happily, there is a growing tradition of right rule
and of great rulers—of men who have no other idea
than to govern well the province or the people placed
under their charge—and, as part of that tradition, is
growing the conviction that the less people are gov-

erned the more surely they are governed. Half the troubles that have befallen the British as a ruling race have arisen from over-governing—from trying to make the subject people be or do something that is alien to their nature. If they had always been content to let the old ones die off, bestowing their chief attention upon the young, the task would have become comparatively easy. All, perhaps, are not so easy of government as the Basutos; but what has been done with them may in a measure be effected with others.

Mr. Poultney Bigelow, in giving, in *Harper's Monthly*,[1] an account of a visit he made to the British Protectorate of Basutoland, describes with confessed surprise an achievement in government which shows the best traditions of British rule at work. "At last," he says, "in the midst of most complete savagery, was an English home presided over by an accomplished and amiable English lady, whose husband held imperial rule over a quarter of a million naked negroes, not one of whom, probably, could explain by what means Mr. Lagden exercised his extraordinary authority. There was not a single redcoat to shield them against insurrection; there was not a single white policeman to guard their door. The Lagden family in Basutoland is separated from all the world almost as completely as though on a rock in the ocean. If a single chief refused to obey the order of the British Resident, there is no visible force at his command by which he could bring that chief to his knees."

[1] March, 1897.

The writer goes on to explain the secret of Mr. Lagden's rule. " But, fortunately, there are invisible forces which even the negro can understand. Every chief in the Basuto country, and through him every black warrior—I might almost say every black man from the Zambesi to the Cape—is brought up to the faith that there is far away a white Queen, who, like a goddess of the ancients, can be invoked for the protection of the black. English rule in Africa has been rough and ready in many cases, but, so far as the black man is concerned, it has been vastly more humane than that of the black man towards his fellow-blacks. Even to-day the black man prefers English rule to that of Portugal, France, or Germany, and this not merely because the English Government has more jealously guarded the rights of the black natives, but because England is credited with greater powers of enforcing her wishes than any other government."

That is an instance of what may be done with the African—which might have been done with the Mashona and the Matabele, possibly that may be done still. Anyway, the wise ones amongst us are coming more and more to perceive that the real art of governing consists in so training men and women as to develop the essential principles of government that are within.

Every self-governing nation that Great Britain has thrown out is sending home that message to the old mother. Spend all you can on the education of your children, and on your young men and maidens, and they will pay you back fourfold in good behaviour and easy government,—in added strength and endurance to the fabric of the Empire. America was the first to apply the lesson. The New England colonies in their very infancy made education compulsory, and they had their reward. Most of the colonies have followed in their wake, putting primary education, largely free and wholly unsecular, in the forefront of their policy. After their first—under the circumstances almost pardonable—mistake, the Americans decided to leave religion free from State control. In that, too, the colonies have followed their lead. They failed to see how a church, any more than a plant, could become strong and independent if parasitic; and so far they have had no reason to question their wisdom in so doing.

There are many other questions connected with the future of the Empire that are now, as it were, in the melting-pot, and that will have to take form and shape within a few years. They are at present in the brooding stage in men's minds, and must come to birth of some sort ere long; but what their ultimate effect will be no one can possibly forecast. The English are for the most part a slow, plodding race, albeit not by any means so destitute of imagination as they are sometimes held to be—perhaps, indeed, the most imaginative of races, if we may judge from their achievements in literature and art, in the domain of science, and in practical affairs. For it takes imagination of the highest order to win results like those of Bacon, Newton, Locke, Priestley, Herschel, Adam Smith, Adams, Darwin, and Spencer, to say nothing of such conquests as were made by the Watts, the Stephensons, the Arkwrights, the Davys, the Faradays, the Maxwells, the Thompsons, and other way-breakers like them.

Nor is there, perhaps, much less of the quality of imagination in men of affairs of the grasp and character of Sir John Pender, to whom we owe so much in connection with the uniting of the various parts of the Empire by the electric wire, an achievement on the colossal scale; and of similar calibre are the men who pioneered the way in ocean-bridging by the building and floating of steamship palaces such as now make travel round the world a holiday and a recreation.

In like manner the conceptual faculty has not been lacking in the field of politics. The British Constitution—at once the admiration and exemplar of the world—has been the piecemeal growth of centuries; but it was not so wrought out, so shaped to the needs of a developing people—" bodied forth," in Shakespeare's pregnant phrase—without the aid of a quick and teeming imagination. That "faculty divine," however, has at all times been wedded to a plodding and common-sense intellect—an intellect that has too lively an appreciation of the evil of losing a solid foot-grip on things to launch forth wildly into the vague. Hence the pace has been slow but sure.

One infers that this combination of the practical and the creative powers may have arisen from the mingling of the Roman with the Celtic blood during the four centuries of Latin rule, on the top of them coming the plastic Teuton races with their enormous vitality, their adaptability, and their easy assimilation to surrounding conditions. The Celt gave ideas, the Roman grip and the power to take and hold,—the building vein,—while from the Scandinavo-Teuton came the swarming, land-loving, autochthonic, amphibious instincts of the race.

But the prevalence and supremacy of the stock have not depended on these things alone. Other qualities have had their say and do, not the least influential of these being an innate sense of justice. Often enough in practice that quality has shown itself but a rough working ideal; nevertheless, it has been there, and in its quiet way has shaped the nation's purposes and ends amid a welter of inchoate forces, and so has tended to strength and endurance. For, however much men may think to the contrary, the good mystic's words hold true—

> "Whoever fights, whoever falls,
> Justice conquers evermore."

It is, indeed, the only permanently conquering force. And what of stability and endurance there is in the Empire it owes, and will owe, to an inborn sense of right translating itself into the rightwise act. Therein lies Britain's hope for the future. Men may intrigue, fight, work for low and sordid ends; but not a thought or an act will tell for permanence unless put in the right place and in the right manner. The building of an Empire is very much like the building of a house—everything depends upon the plumb and square. The best material goes for nothing without those tools, which are not only tools, but symbols of underlying and eternal principles. Let but that idea take thorough hold of the British people, and the future of the Empire is secured, so far as there is any security in sublunary affairs. And even if, amid the endless change and mutability of things, it should come to pass that this noble structure must fall and become a record and a recollection merely, it would still leave a glorious and imperishable inheritance for all time, from which the nations to come would not be slow to draw and benefit, as we, the people of to-day, have drawn and benefited from the moral and intellectual output of the Greeks and Romans, and other peoples of the time that was and is not.

But these things are not for the doing of kings or statesmen alone, nor perhaps for any stipendiary person. They depend on thought and act working in and through the people. There have been times, as this record has attempted to show, when the British name has seemed on the point of sinking so low as almost to suggest the broader penultimate vowel and a discarded glory. Heaven forbid that, with such a possible future as lies ahead of us, the like declension should ever occur again!

But that future will not be secured except at the price of enormous effort. If, however, the task is a great, it is also a noble one. It is one that might well inspire the best and highest there is in men. One is not without hope that it may. Hitherto, when the need has arisen, England—Britain—has produced men equal to the emergency, men who have seen the present need, the forward and upward path, and have won to it. Such a time is now with us. There is a call for further advance, for a going forward to higher levels of achievement. That way lies safety—ever on the upward path. For a nation, as for an individual, there is no going back, if retrogression means descending to a lower ideal.

There are those who imagine that it is possible to stay; who would arrest the stars in their grand ecliptic roll, and have the solemn march of the ages lag to the tune of their buttery-hatch. They would still keep the good new wine in the old bottles, like the fond old grandmother by the ingle-nook, even at the risk of ruining the whole vintage. Best lay the old tackle aside, and go to work like thrifty husbandmen and make fresh bottles, and so preserve the bubbling must to make the evening glad. One cannot be too grateful to the makers of the new bottles in the past—to the grand old conservators of all that is best and greatest in this commonweal of ours. But for them—battling as they did with those who love to sit, blind and unthrifty, with the old skins at the foot of the tree of life, refusing to let its roots be stirred or watered, or any movement be set agog for health and fertility—but for them what a ruin and a desolation there would have been in place of this most generous growth of time!

Fortunately, in Chatham's prophetic phrase, a new world has again tended to readjust the balance of the old. New men, away from the deadening influences of old ideas and corrupt institutions, have seen and gone a great length beyond what was, and still is, thought possible here, and again wisdom has been justified of her younger children. Humane men, judging by their own hearts, have trusted humanity, confident in its inherent yearnings for the foundation of a deeper and truer civilisation. Thus far they have seen no reason to turn back, but every reason to go forward; and so year after year witnesses some fresh advance. Australia and New Zealand have thus far led the step, pioneered by such men as Sir George Grey and Sir Henry Parkes, the latter a man of whom not only New South Wales, but England, his birth-land, may well be proud. With the meagre and imperfect education which was alone possible for a poor man's child in the early half of the century, helped out by such reading as he could get during his bread-winning, he rose to be the leading statesman in his chosen colony, and the author of measures that gave points to the mother-country, notably his Education Act of 1866, which furnished ideas to Mr. W. E. Forster in the preparation of his epoch-marking Bill.

Notwithstanding the faults of a partially and self-educated person, Parkes possessed elements of undoubted greatness; and he is the type of a class of men coming more and more prominently to the front every year in the colonies—men who in different ways and with different ideas are leading the van of progress in the new nations that are springing up under the broad ægis of the Empire, and whose opinions and doings are destined to react upon the home land in a thousand various ways, broadening the base and bounds of its freedom, enlarging its patriotism and its humanity, shaming it out of its

THE LATE SIR HENRY PARKES.

inequalities, strengthening it by links of confederation and sympathy, but above and beyond all, helping it towards that higher and deeper consciousness of right which is the one pre-eminent possession that no noble mind, amid its sheaf of noble furnishings, can afford to be without, especially in its relation to inferior races and the less generously endowed children of the common Father.

INDEX.

A

Abercrombie, General Sir Ralph, 245
Abolition of slave trade, 282
Aboukir, battle of, 244, 248, 300
Acadia, 15, 39, 54
Acapulco, 48
Adamawa, 421
Adams, Samuel, 158
Addington, 267
Adelaide, 338, 340
— Plains, 340
Adventure, 219
Afghanistan, 313
Afghans, 27, 245
Agra, 21, 254, 260
Ahmadnagur, 257
Ahmed Abdali, 28
Akassa, 423
Akbar, 31
Alexander of Russia, 288, 291
Alighur, 260
Aliveray Khan, 106, 125
Alleghany Mountains, 40, 50
Amazon River, 36
Ambitious, 6
Amboyna, 246, 311
American commerce, 278
— war, 230, 240, 279
Angria, 105
Anguilla, 318
Annapolis, 40, 45
Anne, Queen, 12, 43
Anson, Commodore, 47, 48, 214
Antwerp, 287

An'war-ad-Dien, 71, 72
Arab slave-traders, 433
Arcot, 33, 72, 78
Arkwright, Richard, 211
Armed neutrality, 184
Armenians, 58
Arni, 80
Arnold, General, 180
Asaba, 423
Assaye, battle of, 258, 259, 299
Asserghur, 260
Auckland, 346, 350
Aurengzebe, 20
Austerlitz, battle of, 268, 272
Australasia, 319
Australia, 17, 454 ; (New South Wales), 454; (Western), 434, 445 ; (South), 444
Austria, 268
Austrian Netherlands, 236
Azim Ooshaun, 23
— Shah, 21

B

Bahadur, Shah, 21, 22
Bahamas, 38, 318
Bahar, 117
Baillie, Colonel, 199
Baines, 211
Baird, Sir David, 304
Banda, 246
Bank of England, 13, 14
— Scotland, 14
Banks, Sir Joseph, 216
Barcelona, 8
Barfleur, battle of, 6

457

458   INDEX.

Barker, Captain, 338
Barlow, Sir George, 313
Barré, Colonel, 148, 160, 173
Bass, George, 323, 327
Bassein, treaty of, 254
Basutoland, 447
Batavia, 312
Bathurst, 328
Baudin, 326
Bautzen, battle of, 290
Bay of Biscay, 238
— Islands, 343, 348
— La Hogue, 7
Beau Sejour, fort, 53
Bechuanaland, 430
Behar, 120, 127
Beira, 432
Belgium, 291
Bell, Henry, 277
Benbow, Captain, 7
Bengal, 106, 111, 117, 120, 125, 127
Benin, 426
Benué River, 420, 422
Berar, 262
Berlin Decree, 284
Bermudas, 318
Bernard, Governor Sir Francis, 141, 155
Beroach, 262
Bharpur, 312
Bhoonsla, Rajah of Berar, 257, 261, 312
Bida, 423, 426
Bigelow, Poultney, 441, 447
Bijapur, 20, 22
Bill of Rights, 2, 361
Black Hole of Calcutta, 108
— War, 327
Blantyre, 432, 433
Blenheim, battle of, 299
Bligh, Captain, 321, 322
Blockade of Boston, 179
Blücher, General, 291, 294
Blue Mountains, 327
— Nile, 427
Board of Admiralty, 153
— Control, 364
Boers, 307, 311, 405
Bombay, 29, 249, 319

Bonaparte, Napoleon, 238, 244, 248, 265, 294, 302, 319
Bonavista, 42, 44
Borgu, 420
Borneo, 412, 414, 416
Borodino, battle of, 289
Boscawen, Admiral, 53, 67, 72
Boston, 139, 146, 147, 155, 164, 169, 170, 178
— Neck, 165, 170, 175
— Port Bill, 161, 164
Botany Bay, 218, 223
Boulogne, 270
Boulton and Watt, 275, 277
Bounty, 215
Bourbons, 206, 236, 296, 298
Bourke, Sir Richard, 329, 331, 332, 344
Bowen, Lieutenant, 326
Braddock, General, 53
Bread riots, 274
Brest, 8, 270
Brindley, 213
Brisbane River, 328, 334
— Sir Thomas, 328, 334
British and Foreign School Society, 354
— Central Africa, 430
— common sense, 449
— Constitution, 230, 234
— East Africa, 427
— Honduras, 318
— North Borneo, 412, 414
— Nyassaland, 430
— South Africa Company, 428
— South Africa Protectorate, 423
— trade and manufactures, 139, 151, 192, 211, 212, 275, 279, 297, 302
Brittany, 267
Brooke, Sir James, 412, 413, 414
Brougham, Lord, 355
Brown, Colonel, 250
Brownrigg, Sir Robert, 316
Brunei, 414, 416
Bryant, 158
Budge-Budge, 108
Buffalo River, 306
Bulawayo, 430
Bunker's Hill, 179

INDEX.   459

Burghash, Sultan, 413
Burhampoor, 260
Burke, Edmund, 148, 160, 171, 173, 234
Burmah, Lower, 410
— Upper, 440
Burmese War, 410
Bushmanland, 306
Bushmen, 306, 307
Bussy, M., 75, 111
Bute, Lord, 123
Byron, Admiral, 215
— Islands, 215

C

Cabul, 21, 27, 28, 245
Cadiz, 10, 270
Cairo, 248
Calcutta, 29, 32, 106, 110, 125, 126, 194, 318
— Council of, 125
Cambay, Gulf of, 201, 257
Cambridge, 151, 165, 170, 175
Campbell, Sir Colin, 411
Camperdown, battle of, 240
Canada, 36, 38, 50, 123, 162, 180, 318
Canara, 252
Canceau, 46
Candahar, battle of, 245
Cape Colony, 405, 408
— Comorin, 69, 75
— François, 188
— Good Hope, 215, 224, 246, 304, 308, 442
— St. Vincent, 7, 184
— —, battle of, 240
Carbonier, 42, 44
Carnatic, 70, 74, 80, 104, 120, 198, 252
Carolina, 150
Carpentaria, Gulf of, 325
Carteret, 215
Cartwright, Edmund, 212
Cauvery River, 68, 76
Cawnpore, 411
Ceylon, 121, 246, 304, 316, 319
Chandernagore, 59, 110, 113
Channel ports, 270

Charles River, 165, 175
Charlestown, 160
— Neck, 178
Chartered Companies, 412 *et seq.*
"Chartism," 445
Chatham, Earl of, 123, 143, 171, 178, 182, 360
Chebucto, 48, 50
Chili, 47
China, 226, 311
Chingleput, 82
Chunda, Sahib, 71, 77, 104
Church Missionary Society, 343
Chutanuttee, 33
Clarence, 336
Clark, Captain, 219
Clarkson, 208
Clermont, 277
Clive, Robert, 69, 77, 83, 105, 122, 124, 128, 194
Coalition Cabinet, 202
Cobden, Richard, 413
Coleroon, 68
Collingwood, Admiral, 270
Collins, Colonel, 308, 326
Colonial manufactures, 152
Colville, Lord, 45, 216
Comet, 277
Commercial legislation, 359
Common man, the, 443
Common sense, British, 449
Concord, 170, 176
Congo Free State, 347
Congress at Philadelphia, 166, 173
Conjeveram, 80
Continental Congress, 167
"Continental System," 284, 288, 302
Convention, 236
Convention of Wargaum, 198
Convicts, Australian, 223, 226, 229
Cook, Captain, 216, 222
Coote, Major Sir Eyre, 113, 120, 200
Copenhagen, bombardment of, 286
Corah, 126, 127
Cornwallis, Hon. Edward, 50

Cornwallis, Lord, 186, 204, 245, 313
Coromandel coast, 75
Corps Legislatif, 287
Corsica, 237
Cort, Henry, 213
Cossim, Ali Khan, 125
Cossimbuzar, 113
Cotton, 422
Count d'Aché, 121
— de Grasse, 186, 188
— d'Orvilliers, 182
— de Vaudreuil, 39
— Lally, 121
Court of Admiralty, 134, 138
— Berlin, 268
— Madrid, 182
Crimean War, 409
Crompton, Samuel, 212
Crown Point, 53
Cuddalore, 64, 66
Culloden, battle of, 244
Customs Board (of Boston), 143
Cutwa, 113

D

Dalhousie, Lord, 410
Dampier, Wm., 215, 217, 218
Dance, Captain, 278, 279
Danes, 278, 286
Dardanelles, 10
Darien, Isthmus of, 14, 16
Darling Downs, 334
— River, 332
— Sir Ralph, 328
Darwin, port, 418
Daudpore, 74
D'Auteuil, M., 71
Davy's safety lamp, 358
De Bienville, 51
Deccan 20, 26, 33, 71, 104, 249, 260
Declaration of Independence, 280
Declaratory Act, 140, 141, 156
Delaval, Admiral, 7
Delaware Colony, 150
Delhi, 26, 104, 245, 254, 260
Demarara, 186

Derwent River, 326
Devicotta, 68
De Villiers, 52
Dieppe, 8
Dingan (Zulu chief), 375
Directory, French, 242, 247
Discovery, 219
Diu, 33
" Divine right," 1
Dominica, island of, 188, 318
Dominion of Canada, 404
Doondiah, 253, 256
Douab, 127
D'Oyly, John, 316
Dresden, battle of, 290
Duchambon, 40
Duncan, Admiral, 240
Dundas, Lord, 277
Dunning, 162
Duplaix, 59, 75
Durham, Earl, 370, 372, 405
Durrains, 28
Dusky Bay, 342
Dutch, 2, 17, 122, 206, 240, 246, 304, 314
— East India Company, 34
— East Indies, 311

E

Earl Percy, 178
East Africa Company, Imperial, 426
East India Company (British), 10, 20, 34, 68, 124, 125, 157, 160, 194, 196, 246, 252, 262, 279, 312, 362
East Indies, 364
Education, 354, 357
Egypt, 244, 248, 266
Elba, 291
Electric telegraph, 389
Elizabeth, Augustan age of, 354
— Queen, 297
Elliott, General, 190
Endeavour, 216
England's better destiny, 445
Enterprise, 358
Essequibo River, 186

F

Falkland Islands, 215, 318
Farewell, Lieutenant, 374
Feroksere, 24, 32
Fiji, 436
Fish River, 327
Fitzroy, Captain, 386
Flinders, Matthew, 323, 324, 327, 328
Florida, 123, 193
Flying Post, 16
Forster, W. E., 454
Fort du Quesne, 52
— Necessity, 52
— St. David, 29, 64, 83, 105, 120
— St. George, 58
— William, 106, 119
Fox, 158, 202, 267
Franklin, Dr., 172, 190
Freemantle, 337
Fréjus, 291
French, 4, 13, 35, 82, 110, 123, 148, 182, 184, 188, 206, 238, 247, 250, 255, 270, 278, 284, 286
— East India Company, 104
— Revolution, 230, 235, 238, 272, 296
— West India Company, 35
Frontignac, Governor, 38, 39
Fulahs, 420, 421
Fulton, Robert, 277
Furneaux, Captain, 219

G

Gage, General, 162, 166–169, 170, 175, 179
Gaika, 310
Gando, 423
Ganges, 27, 201, 266
Gaspereaux, 53
Gawilghur, 266
Gawler, Lieutenant-Colonel, 340
General Assembly of Virginia, 137, 150, 164
George II., 123
— III., 123, 129, 267, 300

George IV., 360
— Town, 327
— Washington, 53, 54
Georgia, 130, 135, 138, 167, 318
Geriah, 105
Ghent, 291
Gibraltar, 10, 13, 184, 190
Gillespie, Colonel, 313
Gingee, 74
Glenelg, Lord, 377
Goa, 58
Godavery River, 257
Goddard, Colonel, 196
Gold (in Australia), 390
Goldie, Sir G. T., 426
Gordon, Lord George, 353
— Sir Arthur, 438
Gourkhas, 315, 368
Government of Madras, 198
Governor-General of India, 261
— Shirley, 46
Graham, Colonel, 309
Graydon, Admiral, 43
Great Australian Bight, 325
— Fish River, 304, 309
— Java, 17
Greathead, 276
Grenada, 318
Grenville, Mr., 132, 140, 267
Grey, Sir George, 341, 406, 408, 454
Griffin, Admiral, 65
Guadaloupe, Island of, 237
Guaria, Admiral, 272
Guiana, 318
Gulf of Guinea, 420
— Mexico, 35
Guzerat, 33, 196
Gwalior, 198

H

Habeas Corpus Act, 274
Halifax, 48, 146
Hamburg, 287
Hamilton, Dr., 32
Hanover, 267
Hanson, Lieutenant, 342
Hargraves, E. H., 391
Hargreaves, James, 211

Harponelly, 252
Harris, General, 249, 255
Hastings, Marquis of, 314, 368
Havre de Grace, 8
Heligoland, 287
Henry, Patrick, 136
Herbert, Admiral, 3, 4
Himalaya Mountains, 319
Hindmarsh, Captain, 340
Hindus, 21, 26, 28, 58, 63
Hobart, Lord, 246
Hobson, Captain, 349, 350
Hokianga River, 344
Holland, 237, 267, 277
Holy Alliance, 296
Home, Lord, 238
Hong Kong, 416, 419
Hood, Sir Samuel, 186
Hottentots, 309
Hougomont, 292, 295
Housas, 433, 436
House of Commons, 1, 16, 131, 202, 208
Howard, John, 207, 223
Hudson River, 14, 277
Hudson's Bay, 10, 36, 318
—— Company, 402, 404
Hugli, 110, 122
Hulls, Jonathan, 276
Humboldt, 19
Huskisson, 359
Hutchinson, 155, 158
— Governor, 155, 158
Hyderabad, 20, 22, 75
Hyder Ali, 196, 201, 250

I

Idolatry of wealth, 440
Illinois, 38
Illorin, 421
Imagination, English, 448
Imperial East Africa Company, 426
— Guard, 295
India, 20, 34, 56, 183, 194, 244, 248, 249, 363, 364
Indian allies, 40
Indian Mutiny, 410, 411
Indus River, 262

Infant schools, 354
Ireland, 240
Iroquois, 38
Isle of Bourbon, 59
— France, 59, 248
Italy, 236

J

Jacobite conspiracy, 7
Jaffier Khan (Mir Jaffier), 125
Jamaica, 15, 188, 318, 366, 367
James II., 7
Jameson, Dr., 430
Java, 215, 311, 313, 366
Jehander Shah, 24
Jervis, Sir John, 240
Jingoism, 442
Johnson, Captain, 358
Juah River, 258
Jugget Seit, 118
Justice, 451
Justinia, 228

K

Kaffirs, 308, 310, 379, 380
Kanawha, 50
Kandy, king of, 314, 316
Kangaroo Island, 325, 339
Kauraki Gulf of, 350
Kendall, 343
Kennebec River, 45
Kent, Mr., 339
Keppel, Admiral, 182
King, Captain, 338
— Lieutenant, 225
Kipini, 427
Kistna River, 74, 75, 257, 258
Knights of St. John, 265
Koh-i-noor, 409
Kojesteh, 23
Kororareka, 348, 386

L

Labourdonnais, 56, 58, 61, 62, 64
Labrador, 216
Labuan, 413, 414
Lachlan River, 328

INDEX. 463

Lagden, Mr., **447**
Lagos, 424
Lahar, 190
La Haye, 292
—— Sainte, 292
Lahore, 122, 128, 245
La Jonquière, 49
Lake Erie, 51
— General, 260, 261, 312
— Nyassa, 432
— Tanganyika, 430
— Tchad, 420, 423
Lander, Richard, 423
Lansdowne, Lord, 355, 359
La Salle, 36
Laswari, 261
Launceston, 332
Law, M., 120
Lawrence, Major, 69, 73, 74, 81
— Sir Henry, 411
Leake, Sir John, 43
Leslie, Colonel, 196
Lexington, battle of, 176, 178
Licencing Act, 16
Lifeboat, invention of, 276
Ligny, battle of, 291
Limpopo River, 405
Linois, Admiral, 278
Liverpool Plains, 332
Livingstone, Dr., 432
Lockyer, Major, 334
Lokoja, 423
London, port of, 280
Lord North, 151, 158, 161, 172, 173, 180, 181, 196
Louis XIV., 4, 12, 13, 42
— XVI., 231, 275
Louisburg, 46
Louisiana, 36, 50
Low Archipelago, 215
— Countries, 49
Lucknow, 411
Lutzen, 290

M

Macarthur, John, 321
Macartney, Lord, 200
Macaulay, Lord, 112, 118, 123, 355

Machinery, 274
Mackinnon, Sir William, 426
Mackintosh, Sir James, 315
Macquarie, General, 322, 323, 328
— River, 328
Madras, 56, 61, 63, 67, 78, 82, 105, 108, 121, 128, 246, 319
Mafeking, rail to, 432
Maharajah Krishna Ondawer, 252
Mahomed Ali, 65, 72, 76, 80, 104
— Shah, 24, 28
Mahomedans, 26, 58
Mahrattas, 20, 26, 78, 105, 126, 127, 196, 247, 248, 254, 312, 314
Maine, 135
Maitland, Sir P., 380
— Sir Thomas, 315
Major Lawrence, 74
Malabar coast, 104, 249
Malacca, 246
— Strait of, 246, 311
Malay Peninsula, 311
Malcolm, Major, 257
Malplaquet, battle of, 299
Malpoorba, 253
Malta, 265, 304
Malwa, province of, 312
Manchester massacre, 353
Manila, 48, 246
Manuel Godinho de Eredia, 17
Manukau Harbour, 350
Maoris, 342, 343, 384, 385
Maphuse Khan, 65
Maria Theresa, 49
Marie Antoinette, 231
Maritime trade, 10
Marlborough, Duke of, 12, 32, 44
Marquis of Rockingham, 140
Marsden, Samuel, 343
Martin, Admiral, 48
Maryland, 50, 141, 150
Mashonaland, 430
Massachusetts, Act for Government of, 169

Massachusetts, Assembly of, 137, 141, 144, 150, 163, 164, 179
— colony, 37, 44, 134, 139, 145, 154, 155, 161, 169
Masulipatam, 33, 69, 74
Matabeleland, 430
Matabele War, 377
Mauritius, 56
Maxwell, Lieut.-Colonel, 259
McBrian, James, 390
McDonald, Sir R., 400
McIllwraith, Sir Thomas, 438
Melbourne, 333, 334, 392, 393
Melville, Lord, 268
Mercury, 216
Mexico, Gulf of, 36
Miller, Patrick, 276
Minorca, 13
Mint at Calcutta, 119
Minto, Lord, 313
Miquelon, 44
Mir Jaffier, 113, 116, 117, 122
Mirzapha Jung, 71, 73, 75
Mississippi River, 36, 37
Mitchell, Sir Thomas, 332
Mogul, 27, 63, 254
Moguls, empire of the, 26, 28, 74
Moiz ad Dien Khan, 23
Monckton, Colonel, 53
Monongahela River, 50
Monson, Colonel, 312
Montego Bay, 366
Montgomery, General, 180
Montserrat, island of, 318
Moorshedabad, 110, 119, 125, 194
Moravians, 208
Moreton Bay, 334
Mornington, Earl of (Marquis Wellesley), 247, 248
Moscow, 289
Mule-jenny, 212
Munro, Sir Hector, 199
Murray River, 332, 338
Murrumbidgee River, 328
Mussulmans, 28
Mutiny Act, 142
Mysore, 198, 252, 253

N

Nadir Shah, 26
Napier, 384
Naples, 236
Natal, 374, 376
National debt, 207
— education, 354
— Society for the education of the poor, 284
Naval mutiny, 242
Navy, 4
Nawab of Arcot, 63
Nazir Jung, 72, 73
Negapatam, 200
Nelson, Admiral, 242, 244, 270
Neptune, 384
Nerbudda River, 257
Nevis, 318
New Britain, 215, 341
— Brunswick, 53, 318, 370, 404
— Caledonia, 219, 402
— Edinburgh, 14
— England, 35, 38, 42, 129, 145, 146, 170, 174
— Guinea, 17, 218, 437, 439
— Hampshire, 137
— — Assembly of, 138
— Hanover, 215
— Hebrides, 219
— Ireland, 215
— Lanark, 354
— Orleans, 51
— South Wales, 217, 222, 223, 259, 323, 328, 329, 338, 342, 344, 381, 391, 399, 439, 444, 454
— York, 38, 54, 137, 150, 173
— — Assembly of, 142
— Zealand, 216, 219, 341, 342, 350, 383, 385, 401, 444, 454
Newfoundland, 13, 39, 42, 174, 216, 318, 404
Newspaper press, 357, 389
News-sheets, 16
Ney, Marshal, 291
Niagara, 53
Nicholson, General, 40
Niger, 419, 421, 425
— Company, Royal, 420, 424, 425

Niger Protectorate, 426
Nigritia, 421
Nizam-ul-Mulk, 26, 70, 71
— of the Deccan, 247, 249, 252
Nootka Sound, 219
Norfolk Island, 225, 227, 342
North America, 219
— Carolina, 138, 164
Northern Circars, 199
Northumberland, 216
North-West Territory, 404
Nova Scotia, 38, 39, 123, 162, 318
Nun River, 423
Nupe, 426
Nyassaland, British, 342

O

Ohio Company, 50
— River, 50
Oil Rivers, 424
Old Calabar, 420, 424
Opium War, 418
Orange Free State, 380, 405, 408, 441
— River, 380, 405, 406
Orient, 244
Orissa, 117, 127
Oudh, 27, 196
Owen, Robert, 354

P

Pacific Ocean, 215, 216, 222
Paita, 47
Palliser, Sir Hugh, 182
Palmerston, Lord, 408
Papelotte, 292
Paris, 290
Parker, Sir Hyde, 186
Parkes, Sir Henry, 454
Parliament, 2, 131, 133, 140, 141, 156, 160, 161, 168, 171, 174, 201, 274, 281, 268
Patans, 74, 75
Paterson, William, Colonel, 326
Patlee, 113
Patna, 60, 125

Peace of 1763, 128
Peel, Sir Robert, 413
Peepulquon, 258
Penal settlement in New South Wales, 223
Penang, 246, 318
Pender, Sir John, 450
Peninsular War, 287
Pennsylvania, 50, 52
Periapatam, 250
Perron, 260
Persia, 343
Persians, 26, 216
Perth, 337
Peru, 47
Peshwa of Mahrattas, 105
— Mysore, 247, 248, 252, 257
Philadelphia, 163
Philip, Governor, 323
Philippine Islands, 215
Philips, Captain Arthur, 223, 225, 228
Phipps, Sir William, 35, 39
Pindarees, 314, 369
Pitcairn, Major, 175
Pitcairn's Island, 215
Pitt, William, 215, 230, 233, 238, 267, 272
Placentia, 43
Planchenoit, 295
Plassey, battle of, 114
Pococke, Admiral, 121
Point Riche, 44
Poland, 236, 275
Pollock, General, 370
Pondicherry, 56, 59, 64, 73, 120, 121, 198, 255
Poona, 254, 255
Pope, the, 236
Popham, Captain, 196
Port Chalmers, 384
— Dalrymple, 326
— Jackson, 218, 224, 226, 319
— Lyttleton, 384
— Moresby, 438
— Nicholson, 344
— Philip, 325, 326, 332, 374, 382
— Royal, 39, 40
Portland Bay, 332

VOL. II.—30

Porto Bello, 47
— Novo, 200
Portugal, 287
Portuguese, 17, 31, 68
Poulett Thomson, 359
Power-loom, the, 212
Presidency of Bombay, 31, 32
— Calcutta, 31, 32
— Madras, 31, 32
President of Board of Control, 202
Pretaupa Sing, 68, 70
Pretoria, 376
Prince Edward Island, 48, 404
— Eugene, 12, 44
Privateers, 49
Protestant League, 17
Providence, 154
Prussia, 236, 268
Punjab, 28

Q

Quakers, 208
Quatre-Bras, 291
Quebec, 38, 39, 166, 180
— Act, 370
— battle of, 299
Queen Victoria, 373, 435
Queensland, 328, 397, 401, 439, 445
Quiros, 215

R

Rabba, 423
Raffles, Sir Stamford, 311
Railways, 388
Rajah Sahib, 77
Rajmahal, 119
Rajpoots, 22
Rajputana, 312
Ramnarrain, 120
Rana of Gohud, 198
Ranier, Admiral, 246
Rao Holkar, 126, 254, 255, 312
Read, Colonel, 250
Reclus, 422, 424, 425
Reform Act, 360
— Bill, 444

Regulation Act, 157
Resolutions of General Assembly of Virginia, 136
Restoration, 16
Retrogression, 454
Rhine, river, 236
Rhode Island, Assembly of, 142
Roads, 213
Robinson, 239
Rockingham, Marquis of, 186
Rodney, Sir George, 184, 188
Roh, 27
Rohillas, 27, 245
Rotumah, 436
Ruffeh Ooshaun, 23
Russell, Admiral, 6, 10
Russia, 239, 268, 288, 290

S

Sahara, 421
Salabut Jung, 76, 111
Salamanca, 299
Salem, 163, 169, 175
—, Assembly of, 170
Salisbury, 430, 432
Sandwich Islands, 215, 219
San Tomé, 67
Sarawak, 413, 414
Sardinia, 236
Savoy, 236
Science, 357
Scindhia, 198, 247, 248, 252, 254, 261, 312, 313
Scurvy, 226
Senegal, 123
Serhind, 28
Seringapatam, 204, 248, 250, 255
Seringham, 76
Seven United Provinces, 236
Seymour, Hon. Henry, 132
Shah Alum, 21, 126, 260
Shelburne, Earl of, 190
Shore, Sir John, 245, 247
Siam, 311
Sierra Leone, 319
Sikh War, 409
Sinclair, Sir John, 192
Singapore, 311

Sirius, 177, 178
Slave Trade, 13, 208, 222, 362, 364, 365
Smith, Adam, 359
— Colonel, 377, 378
— Lieutenant-Colonel, 175
Smohain, 292
Sokoto, 420, 423
Solander, Dr., 216
Solomon Islands, 439
Somerset, Lord Charles, 310
Soult, Marshal, 294
South Africa, 405
— African Republic, 405
— Australia, 338, 339, 341
Spain, 123, 184, 206, 215, 219, 240, 265, 270, 286
Spaniards, 14, 47, 188
Spanish colonies, 135, 302
Spinning-frame, 211
— jenny, 211
Spurrman, 306
Stamp Act, 134, 138
Stanley, Lord, 385
St. Christopher Island, 13
Steam, development of, 277, 358, 388
St. Eustatia, island of, 184, 318
Stevenson, Colonel, 258, 260, 262
Stewart, Sir J. D., 359
Steyne, President, 441
St. George's Bay, 215
— — Island, 215
— — Sound, 334, 337
St. Helena, 319
Stirling, Captain, 334
St. John, 42, 43
St. Kitts, 318
St. Lawrence River, 39, 51, 216
St. Lucia, 188
St. Malo, 8
St. Ovide, 43
Strzelecki, Count, 391
Stuart, Captain, 338
— General, 249, 255
St. Vincent, 318
Subahdar of Bengal, 33
— Oude, 246
Subercase, 40

Suez, 248
Sullivan's Cove, 326
Sunda, Strait of, 311
Supply, 226, 227
Surajah Dowlah, 106, 117, 119, 126, 194
Surat, 29
Sutlej River, 23, 28
Swallow, 215
Swan River, 333, 337
Sydney, 382
— Cove, 224, 227
Symington, William, 277

T

Tahiti, island of, 215, 216
Talmash, General, 8
Tangore, 68-72
Tasmania, 324, 327, 332, 334, 345, 399
Tchaka, 374
Tea ships at Boston, 158
— tax, 152
Thames River, trade of, 279
Thorn, Major, 261
Thugs, 369
Tippoo Sultan, 198, 200, 204, 245, 254
Tobago, 304, 318
Topazzes, 31
Torres, Strait of, 17, 438
Toulon, 10
— fleet, 237
Tourville, Admiral, 4
Trade, 42
— of American colonies, 134
Trafalgar, battle of, 268, 300
Transvaal, 430
Treaty of Aix-la-Chapelle, 49, 67
— Amiens, 255, 265, 266, 278
— Bassein, 255
— commerce, 230, 233
— Fontainebleau, 123
— Presburg, 268, 272
— Ryswick, 39-42
— Tilsit, 288
Trichinopoly, 72, 73, 76, 80
Trincomalee, 200

INDEX.

Trinidad, 318
Trivadi, pagoda of, 74
Tuileries, palace of the, 168
Turgot, 222
Tuscany, 10

U

Uganda, railway to, 428
Ulm, surrender of, 268
Umpada (Zulu chief), 376
Underdown, Captain, 43
Union of New England colonies, 141 et seq.
United Provinces, 246
— States, 180, 289, 302

V

Vaal River, 405
Vancouver, 402, 403
Vansittart, 125
Vaudreuil, 39
Vellore, 78, 249, 313
Vengeur, 238
Venice, 10
Vernon, Admiral, 47
Victoria, 439
— Lake, 338
— Nyanza, 427, 428
— Queen, 373
Villeneuve, 270, 272
Virginia, 50-52, 54, 134, 136-138
Viscount Gooderich, 344

W

Wakefield, Edward Gibbon, 339, 347
Wallis, Captain, 215
Walpole, Sir Robert, 47, 56, 319
Wandewash, 121
Wanga, 428
Wangaroa, 343
War of Spanish Succession, 39
— with Holland, 186
Warren, Admiral, 46, 49
— Hastings, 194, 196, 199, 203, 246

Washington, General, 179, 186, 208
Waterloo, battle of, 263, 291, 299
Watson, Admiral, 104, 108, 112, 120
Watt, James, 211
Way-breakers, 450
Wellesley, Colonel, Sir Arthur, 245, 249, 253, 261
— Marquis (Lord Mornington), 247, 313
— Province, 319
Wellington, Duke of, 291, 294
Wesley, John, 207
Wesleyans, 343
Western Australia, 334, 337, 434, 445
West Indies, 13, 193, 270, 366, 367
Whitbread, William, 282
Whitefield, 207
Whitney, Eli, 210
Wilberforce, William, 208, 282
William III. (Prince of Orange), 1, 17, 35
Williamsburgh, 104
Winthrop, General, 38
Wood, John, 277
Worcester, 175
Wordsworth, 274
Wouldhave, William, 276
Wurno, 421
Wyatt, John, 211

Y

Yakoba, 423
Yorktown, 186
Yoruba, 424
Young, Arthur, 213

Z

Zambesia, 430, 433
Zanzibar, 428
Zemoun Shah, 246
Zoutman, Admiral, 186
Zulfeccar Khan, 23, 24
Zulus, 374, 375

The Story of the Nations.

MESSRS. G. P. PUTNAM'S SONS take pleasure in announcing that they have in course of publication, in co-operation with Mr. T. Fisher Unwin, of London, a series of historical studies, intended to present in a graphic manner the stories of the different nations that have attained prominence in history.

In the story form the current of each national life is distinctly indicated, and its picturesque and noteworthy periods and episodes are presented for the reader in their philosophical relation to each other as well as to universal history.

It is the plan of the writers of the different volumes to enter into the real life of the peoples, and to bring them before the reader as they actually lived, labored, and struggled—as they studied and wrote, and as they amused themselves. In carrying out this plan, the myths, with which the history of all lands begins, will not be overlooked, though these will be carefully distinguished from the actual history, so far as the labors of the accepted historical authorities have resulted in definite conclusions.

The subjects of the different volumes have been planned to cover connecting and, as far as possible, consecutive epochs or periods, so that the set when completed will present in a comprehensive narrative the chief events in the great STORY OF THE NATIONS; but it is, of course, not always practicable to issue the several volumes in their chronological order.

The "Stories" are printed in good readable type, and in handsome 12mo form. They are adequately illustrated and furnished with maps and indexes. Price, per vol., cloth, $1.50. Half morocco, gilt top, $1.75.

The following are now ready:

GREECE. Prof. Jas. A. Harrison.
ROME. Arthur Gilman.
THE JEWS. Prof. James K. Hosmer.
CHALDEA. Z. A. Ragozin.
GERMANY. S. Baring-Gould.
NORWAY. Hjalmar H. Boyesen.
SPAIN. Rev. E. E. and Susan Hale.
HUNGARY. Prof. A. Vámbéry.
CARTHAGE. Prof. Alfred J. Church.
THE SARACENS. Arthur Gilman.
THE MOORS IN SPAIN. Stanley Lane-Poole.
THE NORMANS. Sarah Orne Jewett.
PERSIA. S. G. W. Benjamin.
ANCIENT EGYPT. Prof. Geo. Rawlinson.
ALEXANDER'S EMPIRE. Prof. J. P. Mahaffy.
ASSYRIA. Z. A. Ragozin.
THE GOTHS. Henry Bradley.
IRELAND. Hon. Emily Lawless.
TURKEY. Stanley Lane-Poole.
MEDIA, BABYLON, AND PERSIA. Z. A. Ragozin.
MEDIÆVAL FRANCE. Prof. Gustave Masson.
HOLLAND. Prof. J. Thorold Rogers.
MEXICO. Susan Hale.
PHŒNICIA. Geo. Rawlinson.
THE HANSA TOWNS. Helen Zimmern.
EARLY BRITAIN. Prof. Alfred J. Church.
THE BARBARY CORSAIRS. Stanley Lane-Poole.
RUSSIA. W. R. Morfill.
THE JEWS UNDER ROME. W. D. Morrison.
SCOTLAND. John Mackintosh.
SWITZERLAND. R. Stead and Mrs. A. Hug.
PORTUGAL. H. Morse Stevens.
THE BYZANTINE EMPIRE. C. W. C. Oman.
SICILY. E. A. Freeman.
THE TUSCAN REPUBLICS. Bella Duffy.
POLAND. W. R. Morfill.
PARTHIA. Geo. Rawlinson.
JAPAN. David Murray.
THE CHRISTIAN RECOVERY OF SPAIN. H. E. Watts.
AUSTRALASIA. Greville Tregarthen.
SOUTHERN AFRICA. Geo. M. Theal.
VENICE. Alethea Wiel.
THE CRUSADES. T. S. Archer and C. L. Kingsford.
VEDIC INDIA. Z. A. Ragozin.
BOHEMIA. C. E. Maurice.
CANADA. J. G. Bourinot.
THE BALKAN STATES. William Miller.
BRITISH RULE IN INDIA. R. W. Frazer.
MODERN FRANCE. André Le Bon.

Heroes of the Nations.

EDITED BY

EVELYN ABBOTT, M.A.,

FELLOW OF BALLIOL COLLEGE, OXFORD.

A SERIES of biographical studies of the lives and work of a number of representative historical characters about whom have gathered the great traditions of the Nations to which they belonged, and who have been accepted, in many instances, as types of the several National ideals. With the life of each typical character will be presented a picture of the National conditions surrounding him during his career.

The narratives are the work of writers who are recognized authorities on their several subjects, and, while thoroughly trustworthy as history, will present picturesque and dramatic "stories" of the Men and of the events connected with them.

To the Life of each "Hero" will be given one duodecimo volume, handsomely printed in large type, provided with maps and adequately illustrated according to the special requirements of the several subjects. The volumes will be sold separately as follows:

Large 12°, cloth extra $1 50
Half morocco, uncut edges, gilt top . . . 1 75

The following are now ready:

Nelson, and the Naval Supremacy of England. By W. CLARK RUSSELL, author of "The Wreck of the Grosvenor," etc.

Gustavus Adolphus and the Struggle of Protestantism for Existence. By C. R. L. FLETCHER, M.A., late Fellow of All Souls College.

Pericles, and the Golden Age of Athens. By EVELYN ABBOTT, M.A.

Theodoric the Goth, the Barbarian Champion of Civilisation. By THOMAS HODGKIN, author of "Italy and Her Invaders," etc.

Sir Philip Sidney, and the Chivalry of England. By H. R. Fox BOURNE, author of "The Life of John Locke," etc.

Julius Cæsar, and the Organisation of the Roman Empire. By W. WARDE FOWLER, M.A., Fellow of Lincoln College, Oxford.

John Wyclif, Last of the Schoolmen and First of the English Reformers. By LEWIS SERGEANT, author of "New Greece," etc.

Napoleon, Warrior and Ruler, and the Military Supremacy of Revolutionary France. By W. O'CONNOR MORRIS.

Henry of Navarre, and the Huguenots of France. By P. F. WILLERT, M.A., Fellow of Exeter College, Oxford.

Cicero, and the Fall of the Roman Republic. By J. L. STRACHAN-DAVIDSON, M.A., Fellow of Balliol College, Oxford.

Abraham Lincoln, and the Downfall of American Slavery. By NOAH BROOKS.

Prince Henry (of Portugal) the Navigator, and the Age of Discovery. By C. R. BEAZLEY, Fellow of Merton College, Oxford.

Julian the Philosopher, and the Last Struggle of Paganism against Christianity. By ALICE GARDNER.

Louis XIV., and the Zenith of the French Monarchy. By ARTHUR HASSALL, M.A., Senior Student of Christ Church College, Oxford.

Charles XII., and the Collapse of the Swedish Empire, 1682-1719. By R. NISBET BAIN.

Lorenzo de' Medici, and Florence in the 15th Century. By EDWARD ARMSTRONG, M.A., Fellow of Queens's College, Oxford.

Jeanne d'Arc. Her Life and Death. By MRS. OLIPHANT.

Christopher Columbus. His Life and Voyages. By WASHINGTON IRVING.

Robert the Bruce, and the Struggle for Scottish Independence. By SIR HERBERT MAXWELL, M.P.

Hannibal, Soldier, Statesman, Patriot; and the Crisis of the Struggle between Carthage and Rome. By W. O'CONNOR MORRIS, Sometime Scholar of Oriel College, Oxford.

Ulysses S. Grant, and the Period of National Preservation and Reconstruction, 1822-1885. By LIEUT.-COL. WILLIAM CONANT CHURCH.

Robert E. Lee, and the Southern Confederacy, 1807-1870. By PROF. HENRY ALEXANDER WHITE, of the Washington and Lee University.

The Cid Campeador, and the Waning of the Crescent in the West. By H. BUTLER CLARKE, Fellow of St. John's College, Oxford.

To be followed by:

Moltke, and the Military Supremacy of Germany. By SPENCER WILKINSON, London University.

Bismarck. The New German Empire, How it Arose and What it Displaced. By W. J. HEADLAM, M.A., Fellow of King's College.

Judas Maccabæus, the Conflict between Hellenism and Hebraism. By ISRAEL ABRAHAMS, author of the "Jews of the Middle Ages."

Henry V., the English Hero King. By CHARLES L. KINGSFORD, joint-author of the "Story of the Crusades."

G. P. PUTNAM'S SONS, NEW YORK AND LONDON.

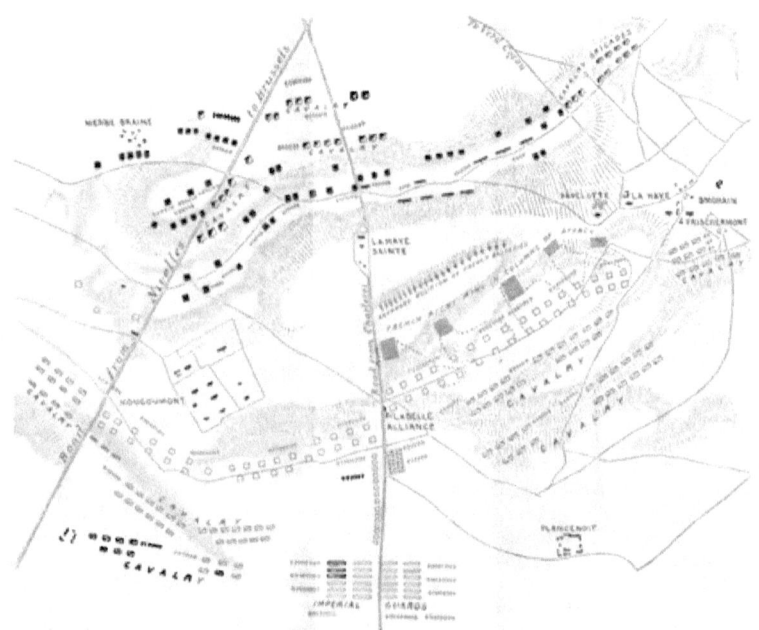

FORMATION OF THE LINES OF BATTLE AT WATERLOO.

www.ingramcontent.com/pod-product-compliance
Lightning Source LLC
Chambersburg PA
CBHW021425300426
44114CB00010B/655